The Fields and Methods of Social Planning

The Fields and Methods of Social Planning

Edited by
James Midgley and David Piachaud

St. Martin's Press · New York

© Individual authors list in Contents in each chapter;
all other matter, James Midgley and David Piachaud, 1984

All rights reserved. For information, write:
St. Martin's Press, Inc., 175 Fifth Avenue, New York, NY 10010
Printed in Great Britain
First published in the United States of America in 1984

ISBN 0-312-28841-7

Library of Congress Cataloging in Publication Data
Main entry under title:

The Fields and methods of social planning.

   Bibliography: p.
   Includes index.
   1. Social policy—Addresses, essays, lectures.
2. Public welfare—Addresses, essays, lectures.
3. Social service literature—Addresses, essays,
lectures.   I. Midgley, James.   II. Piachaud, David.
HV31.F54   1984   361.2 '5   83-40630
ISBN 0-312-28841-7

Contents

The Contributors

Tony Cornford   Lecturer in Computing at the London School of Economics. He has worked as a Research Officer at the Centre for Labour Economics and acted as a consultant to a number of studies in labour economics, health and income distribution.

Derek Diamond   Professor of Geography with special reference to Urban and Regional Planning at the London School of Economics. He has been an adviser to regional planning authorities in Scotland and overseas and has made a special study of the application of social science to settlement planning. He is editor of *Geoforum* and *Progress in Planning*.

Howard Glennerster   Reader in Social Administration at the London School of Economics. He has written widely on social and educational planning and social service finance and expenditure. He is undertaking research on the planning of services for the elderly and mentally handicapped. He is author of *Social Service Budgets and Social Policy, Planning for the Priority Groups* and contributed to the volume *Planning for Welfare*.

Margaret Hardiman   Senior Lecturer in Social Administration at the London School of Economics until her retirement in 1983. She lectured at the University of Ghana from 1968 to 1971 and has undertaken consultancies in Nigeria, Sierra Leone, Swaziland and India. She is co-author (with James Midgley) of *The Social Dimensions of Development*.

James Midgley   Lecturer and Convener of the Social Planning Courses at the London School of Economics. He previously taught at the University of Cape Town and has been a consultant to several social development projects in the Middle East and West Africa. He is the author of *Children on Trial: A Study of Juvenile Justice, Professional Imperialism: Social Work in the Third World* and (with Margaret Hardiman) *The Social Dimensions of Development*. He is co-editor of *Crime and Punishment in South Africa* and editor of a series of books on *Social Development in the Third World* which is published by John Wiley & Sons.

David Piachaud Reader in Social Administration at the London School of Economics. From 1974 to 1976 he was Social Policy Adviser to the British Prime Minister. He has been consultant to WHO, EEC and OECD. He is author of *The Distribution and Redistribution of Incomes* and (with others) *The Causes of Poverty* and *Child Support in the European Community*.

Jonathan Rosenhead Senior Lecturer in Operational Research at the London School of Economics. Previously, he worked in industry and for a firm of consultants; current interests are in strategic planning and social service planning in particular. He is joint author of *The Technology of Political Control* and an active member of the British Society for Social Responsibility in Science.

Introduction

Although not new, the belief that knowledge can be applied to deal effectively with social problems has become more widely accepted during the latter half of this century; it has been a recurrent theme in western social philosophy and especially in the writings of utopian thinkers. Similar ideas are to be found in the works of philosophers of other cultures. Although their prescriptions for the improvement of society have not always been welcomed by those in political authority, current social scientists have been able to persuade decision-makers that they have a valuable contribution to make, and they have done this so successfully that they have achieved a degree of recognition undreamed of by their predecessors. Those in academic employment regularly study the actions of government, evaluate their programmes and assess their effects on social conditions; they are frequently commissioned to advise governments on a variety of matters and on the formulation of social policies. Others exert influence on the social policy process through the studies they undertake in independent research organisations or in bodies established within governments specifically for this task. Still others are directly employed in administrative and policy-making positions in government where they bring the knowledge of the social sciences to bear on social problems. Some social scientists even become career politicians and apply the perspectives of their disciplines to many of the decisions they make.

Social science involvement in public policy-making has taken many forms and has involved a variety of social science disciplines, but in recent years there has been a considerable interest in the application of planning principles to social problems and issues of social welfare. The term social planning has gained much currency and many academic articles and books on the subject have been published. This has been accompanied by the development of courses in social planning at universities and other tertiary educational institutions in the industrial countries, and especially in Britain and the United States where social planning became a relatively popular subject during the 1970s. Social planning courses are also taught in other industrial countries and to some extent in the Third World where the United Nations has promoted its expansion.

In spite of these impressive developments and a now substantial literature on the subject, there is still a great deal of confusion about the nature of social planning and about the role of techniques and methods in social planning and the responsibilities those who are qualified in social planning are able to undertake. Because these and other defects have become apparent to us and our colleagues who are responsible for teaching courses in social planning at the London School of Economics, we have attempted to survey the field and identify gaps and ambiguities in the literature that has been published on the subject. Accordingly, we have written and compiled this volume in a way which seeks to respond specifically to these deficiencies. A review of what we regard to be the most serious shortcomings of the literature will help to explain how this book has been structured and what it hopes to achieve.

Firstly, we believe that the existing literature has failed to define social planning adequately. The use of the term social planning to denote the application of planning activities to different fields of social concern has caused a great deal of confusion. However, the absence of a standard definition or approach to social planning is not the most serious difficulty; indeed, planning procedures can be applied legitimately to deal with different problems. The real difficulty is that no attempt has been made to categorise these various definitions and to compare their application in various fields. One objective of this book, which is pursued in the first chapter, is to identify and examine the different ways in which the term social planning has been used.

A second problem is that much of the literature is vague about how the ideals of social planning are to be realised. There is no shortage of suggestions on what social planning should seek to achieve: improvements in human welfare, a greater measure of social justice, social structural change, the realisation of the individual's full potential and better standards of social service delivery are frequently mentioned as the goals which social planners should strive to attain. But few works on the subject specify, in any detail, how these goals are to be realised in practical, organisational and administrative terms. Because social welfare, equity and opportunities for the realisation of human potential do not magically appear from nowhere, but are the results of the organised efforts of human beings, the attainment of these ideals through social planning requires a discussion of organisational arrangements and professional responsibilities for social planning personnel, both of which need to be clarified if these abstract ideals are to be translated into practical agendas for action. The issue is discussed in chapter 1 of this book, which seeks to review proposals for the deployment of social planning personnel in particular organisational settings in the different fields of social planning which are described in the literature. Where clear statements about the roles social planners are expected to play are not provided, an attempt has been made to identify the implicit proposals contained in the literature. This review is compatible with the chapter's central argument that there is an urgent need to clarify practical fields and professional responsibilities in social planning.

A third problem is that much of the available literature is so specific to Britain or the United States that it cannot be used meaningfully elsewhere. For example, some of the most widely prescribed textbooks on social planning, such as those by Kahn (1969a), Mayer (1972) and Perlman and Gurin (1972) are so specifically concerned with conditions in the United States that they are of little use to students in European and other industrial countries, let alone the developing countries. Similarly, books about social planning in Britain, such as Falk and Lee's (1978) account of social planning in the British social services or the collection of articles edited by Booth (1979) on the subject are of little relevance to readers in the United States and other countries. Although these books are of obvious value to students of social planning in Britain and America, they are not suitable for general readership. And yet, we are aware that these and similar works are prescribed on the reading lists of universities in the Third World where they must be almost totally unintelligible to the student. For this reason we have attempted to provide a broad, comparative account of social planning in this book and have, in particular, sought to use case studies to show how social planning methods have been employed in different countries in both the industrial and developing worlds. The account of the fields of social planning provided in chapter 1 also contains a section about social planning in developing countries and the discussion of issues in social planning is not related specifically to events in any one society. We hope that these efforts will make the subject comprehensible to students in many countries and be relevant to their needs.

A final shortcoming in the available literature is that the use of planning methods is neglected. Although authors of social planning books invariably emphasise the need for rational planning and for the adoption of formal decision-making tools in the policy-making process, few describe the techniques that are available to social planners and of the few that do, most do not demonstrate how these can be applied to specific problems. Although this may be attributed partly to the fact that social planners have not developed any planning tools which they can call their own, a variety of techniques have been devised in fields such as economics, operations research and public finance which can and have been applied in social planning. A few generally advanced works which describe how some of these methods can be employed to facilitate social planning tasks have been published (Sugden and Williams, 1978; Boldy, 1980; Carley, 1981), but they concentrate usually on only one technique and focus on its application to a particular area of social planning. Because we believe that there is an urgent need for a work which brings these various methods together and demonstrates how they can be applied in different fields of social planning, we have devoted the greater part of this book to a discussion of the role of methods in social planning. The term 'method' is used broadly and encompasses data collection as well as decision-making techniques. Each chapter in the second part of the book focuses on a particular method, describing its relevance to one or more fields of social planning as well as its strengths and weaknesses; case study material, drawn from different countries, is provided to illustrate these accounts.

Controversies in social planning

Although this book has been compiled in a way which is intended to meet the inadequacies of the existing literature, it does not attempt to provide a detailed account of the many controversial issues which attend the idea of social planning. These include disagreements about the role of techniques in social planning, the desirability of professionalism and public participation and the values and ideological assumptions which are reflected in the literature on the subject. A proper discussion of these complex issues not only would require a separate volume but would detract from the primary purpose of this book which, as indicated already, has been compiled to review the major fields and methods of social planning. Also, many of these issues have been discussed already in various journal articles and other publications. Nevertheless, methodological controversies and disagreements about the broader social and political issues that arise from the use of social planning are too important to be ignored entirely, especially in a book which advocates the greater use of rational decision-making techniques in social policy. Since it is desirable that the problems associated with the use of social planning methods be recognised, a brief discussion of some of the more important controversies in social planning and indeed, in planning as a whole, will be attempted. While not seeking to resolve the different views which have been expressed on these issues, the disposition of the editors and contributors will become evident. Some of these controversies cannot be reconciled easily, but by discussing them, it is hoped that readers will more readily appreciate the complexities as well as limitations of social planning.

A major controversy, which applies not only to social planning but to planning in general, concerns the nature of planning itself. Chapter 1, which attempts to examine the meaning of social planning, will also show that conceptions of planning vary considerably. They range from definitions which treat the planning process no differently from decision-making in general to those which regard planning as a precision task involving a high degree of skill and a detailed knowledge of techniques such as those described in Part II of this book. These different views are associated with two major traditions in administrative science which are known as the rational–comprehensive (or synoptic) and the disjointed–incrementalist approaches. Advocates of the former stress the need for rationality, goal directed action and comprehensiveness in the planners' knowledge of the field and their efforts to direct it. Adherents to the latter approach claim that these are unattainable; planners neither can direct action entirely, nor can they hope to have full information about the field within which they are operating. They argue that planners should be more aware of their limitations, be more attuned to the politics of decision-making and responsive to the changing realities of the policy process. Although they correctly stress the need for flexibility in planning and are properly concerned with day-to-day decision-making, the former approach is attractive because it formalises the planning process, lays stress on ultimate objectives and attributes features to planning which distinguish it from routine administration and policy-making. Since policy-making and planning are often confused, most writers who regard planning as a distinctive professional activity tend to favour the rational–comprehensive interpretation. Although most recognise the limitations of this approach and accept one of several proposals for its more flexible reformulation, the synoptic tendency can be identified in much of the literature on planning today and, indeed, is reflected in the subsequent chapters of this book.

These two approaches in administrative theory are also associated with differences of opinion about professionalism in planning and the role of planning techniques in decision-making. Incrementalists tend to be sceptical, both of professionalism and of the use of planning tools. They believe that policy-making is an essentially political activity which evolves through a gradual process of bargaining and compromise. In this process, advocates of particular views compete with others to have their ideas adopted; political astuteness and the weight of interest groups rather than the application of planning technology determines the outcome of events. They reject the notion that plans can be formulated by hired professionals whose use of decision-making techniques somehow transcends the pluralism of the planning process. Some proponents of this approach view policy-making as a strictly non-technical activity which does not require the gadgets and methodologies of the technicians of planning. On the other hand, some authorities take an extreme synoptic view of planning in which the use of techniques is pre-eminent. They ignore the political realities of decision-making and define planning as no more than the application of, for example, cost-benefit analysis to the allocation of budgetary resources or the use of critical path analysis in the implementation of a project.

Differences of opinion on this question have accompanied the increasing professionalisation of planning since the Second World War. The expansion of specialist training courses for planners, the creation of professional associations and the increasing sophistication of planning techniques have tended to divide policy-makers between the exponents of planning technology and those of a more traditional persuasion who have viewed these developments with some disquiet and have often overestimated the threat they present to secure and well tried office routines. Senior administrators who do not have formal qualifications in planning are often suspicious of those who do and tend to denigrate their skills. At the same time, the practitioners of planning are often resentful of those with authority who do not share their professional orientation, and they cope by seeking solace in the technical sophistication of their art. It is for this reason that the two opposing views about the role of techniques in planning described earlier should not be dismissed as too extreme to merit full discussion; although they may be reconciled in the cloisters of reasoned argument, they are actual alternatives in the real world of administration and policy-making.

It is likely that this debate will become more relevant to social planning in the future as greater use is made of planning techniques in social policy and administration and as more professionally trained social planners find employment in organisations concerned with the social services and the implementation of other social policy measures. It is partly in an attempt to foster a greater appreciation and understanding of the use of planning techniques in social policy that so much space has been devoted to them in this book. Although it is recognised that planning techniques have many limitations (and these are referred to by the authors of the subsequent chapters), we believe that they are helpful aids to policy-making which enhance objectivity and efficiency. To reject their use is to legitimise Machiavellian tendencies and traditionalism in organisational politics and to deny the need for greater rationality in decision-making.

Another issue which is frequently debated in social planning is the question of popular participation in the planning process. In some fields of planning, such as urban planning, attempts have been made to create opportunities for public involvement and in some countries, the right of public consultation has become a routine requirement in town planning. Calls for the greater involvement of ordinary citizens in social planning have been made on numerous occasions but more attention has been focused on the desirability of public participation than on the difficulties of establishing tangible opportunities for public involvement.

Many advocates of citizens' participation in social planning refer to democratic ideals when presenting their case, arguing that since social planning is for ordinary people, they should be actively involved in the social planning process. It has been argued also that public participation can effectively check the arrogance of professionalism. As planning becomes increasingly technical and sophisticated, planners become preoccupied with their skills and are less likely to recognise their limitations or to indulge in healthy self-criticism. Planning disasters can be avoided by involving members of the public who are more attuned than planners to the practical realities of everyday life. Other proponents of public participation in planning have been more utilitarian, arguing that participation facilitates efficiency; if ordinary people are actively involved in planning, less resistance to the implementation of planning decisions is likely to be encountered. A less instrumental version of this argument is that participation contributes constructively to the planning task since local people are able to identify constraints and help planners anticipate and overcome obstacles to implementation.

The case for popular participation in planning is often taken for granted but it has been questioned on several grounds. Some have claimed that far from promoting efficiency, participation retards the planning process since it subjects the planner's expertise to interminable scrutiny and review; these delays and the creation of proper channels for citizens' involvement are also very expensive. The question of expertise has also been used to criticise the idea of popular participation. Some have argued that public participation in planning is a contradiction of terms: because planning requires technical skills and knowledge that ordinary citizens do not possess, there is little they can contribute. Another argument is that participation is likely to dilute the most efficient and rational course of action proposed by planners. Since participation is an invitation to pressure group politics, compromises and re-negotiated decisions are inevitable and these are likely to be less effective than plans formulated by dispassionate professionals. This argument is similar to the view that popular participation does not in fact provide much scope for the views of ordinary people to be taken into account. Generally, procedures for involving the public in the planning process are dominated by the most articulate, active and influential sections of the community and their views, rather than those of ordinary citizens, are likely to be accepted.

The debate about popular participation in planning is one of several which evokes value and ideological viewpoints. Indeed, the idea of social planning is itself ideological in nature since it involves beliefs about the best way of organising society and dealing with social ills. However, some would reject this view, arguing instead that by shifting the responsibility for decision-making to those with political authority, social planning is a politically neutral activity. This is a distinctly Anglophone conception of public administration which regards the planner as a civil servant who is bound by decisions made in the other world of political action. In this interpretation of the social planner's role, values and ideologies play no part; instead, they are the passive and obedient recipients of political instructions. This view of social planning separates technical and political activities and argues that planners do not take decisions but provide opportunities for politicians to make rational choices between competing alternatives. On the basis of objectives and targets set by those in power, social planners identify different courses of action and compute their advantages and disadvantages, costs and benefits and feasibility and constraints; they also prepare schedules for the implementation of different potential policies. Planners remain politically mute while the politicians choose between different policy options.

Many have challenged this view of the social planner's role as being a naive account of a state of affairs which is seldom if ever attained in practice. Social planners, they argue, are bound to favour certain courses of action rather than others and they are likely to enter the political bargaining process to have their views accepted. In doing so, they inevitably promote their own interests or the interests of others whose interests are compatible with their own. This, it is argued, also takes place on another level which transcends administrative politics; consciously or unconsciously, social planners reflect the views of dominant groups in society since they themselves are members of these groups. A less cynical interpretation holds that social planners, like other human beings, have personal values and beliefs which they inevitably reflect in their work and in the policies they advocate; even if it were desirable, ethical neutrality is both unrealistic and unattainable.

Although many writers accept that the idea of ethical neutrality in social planning is an illusion, they have not adequately debated the logical consequence of this conclusion, namely that if social planners cannot practise professional detachment, they should declare their values. Few authorities on the subject have considered this issue in any depth, let alone attempted an exposition of social planning's value commitment; nevertheless it is clear that many of them have values which are associated with a particular ideological stance. The notions of humanitarianism, progress, welfarism, equality, state intervention and planning itself, which pervades their writings, are a reflection of broader collectivist values.

It is not surprising therefore that many critics of social planning are radical conservatives who reject collectivist ideals and instead espouse the values of individualism, *laissez-faire* and competitive enterprise. The philosophy of planning, let alone its application to matters of social policy, is firmly rejected by proponents of these ideas. They argue that social planning amounts to an extreme form of state interference in social and economic life which is bound to have disastrous consequences. Progess, they believe, lies not in centralised direction by the state but in liberating the natural productive urges in society which, if nurtured in a climate of competition and unrestricted opportunity to pursue self-interest, brings prosperity. Social planning stifles these urges and engenders a complacent dependency on the state which is inimical to economic and social development. Stupified by a generous welfare system, people lose their capacity for work and self-betterment through their own efforts.

In spite of the fact that they subscribe to collectivist ideals, many of those on the radical left are also opposed to social planning or at least to the idea of social planning in any society which is not ruled by an avowedly Marxist party. Social planning, they argue, can only be meaningful in the context of the dictatorship of the proletariat and its use in any other should be condemned. While Marxian writers have supported this argument on several grounds, a common belief is that social planning in the western industrial countries and the Third World is an attempt to halt the historical process of revolutionary change which leads to the overthrow of capitalism and the creation of a socialist society. Social planning in these countries should be resisted because it amounts to little more than a thinly disguised conspiracy initiated by those with political and economic power to suppress the legitimate aspirations of the masses in their efforts to create a just and equitable social order. It is sometimes claimed that social planners are willing participants in this conspiracy which is designed to appease revolutionary fervour through the introduction of minor social reforms and welfare services which maintain the *status quo*.

As these arguments reveal, the apparently straightforward idea that planning principles and techniques can be usefully applied in social policy and administration is a complex one which raises many controversial issues. Questions about values and ideologies, professionalism, the role of techniques and public participation in planning have not been dealt with adequately in this brief review, but it has attempted to demonstrate their relevance to those who seek to use the methods of social planning and to encourage them to consider their wider implications.

The design of this book
As indicated previously, this book seeks to respond to the inadequacies of the existing literature on social planning by firstly, reviewing major fields of practice in which social planners are presently engaged and secondly, demonstrating how decision-making and data collection

techniques can be applied to problems of social welfare. Also, it attempts to do so by referring to a number of different countries instead of focusing on just one country as is usually the case in the British and American books on the subject.

This volume has been divided into two parts which deal respectively with the fields and methods of social planning. Part I consists of just one chapter which attempts a broad review of the literature and reveals that the notion of social planning has emerged in several practical and disciplinary contexts as well. These are described and an attempt is made to identify the recommendations contained in these different authoritative accounts for the professional deployment of social planning personnel. Part II reviews several data collection and decision-making techniques and shows how these have been applied in the field of social policy and administration; their usefulness and limitations are also described. These 'methods', as they are loosely described, include the use of official statistics and indicators, social surveys, cost-benefit analysis, budget planning, spatial analysis methods, operations research and computers. Hopefully, these chapters will not only demonstrate the relevance of these techniques to social policy-making but help remove the mystique which far too often attends their use. Although this book is not intended to serve as a manual which will qualify readers to apply planning methods with proficiency, it seeks to familiarise them with these techniques and to show how they can be used.

While this book is primarily intended to be an introductory text, it is hoped that it will contribute in a modest way to the development of social planning. We have attempted to be as comprehensive as possible and to provide a broad perspective on the subject but it has not been practical to cover every aspect of the field in detail. Lack of space has also placed a severe constraint on the authors of the individual chapters who have been compelled to cover a large subject matter as concisely as possible and to reduce complex procedures to relatively simple and readily intelligible terms; as will be appreciated, this has not been an easy task, especially since the authors have been asked to limit using mathematical notation and other forms of symbolic representation with which they, but not most readers, are conversant. Also, although some planning techniques have not been included, we believe that we have covered those which have the greatest relevance to social policy. In spite of these shortcomings, it is hoped that by describing the most important fields and methods of social planning, readers will be sufficiently interested in the subject to pursue it further.

Part I
The Fields of Social Planning

1 Fields of Practice and Professional Roles for Social Planners: An Overview
James Midgley

Planning is a feature of everyday life. Ordinary citizens regularly take decisions about the future which are based on a rational consideration of known facts and the likely outcome of different actions and, on this basis, pursue courses of action which are perceived to have the most favourable results. This procedure has many features in common with that used by professional planners who employ standard procedures and several formal decision-making techniques to aid organisations, which include local government authorities, commercial enterprises, state industries, multinational corporations and national governments, to decide their future activities. Apart from the role they play in the commercial sector, planners are involved in many aspects of public policy-making: traffic congestion, the development of social services such as education and health, civic construction, the management of public organisations, the preparation of budgets and the evaluation of public projects are just some of the issues with which they are concerned.

Although planning was formally established and professionalised only during this century, it is very old. Its artifacts are to be found in the monuments of the ancient civilisations which, as admiring tourists usually observe, required a considerable degree of foresight and organisation to construct. Urban planning was well developed in ancient times and many cities were built with orderly thoroughfares and well designed amenities. Planning in the organisational and military spheres was also well established. To maintain empires, extract revenues and mount military campaigns, purposeful, rational and directive action was required; this would readily be described as planning today.

The history of contemporary planning is associated with developments in different fields. Although the antecedents of town planning are much older, many accounts of its history begin with the work of

Ebenezer Howard and Patrick Geddes and their utopian visions of a better urban future. The origins of corporate or organisational planning, and the development of operations research in particular, are usually traced to large-scale military campaigns which were launched during the Second World War. The beginnings of economic planning are generally associated with the first Soviet five-year plan of 1928 and to some extent with the influence of Keynesian demand management economics before and after the Second World War. Since then, planning procedures in these and other fields have become increasingly sophisticated, and this has been accompanied by a considerable degree of professionalisation. Professionalisation has been fostered, in turn, by the development of training courses for planners at universities and other institutions of higher learning and the formation of professional planning associations.

The nature of planning

Today, those who work in different fields of planning have very different responsibilities and they apply different techniques to the planning task. The town planner's brief is very different from the economist's or system analyst's, and it is unlikely that they will be able to use each other's techniques readily. Nevertheless, planning in all fields shares common features even though there is much controversy about what these features should be. Although a detailed review of the different features of planning described in the literature cannot be attempted here, they can be briefly enumerated.

Many authorities use the term planning both as a noun and a verb. *To plan* is an activity or process which usually, but not always, results in the production of a document or design known as *the plan*. This distinction is also recognised in the dictionaries which define the word *plan* both as a design, map or blueprint and as a procedure, activity or undertaking. The relative importance which is attached to these two aspects varies: some writers regard the production of *the plan* as the primary and distinctive feature of planning, as opposed to policy-making, while others claim that this is relatively unimportant; instead they emphasise the *planning process* and argue that planners should be more concerned with on-going decision-making than with the production of formal statements of intended action. These different views reflect the two major positions in administrative theory described in the introduction to this book, namely the rational comprehensive and disjointed incrementalist approaches. Incrementalists place more emphasis on the continuity of the planning process than the preparation of formal plans while those who favour the synoptic interpretation argue that the highly structured set of activities required to prepare the plan document are an essential element in the planning process. Nevertheless, advocates of different views of planning frequently use similar terms to describe the nature of planning.

There are many accounts of the features of planning in the literature as well as numerous formal definitions and descriptions of what the planning process entails. Although many employ the same adjectives, different authors have highlighted different aspects of the planning process and seem to place more importance on some of its characteristics than others. Some of the key terms which have been used by writers who have attempted to define planning require further elaboration and reveal how these writers have approached this complex subject.

Process is a common element in all definitions of planning even though this notion is not always made explicit in the literature. Whether emphasis is placed on the production of a plan document or on the continuity of planning, all writers on the subject of planning imply that planning is a process in which a number of procedures are followed. Some authors go further, pointing out that the process of planning is undertaken by personnel who are employed in *organisational settings*. Although they recognise that individuals and small groups also plan, planning has been developed and formalised largely within organisations where most planners find employment. *Decision-making* involving choices is another element in many definitions of planning. The planning process is primarily concerned with deciding how, when and where organisations should act and planners are employed to assist in making these decisions; as noted previously, they use several formal decision making techniques to help them in this task. Many writers argue that planning is an essentially *goal directed* process in which objectives are clearly and formally defined. Many point out that the planning process is primarily concerned with the *future* and that planning seeks to project organisational behaviour into the future. Planning is also *prescriptive*, attempting to direct action toward the attainment of defined goals. The extent to which this is possible is, however, much debated in the literature.

Also debated is the *comprehensiveness* of planning. Although many writers argue that planners seek to deal with all aspects of the planning task, as noted previously, the extent to which this can be done is disputed. *Rationality* is also emphasised in many definitions of planning. The decision-making process is based on rational choices and, to aid rationality, planners use their techniques to identify the consequences of different courses of action. In this way planning seeks to replace other criteria commonly used in decision-making and this gives it a distinctive quality; intuition, routine, authority and other grounds for policy-making are relegated by the formal adoption of planning. However, the impediments to achieving rationality are often recognised in the literature and some writers have modified this concept by using a more modest definition of rationality. Rationality is closely related to the idea of *efficiency* which is included in some definitions of planning. Believing that decisions based on criteria other than rationality are wasteful of resources, planners claim to be able to optimise resource allocations by ensuring not only that their effectiveness is carefully assessed but that allocations are made in ways which bring the greatest returns. Some writers argue that planning is an essentially *normative* activity. Planners are concerned with values which define good and bad choices. Planning, they argue, does not operate in a vacuum but has consequences which are assessed as being either positive or negative in terms of these values. Many authors on this subject believe that all planning should be concerned ultimately with human welfare. Finally, some authors point out that planning is a *professional* activity undertaken by persons trained for the task. Although many writers do not make this clear, the notion of professionalism is implicit in many descriptions of planning.

The sequence of planning

Most authorities on planning also provide accounts of the sequence of procedures which are generally followed in the planning process. Unlike accounts of the features of planning, there is a greater degree of consensus about the steps which characterise the planning process. Writers in fields as disparate as regional planning, corporate planning and project planning usually point out that planning follows a number of steps beginning with a definition of the problem facing the organisation and finishing either with the production of the plan document specifying how the problem is to be solved or otherwise with the evaluation of the organisation's efforts to deal with it.

Typically, accounts of this sequence involve the collection and analysis of all available information about the problem; this may include special data collection studies such as surveys or analyses of information obtained routinely by the organisation or by other organisations. The definition of the problem is followed by a lengthy process of formulating a solution. This begins by defining the desired end state, when the problem is regarded as solved for operational purposes, and it is followed by an account of different ways in which this end state may be reached. Possible solutions are presented as a number of detailed operational plans or programmes in which the constraints to each possible solution are assessed, their respective costs are computed and comparative effectiveness evaluated. On the basis of choices made by those in authority, the chosen scenario is prepared for implementation and provision is usually made for monitoring and evaluation. The plan document contains an account of the various steps of the process including the definition of the problem and its different possible solutions but emphasis is usually given to the chosen operational plan and the scheduling of its implementation.

This sequence, it is argued, can be applied to a variety of planning tasks and at different levels of operational complexity and different time periods. For example, these procedures may be used, on the one hand, to formulate a simple plan for a small, short-term construction project and on the other, to prepare a complex, comprehensive plan for the affairs of a country for a period of five or even ten years.

Although most textbook accounts of the nature of the planning process outline a similar sequence of procedures, it must be recognised that these are ideal-typical descriptions which are seldom realised in practice. In its implementation, the planning process is far more complicated and does not always follow a linear progressive path. Targets which are clearly defined at the outset may be substantially altered or even abandoned. This is probably inevitable given the complexity of the planning task. Perceptions of the planning problem may change and proposed solutions may be modified in the light of new developments. The fact that the planning process is subject to the influence of different people or groups with different views on which courses of action to follow often results in modifications to the professional planner's conception of the preferred way of proceeding. These are just some of the many reasons why the sequence of steps which are said to characterise planning may not always be followed.

The fields of social planning

Social planning shares most of the features of planning described previously. Most writers point out that social planning is a goal directed process concerned with rational and efficient decision-making and most are explicit about its normative content. Also, most accounts provide descriptions of procedural steps in social planning which are very similar to those given by authors in other fields. However, the advocates of social planning claim that unlike other forms of planning, social planning is exclusively concerned with social reality. Although they do not deny that all planning has social implications, they argue that social planning deals directly with social issues and problems. It is understandable that these authors do not state precisely where the boundaries between social and other concerns in planning lie – no one has yet defined the term *social* to the satisfaction of everyone else and this problem is exacerbated by the fact that it has been given different meanings or emphases in different social science disciplines and subjects. Nevertheless, definitions of social planning imply a unique concern for social issues and the application of the ideals of planning to the direction of social events.

Apart from this, the many academic articles and books about social planning which have been published during the last fifty years differ significantly. Many reviews of the origins, characteristics, methods and shortcomings of social planning are now available but the average reader is likely to be more confused than informed after perusing them. The main reason for this is that different authors use the term to denote the application of planning methodology to very different fields of interest, and unfortunately most writers who have offered authoritative definitions of social planning appear to be oblivious of the fact that others have also done so; if these different formulations had been contrasted and debated, much confusion could have been avoided.

To attempt a detailed analysis of these various accounts would be beyond the scope of this introductory chapter. However, since clarification is urgently needed, it may be helpful briefly to review the different ways in which the term social planning has been used in the literature. This can best be done by identifying the fields of involvement referred to by those social scientists who have written about social planning. They come from academic backgrounds as disparate as sociology, social work, environmental planning, social policy and administration and development studies. All have implicitly or explicitly made suggestions for the practical involvement of social planning personnel in activities of social concern. These activities will be referred to as the fields of social planning in this book and they include the following:

1. Social planning, social change and applied sociology;
2. Social planning, social work and community organisation;
3. Social planning and urban planning;
4. Social planning, social policy and social service planning;
5. Social planning and development planning in the Third World.

Social planning, social change and applied sociology
The notion of social planning has been implicit in sociological writing since the subject emerged in the nineteenth century as a distinctive discipline. Auguste Comte, who is widely regarded as the inventor of the term sociology, conceived of the subject as an applied social science which would be primarily concerned with the improvement of society. Sociologists were also the first to use the term social planning explicitly. It seems that it was first employed by an American sociology professor, Charles North, in a book published in 1932. Like many others writing within the framework of what C. Wright Mills (1943) subsequently called the 'ideology of social pathology', North believed that many social problems, including overpopulation, falling moral standards and increasing family instability were caused by social change. Because sociologists studied how change occurred he argued that they could

discover ways of controlling it; this knowledge could be applied through legislation, education, propaganda and effective leadership to direct change and limit its harmful effects. North's writings are today forgotten, but it is interesting that many subsequent books have expressed very similar ideas on the subject although in a more sophisticated way.

Although social change was a fundamentally important feature of sociological enquiry in its formative years, engaging the thoughts of some of its most influential thinkers such as Marx and Weber, it was subsequently regarded as a subfield within the discipline and usually dealt with in the last chapter of introductory sociology textbooks. This was largely because of the influence of the structural functionalist school of sociology and, like North, many of its proponents believed that social change produced strains or value conflicts which disrupted the natural equilibrium of the social structure. The idea that social planning could correct these dysfunctions was common, but some regarded the prospect of directing change or of 'guiding change', as it was also called, to be desirable in its own right.

This idea owes much to the work of Ogburn in the 1920s and 30s whose influential book *Social Change* laid great emphasis on the study of social change in modern sociology. Ogburn argued that social change could be subjected to sociological investigation and even that it could be measured empirically and, like North, he took the view that it could be technologically directed. In a later collection of articles, Bennis and his colleagues (1961) put forward a similar argument. They defined 'planned change' as the application of social technology, derived from systematic and appropriate knowledge which should be used not only for the purpose of solving specific social problems in society but for 'creating intelligent action and change' (p.3). The belief that planning should be used to strengthen the social fabric of society and to improve social interaction had been advocated previously in the writings of Karl Mannheim and Kurt Lewin, and it is not surprising that many who wrote on the subject of planned change were influenced by these thinkers. Lippitt and his co-authors (1958), for example, dedicate their book to Lewin and acknowledge the influence of his belief that 'science and democracy should merge in a widespread sharing of the rational process of making decisions, taking action and testing consequence' (p. viii).

The literature on the subject is, however, not at all clear on the question of how sociologists are to plan change. Few books attempt a clear statement of the training requirements of these planners, of the techniques they should employ and of the organisational settings in which they should work. In a sociological account of social planning in America, Himes (1954) cites the activities of several government organisations and notably the work of the Tennessee Valley Authority as examples of social planning in action but he says nothing about the role of sociologists in these organisations. Lippitt and his colleagues (1958) write at length about the role of the 'change agent' in planned change but do so in such an abstract way that few practical guidelines are given. Although Bennis and his co-editors (1961) do provide concrete examples, these focus on small group activities in organisational settings and this is a common feature of other works on planned change by Lewin's former students. The examples provided by Zaltman *et al.* (1972) and Mayer (1972) in a widely read book are extensive, but they cover such a wide range of interventions, many of which are taken from fields other than sociology, that prescriptions for sociological involvement are ambiguous. Mayer, for example, used case studies of 'social planners' at work in fields as disparate as urban planning, social work, psychology and politics and proposed an interdisciplinary approach to training even though his definition of social planning as planned social structural change is profoundly sociological. Similarly, Zurcher and Bonjean's (1970) case studies focus on the anti-poverty programme in the United States to such an extent that the reader is bound to wonder why the book was not compiled by social workers or social administrators rather than sociologists.

The failure to identify specific professional responsibilities for sociologists as social planners may be partly attributed to sociology's fear of contaminating its objectivity. The case for a pure sociology is as old as Comte's wish to see sociological principles applied to the improvement of society. Spencer's view that social intervention would interfere with the natural laws of societal evolution and harm social progress was echoed by Sumner at Yale, who persuaded a generation of American sociologists of the desirability of ethical neutrality. As their writings became more widely known, Durkheim and Weber's methodological prescriptions for sociological objectivity added intellectual weight to this argument. There were, of course, influential dissenters such as Ward, who coined the term applied sociology in 1906, and Lynd (1939), Myrdal (1953), Mills (1959) and Gouldner (1961) but generally their plea for an end of what Lynd called the 'sheltering traditions of scientific objectivity' were resisted. This belied the fact that many sociologists were engaged in applying sociological knowledge to practical problems even though they did not acknowledge it. The Chicago ecologists not only investigated urban phenomena but were directly involved in urban renewal. Sociological studies of crime and delinquency were similarly concerned with the improvement of social conditions believed to be aetiologically relevant. Today, criminology, urban sociology, the sociology of organisations, medical sociology, opinion research, industrial sociology and other specialisms continue to study and make evaluative comments and recommendations in a variety of applied fields. That this is still not generally recognised is revealed by the fact that relatively few works on the meta-theory of applied sociology have been published and, as Lazarsfeld and Reitz (1975) reported, there was considerable resistance to the use of the term among members of the American Sociological Association. Although Gouldner (1957) attempted to formulate a basis for applied sociology as long ago as 1957, several writers have shown that it is not at all clearly defined (Crawford and Rokkan, 1976; Rossi, 1981).

Another reason for the lack of an authoritative account of the role of the sociologist as planner is that many sociologists believe that sociological knowledge should be disseminated and diffused through society in a general way. The so-called engineering model, in which the sociologist provides information to clients in response to specific requests, has been criticised by writers such as Janowitz (1971) who argued for an alternative enlightenment approach; he claimed that the impact of sociology is indirect but pervasive, 'not to be measured and judged in terms of specific assignments and specific recommendations, but in the broader intellectual climate it seems to engender' (p. 8). While this may be an accurate description of what many sociologists regard as the proper scope for applied sociology, it is not very helpful to those sociologists in search of jobs as professional planners.

Social planning, social work and community organisation
Social work originated in Europe and North America at the end of the nineteenth century in response to a demand for trained personnel to serve in the numerous philanthropic activities in which the charities had become involved. Subsequently professional social work formalised these activities as three methods of practice known respectively as casework, group work and community work or community organisation as it is called in the United States. The professionalisation of social work was pursued most effectively in America where academic social workers wrote extensively on social work's principles and where various professional bodies were formed to set standards of practice. Casework received most attention and was widely recognised as the primary method of social work and it was not until the 1930s that the National Conference of Social Work commissioned a definitive study of the characteristics of community organisation. This task was undertaken by a number of study groups under the leadership of Robert Lane (1939, 1940) which laid the basis for subsequent developments, including the emergence of community organisation planning in the 1960s.

Lane and his colleagues drew on the limited literature which was available on the subject (Pettit, 1928; Warner *et al.*, 1930) and on the experience of agencies concerned with coordinating social work activities at the local level. Charity organisation, as it was then known, began during the mid-nineteenth century both in Britain and the United States in an effort to harmonise the efforts of the many charities which had been established. The Charity Organization Society was founded in London in 1867 specifically for this purpose. Although it is more usually remembered for being the first to employ paid workers and its efforts to formulate a philosophy of charity, both of which fostered the development of professional social work, its attempts to coordinate the activities of the charities, help new ones to become established and suppress fraudulent fund raising were equally important. However, its successes as leader of philanthropic endeavour were varied: in Britain, it became embroiled in numerous squabbles with independently minded charities and its philosophy was bitterly attacked by the Webbs and the Fabians who favoured centralised state intervention instead of the mobilisation of voluntary effort to deal with the social problems of poverty and deprivation. Conditions were more favourable for its development in the United States where the Society had successfully established itself as the organiser of local community social work services in 92 cities before the end of the century. With the support of the Russell Sage Foundation, it formalised this role and, beginning with the Pittsburgh society in 1908, became known as the Council of Social Agencies.

Other organisations with similar functions also emerged. In some parts of the United States, community organisation was undertaken by the State Boards of Charities while in others, societies which were variously known as community welfare councils, associated charities or social service exchanges were created. After the First World War, the War Chests, which had been established to raise funds for the war effort, became known as Community Chests and they were actively engaged in local welfare fund raising. Community organisation was usually but not always conducted within specific geographic settings: sectarian bodies or charities concerned with particular needy people such as the aged or neglected children, also introduced coordinating and fund raising procedures and established organisations concerned specifically with this task.

Lane's study groups urged that these practices be formally recognised as an integral part of social work and that community organisation be taught in the professional schools. It was, however, only during the 1960s that community organisation was properly established, and this was fostered by the publication of several important books on the subject by authors such as Ross (1955, 1958), Warren (1955) and Harper and Dunham (1959). The development of community work in Britain and other European countries lagged behind and evolved in a rather different way (Kuenstler, 1961; Hendriks, 1964; Gulbenkian

Foundation, 1968; Jones and Mayo, 1974).

The literature on community organisation focused largely on the problems of mobilising, establishing, coordinating and planning the work of local social work agencies emphasising the need to improve the delivery of social work services to the local community. Although this was a dominant theme some writers argued that workers engaged in this field should use community organisation procedures to increase community participation and strengthen community identity; by providing opportunities for local citizens to become involved in welfare activities they could help the community to become more closely integrated and develop a greater sense of community feeling. Ross was a notable exponent of this view. Another theme in the literature was that of community action. Drawing inspiration from the work of Alinsky (1946) and other proponents of neighbourhood activism, some authors argued that community organisation should be concerned primarily with advocacy and with promoting the interests of disadvantaged members of the community (Grosser, 1973). Although this is not a new idea in social work, it was only during the 1960s, as a part of the American anti-poverty programme, that social workers began to support welfare rights and the involvement of needy people in community welfare on a significant scale (Grosser, 1965; Marris and Rein, 1967; Moynihan, 1969; Levine, 1970). There were similar developments in Britain during the early 1970s (Lapping, 1970; Jones and Mayo, 1974; Mayo, 1975). This approach is now more popular in community work but it has not always been translated effectively into practice.

The term planning has been used in the literature of community organisation since the first books on the subject were published, but it was employed loosely and did not connote the application of any distinctive methodologies or techniques which would be identified with planning today. This is the case with one of the first community organisation books (Buell *et al.*, 1952) to use the term planning explicitly in its title. Similarly, Kahn's (1963) call for the adoption of planning in the provision of community services for delinquent children emphasised the coordination function of planning in an effort to reduce inefficiency and duplication. The application of a more formal concept of planning was advocated largely by authors associated with the Florence Heller school of social welfare at Brandeis University such as Morris, Perlman and Gurin. In 1964, Morris pointed out that although community organisation agencies with clear planning responsibilities had been established in several American cities, their impact had been limited. In 1966, he reported that studies of community organisation planning were still fragmentary and that few focused specifically on the role of planners as opposed to administrators and others concerned with general community organisation issues. In an attempt to remedy this defect, Morris and Binstock (1966) published an account of how planning procedures had been applied to develop community services for the aged in several American communities. They emphasised the role of the professional planner in formulating planning goals and implementing and overcoming resistance to these goals; as they pointed out, their book was about 'the attempts of a single actor . . . to change the policies of formal organisations in order to improve conditions of social welfare' (p. 3). This actor had been known in the literature as a community organiser, but because the task of improving community welfare required the adoption of planning, they argued that the term social planner was more appropriate.

Ecklein and Lauffer (1972) took a somewhat different view and attempted to distinguish clearly between community organisation and planning activities. Although they recognised that these were very similar, they argued that planners apply a distinctive methodology to community organisation and that they are more concerned with resources, policies and services than people; the community organiser, on the other hand, works directly with citizens who are engaged in community welfare effort. The many case studies of American community welfare activities which are provided in their book are accordingly categorised separately as community organisation and social planning and this, as the authors demonstrate, has the advantage of accommodating community action which, for obvious reasons, cannot be planned in the formal sense of the word. Perlman and Gurin (1972) were not, however, convinced of the feasibility of distinguishing between organisers and planners and they preferred instead to combine the two and use the phrase 'community organisers and social planners'; although awkward, they believed that 'the accumulated meanings of these terms, taken together, will convey the essence of the practice' (p. 7).

Although Perlman and Gurin are correct in their assertion that the two activities overlap, the essence of American community organisation planning is generally unambiguous. The notion that planning procedures should be brought into the community organisation process is advocated by most authorities and, in this context, the literature suggests that community organisation agencies will either establish planning routines to be used by their own personnel or that they will employ trained planners or even consultants to undertake these tasks. The planning procedures described by these authors generally conform to those outlined previously but techniques are relatively neglected. Most authors who refer to techniques have a limited repertoire and budget planning methods such as PPBS are invariably mentioned. While the question of techniques does require further elaboration by the experts, the field of practice for social planners in American community organisation is reasonably well defined. But, in view of the highly decentralised and privatised nature of the American social services and the emphasis on voluntary effort in American social work, the limited replicability of this approach and restricted usefulness of the literature should be recognised.

Social planning and urban planning

Modern town planning emerged largely as a response to philanthropic concern about overcrowding and squalor in the rapidly expanding industrial cities of Europe and North America. Studies of slum conditions, such as those undertaken by Tuckerman in Boston and by Mayhew and Booth in London, as well as the opportunities provided by the settlement house movement for the middle class to obtain first-hand knowledge of urban deprivation, fostered the provision of sanitary facilities and the construction of schools, recreational centres and other amenities in these areas by both voluntary and public effort. Howard, Geddes and Mumford as well as the proponents of the American City Beautiful movement encouraged aesthetic improvements, and as city governments began to enact land use legislation to control future construction and segregate different types of urban activities, more emphasis was placed on physical than social factors in the planning process. After the First World War, zoning and the preparation of master plans became common in the industrial countries. This type of planning was dominated by engineers and architects and the emphasis which was placed on the enforcement of building and zoning legislation diverted attention from the social aspects of urban planning.

The consequences of neglecting social factors in urban planning became evident after the Second World War when slum clearance and public housing construction was undertaken on a large scale. These were regarded primarily as design tasks to be undertaken by architect planners and engineers; huge faceless blocks of densely packed high rise apartments began to appear in the war ravaged cities of Europe while, in the United States, the 1949 Federal urban renewal programme sanctioned the mass destruction of the inner cities. High-rise living generated new social problems and many estates were characterised by an intolerable degree of vandalism, crime and personal isolation. In America, political resistance to public housing often resulted in little more than the relocation of slum dwellers from inadequate accommodation in the inner city to inadequate accommodation elsewhere (Wilson, 1966). Analyses of these developments gradually stimulated a greater interest in the social, economic and political dimensions of urban planning and it was gradually recognised that urban planning involved a variety of tasks: the creation of jobs through planned investment, the anticipation of the social impact of planning decisions and the involvement of the public in the planning process were just some of the responsibilities which, it was argued, planning authorities should assume. From a narrow architectural focus, urban planning began to draw knowledge from fields such as sociology, economics, social policy and political science. This was accompanied by a broader approach to training. Gans (1968a) reported that the prestigious planning school at the University of Chicago was one of the first to place a greater emphasis on social science knowledge than design skills in the curriculum and other schools soon followed this example. Although a concern with design and land use still dominates the planning process in many places, the other dimensions of urban planning are no longer ignored. This is not the case, however, in most developing countries where urban planning is not well developed and still largely preoccupied with physical design (Stretton, 1978; Taylor and Williams, 1982).

The term social planning emerged in Europe and North America during the 1960s to reflect a new concern for the social aspects of urban planning. It was also used in a more specific sense to refer to tasks undertaken by specialist social planning personnel within the planning agency. The former connotation was recently summarised by Kirk (1980, p. 154) who observed that 'all planning is social planning in that it has social effects – intended or otherwise'. Proponents of this interpretation such as Gans (1968b) argued that because planning was about people, the design, land use and aesthetic aspects of town planning should be subordinated to social concerns. Broady (1968) was equally critical of architectural determinism in planning and argued that urban planning should seek instead to strengthen social institutions, promote human potential and foster social integration by improving social relationships between people.

In spite of defining social planning as the redirection of urban planning towards social goals, these and other writers recognise that there is a role for specialist social planning personnel in the planning process and for the organisational division of different responsibilities. Indeed, distinct professional responsibilities have emerged. Perloff (1963) reported that many American city planning authorities had created social planning divisions and in 1967 Frieden noted that social planning had been placed on a firm footing. Social planning tasks are often undertaken by trained sociologists or social welfare personnel who are brought into the planning team for this purpose or otherwise by town planners who are knowledgeable in these matters. Also close links between urban planners and community organisation personnel working in poor communities were established (Duhl, 1963; Gans, 1968c) and these were strengthened during the years of the anti-poverty programme and the launching of the model city projects (Gans, 1968a;

Gilbert and Specht, 1977a). These links are reflected in the numerous publications about social planning which appeared in the influential *Journal of the American Institute of Planners* during the 1960s and 1970s.

In Britain, as Broady (1968) reported, social planners are usually employed to provide demographic data or to undertake social surveys about social conditions. Although he was critical of this narrow interpretation of social planning, Broady recognised the need for what he called a social development department within the planning authority which would, for example, help people to move into the community, settle down and establish roots quickly, disseminate information about local facilities and promote voluntary activities.

Social planning is now more widely recognised as a specialist activity in urban planning and there is relatively little confusion about the role of social planners in this field. Already in 1963 Perloff identified six tasks which were being undertaken by social planners in American city planning agencies: (i) assessing and monitoring the social impact of urban plans, (ii) preparing long-term social development plans, (iii) undertaking social research, (iv) coordinating community services, (v) helping to locate community facilities and (vi) enlisting grass roots participation in planning. Although subsequent accounts have elaborated and extended on these responsibilities, the role of the social planner in urban planning has not changed significantly since then.

Social planning, social policy and social service planning
State involvement in meeting the educational, health, housing and other social needs of people has increased significantly during this century. Previously, the state's role was negligible, and people generally satisfied their social needs through the market by purchasing health or education or housing as they required and could afford it. Needs that could not be met through the market were dealt with through established institutions such as the family or the church and, increasingly during the nineteenth century, through philanthropy. Although philanthropy undoubtedly fostered governmental participation in the provision of the social services, other factors also contributed to this development. Some authors have argued that the growing strength of the working class movement was perceived as a threat to the established order and that this contributed to the creation of welfare services in an effort to assuage militancy. Although there is some truth in this assertion, the struggles of working people to achieve political representation were equally important; governments that came to power through the enfranchisement of working people did more to improve social conditions and to extend the social services to their constituents than did the representatives of established elites.

Although some have gone further than others, public social services have expanded considerably in most countries during the post-war years. Generally this trend has been most marked in the socialist countries of Eastern Europe which have devoted a considerable proportion of their national incomes to the social services, but they are closely followed and in some cases overtaken by western European nations where public social service expenditures are also substantial; in countries such as Denmark, West Germany, Luxembourg, Norway and Sweden, social service allocations amounted to more than 20 per cent of Gross Domestic Product during the mid-1970s (United Nations, 1979b). Public expenditures on the social services in developing countries have also increased significantly since the war, and this trend continued during the 1970s when, as the United Nations (1979b) reported, allocations to the social services increased faster than total output on goods and services in more than two-thirds of the developing countries for which information was available.

These developments created a greater demand for social service professionals and resulted in the establishment of large public sector bureaucracies responsible for the administration of the social services. In some countries and especially the so-called welfare states of western Europe, these organisations are very large and the managerial demands placed on social service administrators are substantial. The expansion of the social services has been accompanied by academic research into their functioning and in some countries such as Britain, this has been formalised through the creation of university departments of social administration which not only undertake research but train staff to administer the social services.

Planning has become increasingly important both in central and local social service organisations. In Britain, where social service planning was fostered largely by central government, planning procedures were initially adopted to plan the future construction of hospitals, schools and other social service facilities and some attempts at manpower planning were also made. Glennerster (1980) reported that the planning of social service delivery systems began in the 1960s with the introduction of budgetary planning procedures which required the central government social service departments to make forecasts of future demands for services and to set priorities for budgetary allocations in the medium term. In the 1970s, planning procedures were extended to the local authorities responsible for education, housing and social work services and the local administrative divisions of the central government's National Health Service. In some cases, such as the preparation of ten-year plans for social work services, local authorities were instructed to do little more than outline likely future developments in these services but in others, such as the National Health Service, more detailed and prescriptive plans were required and these were accompanied by the introduction of budgetary planning measures at the local level.

Similar planning procedures were adopted by the American government during the 1960s when the Johnson administration, as a result of the RAND Corporation's successes in coordinating the work of the Defense Department, adopted Planning Programming Budgeting Systems, PPBS as they are usually referred to, throughout the Federal government. The introduction of PPBS in the Department of Health, Education and Welfare attracted considerable attention and undoubtedly fostered a greater interest in social planning among social workers in the United States (Drew, 1969; Rivlin, 1970). However, as noted previously, the social services in America are provided to a large extent by voluntary and private agencies and because of the emphasis which is placed on the decentralisation of services, the roles of social service and community organisation planners are frequently blurred in the literature (Ohlin, 1964; Morris, 1966; Stumpf and Granger, 1973).

Some authors on the subject of social service planning use the concept of planning loosely, often as a synonym for social policy-making. As Glennerster (1980) observed, Beveridge described his social security proposals as 'a plan' for social security. Kahn (1969a) is a notable exponent of this view of social planning. He is critical of those who stress formal sequential procedures and the preparation of 'blueprints' in the planning process and instead views social planning as 'policy formulation' consisting of a 'series of generalised guides to future decision and actions' (p. 15). Accordingly, Kahn tends to minimise the importance of techniques in planning and regards them as programming tools for the implementation of social policy decisions. Elsewhere (1969b) he asks whether these are not in fact alternative planning systems to the policy-making process which he equates with social planning.

Other writers have a more definite view of social planning emphasising specific planning tasks in the development of the social services. Reporting on social service planning in Britain, Falk and Lee (1978) welcome the creation of planning departments within social service organisations both at the central and local level and point out that they undertake seven major planning responsibilities ranging from forecasting to performance measurement; two case studies about planning in the National Health Service and the local authority social work departments give insights into the nature of social service planning in Britain while a third provides information about the use of PPBS in the United States. Other accounts of social service planning in Britain and America, such as those by Rein (1968), Glennerster (1980) and Booth (1979) regard the coordination of services and the allocation of resources as the major tasks for social planners in social service organisations, and all stress the importance of budgetary planning procedures as the major instrument for social service planning although, as others have shown, use is also made of techniques such as operations research and cost-benefit analysis (Williams and Anderson, 1975; Boldy, 1980). As a result of these developments, the nature of social planning in the context of social service planning is now reasonably well defined. However, the contribution of social planners to the future development of the social services is less clear, especially in countries such as Britain and the United States where governments have declared their intention to reduce social service expenditures drastically.

Social planning and development planning in the Third World
The adoption of planning in the developing countries after the Second World War was designed to modernise the economies of these countries and to raise the levels of living of their people as quickly as possible. It was believed that the problems of mass poverty could be solved by transferring the bulk of the population from subsistence agriculture to modern wage employment and that this could be done by mobilising capital for industrial development through centralised economic planning.

Waterston (1965) reports that the Asian countries took the lead in this field. The government of the Philippines launched its first development plan in 1947 and India followed in 1952. The Indian leaders were greatly impressed by the achievements of the Soviet Union and believed that centralised planning would accelerate the country's drive toward industrialisation and the abolition of subsistence poverty. Since then, most countries have established central planning authorities which prepare national development plans to direct the process of economic development. However, some countries have been more successful in their attempts at planning than others.

Development planning was for many years exclusively concerned with economic growth and this was compatible with the development philosophy of the time which held that social expenditures were a drain on scarce resources and diverted funds from the overriding objective of mobilising capital for industrial development. During the 1960s, concern for the social problems of underdevelopment such as illiteracy, destitution, landlessness, hunger, disease, underemployment, poor housing and exploitation increased and it became apparent that these could not be ignored by governments. Some had, in any case, begun to respond to the growing demand for the extension of modern health and educational services, while others had made this a major commitment during the independence struggle.

The United Nations encouraged these developments and during the 1960s urged its member states to lay greater emphasis on social planning not only by developing social service planning, but by directing economic planning towards the realisation of social objectives. These ideas were formally expressed in a resolution which was adopted by the Economic and Social Council in 1966, and ratified subsequently by the General Assembly. The idea that governments should, as the resolution put it: 'plan social development in conjunction with economic development with a view to attaining balanced and integrated economic and social development' (United Nations, 1971, p. 4), was laudable, but it lacked operational clarity and there was much uncertainty about how these economic and social objectives could be integrated organisationally in the planning process. The term social planning was also much confused and it was not clear whether specific roles for social planners should be identified and whether training courses for social planners should be established. Although the United Nations encouraged the creation of social planning courses both in the industrial and developing countries, it recognised that the role of social planning in the context of development planning was confused, and in 1968 it convened meetings of experts to clarify the meaning of social planning. These meetings, which were held in 1969 and 1970 did not, unfortunately, succeed in this task.

Both were dominated by well intentioned economists who were critical of the emphasis then given to sectoral social service planning and understandably reluctant to delineate a specific role for social planners as distinct from economic planners in the planning process which they had long regarded as their domain. Their argument for 'unified' socio-economic planning was ambiguous but seemed to suggest that economists would become more concerned about social issues and seek to direct the economic development process in a way which would maximise the welfare of the population; in this sense, social planning may be defined as a socially committed economics.

The idea that economists should be responsible for social planning did not appeal to social development specialists and especially to social workers who argued that, unlike economists whose view of the world was not conducive to an appreciation of social problems, they were uniquely qualified to deal with matters of social welfare. Although this view has been scathingly dismissed by Sovani (1974), it is true that the majority of economists do not have any particular interest in welfare matters. Advocates of the unified approach were also naive in believing that a conventional training in economics is sufficient to provide the skills needed to formulate plans in specific social service fields such as health, education or housing. The belief that these require little more than the application of conventional economic criteria for the allocation of resources is simplistic and denies the need for a multidisciplinary perspective when dealing with issues of social policy. It also fails to recognise that specific organisational procedures for the planning of the social services along sectoral lines had already been established and that this division of responsibilities is inevitable if specific plans and schedules for implementation are to be prepared.

On the other hand, advocates of the sectoral approach were too narrowly concerned with the social services and did not seem to appreciate the need for an overall development strategy which will ensure that economic development plans are directed specifically at welfare objectives; the preparation of sectoral social service plans is clearly not enough if this goal is to be realised. The need for the administrative harmonisation of planning activities is also neglected by the proponents of the sectoral approach who appear to be more concerned with the solitary pursuit of particular social service objectives than with the proper integration of social and economic development activities. Another weakness of this approach, as Midgley (1978) pointed out, is that its advocates have underestimated the complexity of the planning task and have assumed that social service professionals, such as social workers, are automatically qualified to undertake planning responsibilities.

Hardiman and Midgley (1982) argued that social planners must be specifically trained to apply the methodology of planning and the perspective of social policy to problems of social development. They reject the idea that any single discipline can provide the skills required for social planning and claim that the disciplinary origins of those who are selected for training in social planning are relatively unimportant. But, as they put it: 'to be described properly as social planners, they must be engaged in planning and policy-making for social development and should be trained to undertake this task' (p. 24). Their view of what this training should include is propounded in another publication (1980) which suggested that a broad, multidisciplinary, post-graduate education in appropriate social policy formulation at both central and sectoral levels is desirable. They also recommended that students be taught to use planning methods and exposed to a social development philosophy which is committed to the ideals of social progress, welfare, equity and participation and compatible with a humanistic and collectivistic ideology.

As the literature on the subject reveals, personnel trained in social planning have been used in various ways in developing countries and have been given various responsibilities. The first and most obvious of these is sectoral social planning within both central planning organisations and sectoral social service ministries. Here, social planners prepare plans for education, health, social work services, housing and social security and ensure that they are harmonised with broader social and economic policies. A substantial literature on sectoral social planning in developing countries has now been published (Pusic, 1965; Coombs, 1970; Selwyn, 1970; Gerima, 1973; Rys, 1974; Gish, 1975; Psacharopoulos, 1975).

Social planners also work together with economic planners in central organisations to formulate an overall development strategy which is committed to the attainment of social objectives. More economists are today advocating the formulation of economic development plans which will reach the poor (Todaro, 1977; Mehmet, 1978; Streeten, 1981), and social planners are particularly interested in this approach and participating in the preparation of national and regional development plans of this kind.

Research and monitoring are other roles for social planners in development planning (United Nations, 1971). The collection of social information through social surveys and indicators as well as other forms of social research is an important contribution which social planners can make to the planning process. Social research and other techniques can also be used to evaluate the successes of social and economic policies and to assess their impact on the welfare of people. This role is equally important in the field of project planning where, as Conyers (1982) pointed out, social planners are involved both in the initial stages of the project to give advice on its likely social consequences and in the implementation of the project to assess its effects.

A final role for social planners is to encourage the participation of people in development. This has been a particularly popular theme in the United Nations literature (1971; 1979a) which urged social planners to help people become involved not only in local planning but in decision-making at all levels of society. While there can be no quarrel with the idea that participation should be encouraged, it is very difficult to translate into practice; as Apthorpe (1970) observed more than a decade ago, 'The notion of social planning as social participation is particularly elusive, problematic and paradoxical. . . .' This is still the case today.

These developments have fostered a clearer definition of professional responsibilities for social planners in the Third World. Although, as noted previously, some authorities favour an approach to economic planning in which social goals direct the planning process to such an extent that specific social planning roles are not required, this prospect is far from being realised in most countries. Because of this, a concern for the social dimensions of development planning can best be fostered by social planning specialists without whom, it may be argued, there would be no social planning at all.

Problems of defining social planning

Although this review has attempted to identify the major fields in which the idea of social planning has been applied, it should be recognised that some authors do not conform to these categories. Some cross boundaries while others write about social planning without referring to any particular field. The absence of a practical context in discussions on social planning is noticeable in the sociological literature but occurs in others as well. For example, a meeting of social work experts (Morris, 1964) which was held in Weston, Massachusetts in 1963 proceeded without much reference to practical matters, and could have been relevant to any field of planning. This is true also of Gilbert and Specht's (1977b) collection of articles which covers a very broad subject matter. Others use the term social planning in such a general way that its meaning is quite obscure. One example of this is Friedmann's (1979) extraordinary esoteric book which seems to equate social planning with all types of planning and, in spite of the author's background, argued that social planning is antithetical to the notion of the Good Society; as he put it (p. 41): 'Against the "no" of social planning, the practice of the Good Society asserts the "yes" of its commitment to a dialogue in freedom.'

Some writers often refer to more than one field of social planning even though their own disciplinary background dominates the approach they adopt towards the subject. Social workers not only write about community organisation but about social service planning and sometimes about urban planning while urban planners, particularly in America, refer to community organisation. Of course, there is a degree of overlap between these different fields and this is reflected in the research findings and publications of different authors.

There are different emphases in different countries as well. Much of the literature in the United States has been published by social workers, and their writings on community organisation planning are very different from the approach adopted by British authors who generally approach the subject from the perspective of social administration and focus largely on the planning of the social services. Both have, as noted previously, written about the social aspects of environmental planning. Community organisation planning is a uniquely American concept and it is not surprising that social workers in other countries have written little, if anything at all, on the subject; on the other hand, social workers concerned with development issues have contributed significantly to the literature on social planning in the Third World.

Because the idea of social planning has been applied to different fields of social concern, an attempt to synthesise these different meanings is unlikely to succeed. This is not to avoid the problem of formulating a standard definition of social planning but a reflection of the fact that, at present, social planning can only be defined with reference to the different tasks social planners are required to undertake.

Although the different fields of social planning which have been described do share common features, at the present state of the art, social planning will continue to mean different things in different contexts.

Part II
The Methods of Social Planning

2 Social Indicators and Social Planning
James Midgley and David Piachaud

In addition to undertaking specific studies, such as social surveys, to obtain information for planning purposes, social planners use data which are routinely collected through censuses, population registration procedures and the statistical returns of government ministries and other official organisations. These data, which are generally referred to as 'official statistics', not only provide information about the activities of the public sector but report on wider social, economic and other conditions. Statistics about a great variety of topics are now available in the official reports published by government departments of statistics in many countries; they deal with matters such as population growth, traffic flows, voting behaviour, criminal convictions, exports and imports and even the weather.

Official data about social conditions are known as social statistics and they are of great value to social planners. If they are seeking to formulate a policy to deal with a particular social problem such as youth unemployment or hypothermia among the elderly, it is obviously useful for social planners to have information about the incidence of these problems. These data can also help them to measure the impact of their policies on these problems. By using official data, they can see whether the incidence of these problems has declined and assess whether their plans have contributed to this reduction.

Social statistics are useful not only in their own right as *measures* of particular events but as *indicators* of broader social conditions. For example, a particular educational datum, such as the literacy rate, not only provides specific information about the number of people who can read or write but alludes to educational standards in the community as a whole. Similarly, the infant mortality rate not only tells social planners about the number of infant deaths but provides an indication about health conditions in general. Because social planners are concerned not only with planning the social services but with bringing about improvements in levels of living and social welfare in society, they are particularly interested in the use of official statistics as indicators of broader social conditions. Different aspects of social welfare such as health, education and housing are very difficult to measure directly and it is for this reason that social planners frequently use social statistics as social indicators to obtain insights into levels of welfare among the population as a whole. However, it should be noted at the outset that the term social indicators is not always used in this way and that many writers as well as planners and administrators use it to refer to any useful or relevant social statistic. This point will be discussed again later but first it will be useful to have some background information about the historical development of social statistics and indicators.

The development of social statistics and indicators

Social scientists and governments alike have long been concerned with the measurement of social conditions. Public record keeping and the employment of bureaucracies of scribes to record the activities of governments is as old as the ancient civilisations. Enumerations or censuses of the population for various purposes including taxation and military conscription were often undertaken in the ancient world. The first censuses in modern times were also partly motivated by the wish to obtain information for specific rather than routine demographic and other purposes. De Neufville (1975) reported, for example, that the first American census was undertaken primarily to establish electoral registers and that supporters of the unsuccessful English Census Bill of 1753 argued that it would help to determine how many citizens could be recruited into military service in the event of war. Similar justifications for the collection of social statistics had been made previously by Petty in England and Conring in Germany, both of whom believed that statistical record keeping or 'political arithmetic', as Petty called it, would aid government to promote trade or improve the nation's military capabilities.

The development of social statistics was greatly fostered by the eventual acceptance of the idea that censuses should be undertaken at regular intervals to collect information about the population and about social and economic conditions, and not only to obtain information for immediate purposes. Iceland pioneered routine census taking during the eighteenth century and this example was followed by most European countries as well as the United States during the nineteenth century. Another important development was the introduction of official population registration procedures. Baptisms, marriages and funerals had been recorded in parish registers for many years, but it was only when Sweden introduced compulsory registration in the eighteenth century that the state formalised these procedures and began to collect this information centrally. Although the English Bill of

1753 contained a proposal for the compulsory registration of births and deaths, it was almost a hundred years later in 1837 when the General Register Office was established, that this was done.

The ancient art of record keeping developed rapidly in the nineteenth century as governmental organisations began systematically to collect and publish large amounts of statistical information. As De Neufville (1975) observed, a variety of official statistics including data about mineral production, land sales and the acreage devoted to different crops were readily available in the United States at this time. Similar statistics were being compiled in Europe. Previously, the French revolutionary government had actively promoted the collection of statistical information and in the early decades of the nineteenth century, the French took the lead publishing a large number of data on, for example, crime, education, marriages and suicide. These were known as 'moral statistics' and were sufficiently well developed to permit Guerry, an official at the statistical office in Paris to publish a detailed compendium of social statistics in 1833; it attracted widespread attention and greatly facilitated empirical social science investigation.

Although it had long been argued that statistics should be collected for purposes of social science enquiry, it was during the nineteenth century that social scientists made frequent use of official data in their research. Previously, seventeenth century proponents of political arithmetic such as Petty had suggested that the 'sinfulness' of a nation could be measured by calculating the amount spent on alcohol or by recording the number of criminals sentenced by the courts (Cazes, 1972). Bentham made a similar proposal in 1778, advocating the collection of criminal statistics since, he argued, they comprised 'a kind of political barometer' of a country's moral health (Avison, 1972). Although incomplete, population data were used by Malthus in his dismal formulation of a general theory of population growth.

Among the many attempts to employ social statistics in social science enquiry during the nineteenth century, those of Quételet and Durkheim are perhaps the best known. Quételet was an ardent advocate of statistical measurement and among his many empirical studies was a major inductive analysis of European crime statistics which rivalled Guerry's work and related the incidence of crime to age, sex, education, occupation and place of residence. Although he reached some quaint conclusions, such as the notion that crime is related to climatic conditions, many of his findings still apply today. Durkheim's study of suicide is regarded as a major work by modern sociologists not only because of its careful use of statistics and its integration of fact and theory, but because of its wider contribution to sociological knowledge. During the twentieth century, the use of social statistics in sociological research increased rapidly and was actively encouraged by many sociologists, particularly neo-positivists such as Lundberg, Chapin and Ogburn. As Carley (1981) pointed out, Ogburn was an active proponent of the collection of government social statistics and an influential adviser to the Hoover administration on these matters in the late 1920s and early 1930s.

Social statistics were also employed for purposes of formulating government social policies in the nineteenth century; in England, for example, Chadwick and the Webbs made as much use as they could of existing official data. Social statistics were also employed to publicise social conditions for philanthropic purposes in much the same way as Booth and Rowntree's surveys had set out to do. Statistics of the incidence of epidemic diseases, of the number of children employed in factories and of the extent of poor relief not only motivated but armed philanthropists during the nineteenth century. But it was only in the 1920s that an American Presidential Committee, appointed by the Hoover administration, attempted the first thorough examination of the role of social statistics in social policy making. In 1933, after lengthy deliberation, the Committee published a major document entitled *Recent Social Trends* which, reflecting Ogburn's influence, suggested ways of using social statistics in formulating social policies to deal with rapid social change. It also discussed issues such as confidentiality, the standardisation of measurements and the storage and retrieval of data. Although De Neufville (1975) observed that this report had little direct impact, it laid the foundations for subsequent developments in the field.

A major revival of interest in the use of social statistics took place in the United States in the 1960s. One reason for this was the publication of a collection of articles entitled *Social Indicators* (Bauer, 1966) which evolved from a study of the social effects of the American space programme undertaken by the American Academy of Arts and Sciences for NASA, the National Aeronautics and Space Administration. The researchers found that there were numerous methodological problems in attempting to measure these effects and the essays were an attempt to resolve some of them. In addition to discussing these problems, the book succeeded in popularising the term social indicators. A second reason for a revival of interest in social measurement was the appointment of a team of social scientists in the Department of Health, Education and Welfare in 1966 to study the impact of the Johnson administration's 'War on Poverty'. This was to be done through the systematic collection and analysis of social data and in 1967, legislation was enacted to establish procedures for this purpose. In 1969, members of the team published an important document entitled *Towards a Social Report* which called for the further development of social indicators comparable to those providing information about the economy.

These events attracted considerable international attention and facilitated the development of social indicator research in Europe where, as Cazes (1972) noted, the use of official data had been neglected. At this time efforts were also being made to develop appropriate social indicators of Third World development and particularly to find an alternative measure to the ubiquitous GNP per capita which many regarded as inappropriate and misleading. This research was pioneered by the United Nations which had begun publishing social statistics as well as reports on the measurement of levels of living in the 1950s. It also commissioned its Research Institute for Social Development in Geneva to formulate a comprehensive methodology for the measurement of socio-economic development. Various reports on socio-economic indicators, associated with the work of Drewnowski and McGranahan, were published by the Institute (Baster, 1972) and they were complemented by numerous other studies of indicators of levels of living (Adelman and Morris, 1967; OECD, 1976; Morris, 1979).

By the mid-1970s, many governments were collecting and publishing social statistics as well as more detailed social reports which are official publications consisting of useful or interesting social statistics. Carley (1981) noted that these reports are now a major element in social indicator research. The British report, *Social Trends*, first appeared in 1970 and three years later similar documents were issued in France, Germany, Japan and the United States; by 1976, thirty countries had published reports of this kind. More detailed analyses of the methodology of social indicators were also undertaken in the late 1960s and early 1970s; in addition to the work of Bauer and his colleagues, these included studies by Sheldon and Moore (1968), Duncan (1969), Campbell and Converse (1972). A journal, devoted exclusively to social indicators, entitled *Social Indicator Research*, was also established.

The nature of social indicators

Although the development of social statistics and social indicators has been impressive, many experts would agree with Carley's (1981) assessment that researchers in the field have often been over-confident and that the expectations of what indicators could achieve have not always been fulfilled. Apart from the questionable reliability of data collection procedures in many countries and the problems of compiling and presenting these data, the use of social statistics to measure social conditions has been fraught with difficulties. The most obvious problem is that, in spite of a great deal of research and debate, there is, as Moser (1978, p. 206) put it, 'no agreed definition of social indicators'. Although some of the problems of defining indicators are no more than a reflection of semantic difficulties, others reveal the considerable methodological problems involved in measuring social welfare.

Several authorities have suggested that social indicators must be clearly distinguished from *measures* or what social scientists call *operational definitions*. When undertaking research, social scientists use concepts, which are abstract constructs alluding to real phenomena. These are translated into acceptable or standardised operational definitions which permit the quantification, measurement and application of concepts to empirical enquiry. The operational definition must be a reliable, manageable and valid representation of the concept and an accurate measure of the actual conditions, events or phenomena in the real world which the social scientist is seeking to study. Many social statistics are useful operational definitions or measures. For example, the population per physician ratio is a widely recognised measure of the availability of medical personnel in a country. Similarly, the educational enrolment rate is a useful measure of the number of children who are in the educational system. However, as noted previously, these measures can be used also as surrogates or proxies for what Carley (1981) called 'unmeasurable' social concepts such as health, welfare, education or development. Social statistics are in themselves operational definitions of particular events or phenomena but when they are used, as McGranahan (1972) noted 'to point to something else', they are called indicators.

As noted previously, this distinction is not always recognised and the term is often used as a synonym for a social statistic. It is also not clear from the literature whether particular social statistics are being used as measures or indicators. For example, statistics on educational attainment, which report on the educational qualifications of people, may be regarded as a sufficiently valid operational definition to obviate the need for indicators. This is the case also with the urbanisation rate which is a measure of the proportion of the population living in areas designated as urban. It appears from the literature that it is not used as an indicator but as an actual operational definition of urbanisation even though it is frequently associated with other measures relevant to the study of urbanisation.

There are difficulties also with the idea that social indicators are based on social statistics obtained from censuses, registration or the routine collection of information by government agencies. Although most indicators are collected in this way, it should be recognised that data collected through social surveys (which are described in chapter 3) are often used as indicators. Demographic, housing, educational and income distribution statistics are frequently obtained through sample surveys but they feature prominently in the literature on indicators and in government social reports as well.

Another problem concerns the delineation of social as opposed to economic indicators. In the 1960s, many investigators were motivated by a desire to develop a set of distinctive indicators which would measure social as opposed to economic conditions. Although they have been largely successful in finding social statistics which are particularly relevant for social policy purposes and which can be employed usefully as indicators of social conditions, the distinction between social and economic indicators is not always clear. GNP per capita which is an economic measure of the value of the goods and services produced by an economy per head of population is also widely used as a measure of levels of living. Although its use as a social indicator has been severely criticised, it remains, as Hardiman and Midgley (1982, p. 36) observed, 'a convenient, comprehensive and available, albeit crude indicator both of economic and social conditions.' Another example is the rate of residential construction which is widely used as an indicator of housing but it is clearly also a measure of economic conditions. This is true of many other indicators as well; some such as the unemployment rate are very difficult to classify. This problem has been complicated even further by the identification of additional categories of indicators such as those relating to political matters (Taylor, 1972).

There is disagreement also about the normative character of social indicators. The idea that they are measures of 'good' or 'bad' states is contained in many definitions in the literature but it has been argued that these notions reflect subjective value judgements; also what may be regarded as 'good' under certain circumstances may not be applicable in others. One example of this problem is the frequent use of population per hospital bed ratios in poor Third World countries. Although it may be a useful measure of 'good' health conditions in the industrial countries, this may not be the case in developing countries since the concentration of health resources on hospital facilities usually implies a neglect of more pressing rural health problems which can best be dealt with through preventive and public health programmes.

It would be difficult to resolve these difficulties and to reach a concise definition of social indicators which will be acceptable to most authorities. This will not be attempted here and instead the term will be used in a general way to refer to social statistics (derived from various sources) which provide information useful for social policy and planning purposes. While this description is not intended to be a comprehensive or authoritative definition of social indicators, it is compatible with the formal definitions proposed by many leading authorities on the subject. Although indicators should, strictly speaking, not be confused with social statistics, common usage will be followed here and the term will be used as a loose synonym for social statistics which are relevant to the social planner's task.

Types of social indicators

Social statistics and social indicators may be classified in many different ways. They may, for example, be grouped in terms of their origins to distinguish between those obtained from censuses and registration procedures and those which are collected routinely by government organisations in the course of their work; another category includes statistics obtained from sample surveys. Social indicators are frequently classified in terms of their uses in social policy and planning. They may, for example, be grouped into those which provide information about resources and those which refer to performance and targets. Indicators may also be categorised in terms of the level at which they are applied. Many indicators are employed at the national or macro level to refer to social conditions in a country as a whole but they may also be employed at the state, provincial or county level or even at the level of the local community. Another method of classifying social indicators is to distinguish between disaggregated and aggregated or composite indicators. This is an important distinction which refers to the use of separate social indicators on the one hand and a single index on the other which is comprised of a combination of separate social indicators.

Several authorities have argued that the technique of combining separate indicators is a more useful method of measuring social conditions than that of comparing a variety of different indicators. For example, they argue that different social measures of education or health or crime can be combined into a composite index which measures these phenomena more accurately than the crude comparison of separate social statistics by social planners. They also claim that the index is more useful than the single representative indicator; this is a third commonly used method to measure social concepts and is based on the idea that a single measure such as a school attainment datum or urbanisation rate are operational definitions of particular social phenomena.

The technique of devising a composite indicator or index involves a complete set of procedures including the method of weighting its different components. This is designed to combine the various social statistics which comprise the index in a way which accurately reflects their importance or, as Carley (1981) put it, their differential contribution. By weighting, the researcher ensures that the index is not distorted by the excessive influence of one or more of its component parts.

Although there are many examples of composite indicators in the literature, the most difficult and challenging work has been done in the field of measuring levels of living or 'social welfare' in the broadest meaning of the term. Much of this research was pioneered by the United Nations Research Institute in Geneva where investigators sought to invent a unitary measure of social well-being which could be used to compare levels of living between countries. As noted previously, these efforts were associated with the work of Drewnowski and McGranahan and their colleagues, both of whom devised composite indicators based on a very large number of social statistics which were collected by UNRISD over the years. These provided information about many countries, both in the industrial and developing worlds, and included data on life expectancy, newspaper circulation, electricity consumption, primary and secondary school enrolment, urbanisation, animal protein and calorie consumption, agricultural production and many more (Baster, 1972). A more recent and less ambitious attempt to devise a composite index of welfare is that of Morris (1979); known as the Physical Quality of Life Index, or PQLI, it is based on just three basic social statistics – life expectancy, infant mortality and literacy and it has enjoyed a measure of success.

The composite index approach is attractive, but many experts have taken the view that it involves so many methodological problems that its usefulness is limited. As long ago as 1954, a United Nations committee on social statistics concluded that the measurement of welfare could best be approached by examining separate social statistics rather than seeking to devise composite indices. Although UNRISD did not agree with this conclusion, it is clear, as Drewnowski (1970) revealed, that the technical problems of constructing a unitary measure of complex concepts such as 'level of living' and 'social welfare' are formidable. For this reason, many social planners continue to rely on disaggregated indicators which are relevant to their work. Although they sometimes employ just one representative indicator, it is more common for more than one to be used in conjunction with other relevant indicators. For example, a measure of educational attainment, which can be used as a representative indicator of education, is normally employed with school enrolment and adult literacy rates; similarly, the urbanisation rate, which is a representative indicator of urbanisation, is normally used in conjunction with urban growth rates and statistics about the numbers of towns and cities in a country.

Today, most governments have collected a large number of separate social statistics which are used as social indicators. Some are also employed to provide information about economic conditions. Some of these indicators are particularly relevant to the planning and administration of the social services while others are concerned with wider social conditions. Examples of the former include health, education and housing statistics while those of broader significance include measures of income distribution and demographic conditions. Some can be used interchangeably. Although it is beyond the scope of this chapter to describe, let alone discuss, the many social statistics and indicators which are relevant to social planning, Tables 2.1 to 2.5 list some of them. These lists or groups of indicators refer to just some of the major concerns in social planning; some are particularly relevant in the field of social service planning while others relate to issues of broader relevance such as poverty, income distribution and levels of living. Another relevant group provides important demographic data necessary for planning purposes.

Most of these indicators are based on simple enumerations: the numbers of children enrolled at primary schools, the numbers of births and deaths, and the number of people living in towns and cities are examples of enumerations which are used as social statistics. Of course, the enumerations may not refer to people but to events, such as the number of vaccinations undertaken, or to facilities, such as the number of residential dwellings owned by the state. Monetary data are also used as indicators both as measures of income and as budgetary statistics. Although social indicators are often published in a simple numerical form, they are frequently expressed as rates and especially as percentages. For example, information about urbanisation is usually given as a percentage of a country's population living in towns and cities. Many

Table 2.1 Commonly used demographic indicators

Measures of population size and growth
Size of population

Crude birth rate
Fertility rate
Crude death rate
Rate of natural increase

Net migration

Total population growth rate

Age sex ratios

Life expectancy at birth

Measures of population distribution
Population size
Population density

Net migration

Level of urbanisation
Urban–rural distribution

Urban–rural population growth rates
Rural to urban migration

Number of towns/cities over specified size

Table 2.2   **Commonly used social indicators of poverty**

Direct measures
Proportion of the population below
  official national poverty line
  other poverty line(s)

Number of recipients of social assistance benefits

Relative income shares of different income groups
Gini coefficient (or other indices) of income distribution

Indirect measures
Per capita national income
Growth of per capita national income

Life expectancy at birth
Infant mortality rate

Calorie consumption per capita
Animal protein consumption per capita

Unemployment rate

Adult literacy
School enrolment rates

Proportion of population with access to safe drinking water

Proportion of the labour force employed in industry
Contribution of industry to Gross Domestic Product
Level of urbanisation

Physical Quality of Life Index
Drewnowski Welfare Index

---

demographic data are also presented as rates but some, such as those relating to births and deaths, are conventionally expressed per thousand of population and not as percentages; on the other hand, natural population increase, which is the difference between the crude birth and death rates, is given as a percentage. Ratios such as the number of pupils per teacher and arithmetic averages such as the average number of rooms per dwelling are also used. A common practice is for social statistics to be disaggregated by gender, age or other relevant categories. For example, in addition to overall mortality, information about infant and child mortality is often provided. Life expectancy is normally estimated for men and women separately as well as the population as a whole. Another common practice is for national statistical data to be broken down by different types of administrative areas such as states or provinces or municipalities.

Table 2.3   Commonly used social indicators of education

Measures of educational conditions
Proportion of the population
   without formal schooling
   with partial/complete primary, secondary
   and tertiary education

Adult literacy rate

Primary/secondary school enrolment rates
Numbers of students in tertiary educational institutions
Numbers of students in private schools
Increases in educational enrolment
Number of newspapers in circulation

Measures of educational facilities
Number of primary and secondary schools, colleges, universities, etc.
Number of private and public educational facilities

Average size of primary and secondary school classes

Teacher–pupil ratios
Lecturer–student ratios

Measures of educational expenditures
Private and public educational expenditure as a proportion of GNP
Public educational expenditure as a proportion of GNP
Public educational expenditure as a proportion of total public expenditure
Per capita public educational expenditure

Social indicators and the social planning process

As may be seen from the way the indicators in the tables have been categorised, they have different potential applications in social planning. Some allude to existing social conditions while others provide information about resources. These different uses have been recognised by various writers such as Carlisle (1972), Brand (1978) and Carley (1981), all of whom have suggested ways in which social indicators can be employed at different stages of the policy-making process.

It was argued in chapter 1 that many ideal-typical accounts of the planning process as a simple, linear sequence of stages are an over-simplification of the complex procedures involved in planning. Nevertheless, they are helpful in demonstrating how social indicators can be used by planners. These descriptions usually point out that planning begins with the definition of the planning problem and that this is followed by the formulation of a policy designed to solve the problem; different policies are evaluated and the optimal one is programmed for implementation over time. The implementation of the plan is

Table 2.4 Commonly used social indicators of health

Measures of health conditions
Morbidity (prevalence) rates by type of disease

Mortality rates
    Crude death rate
    Infant mortality rate
    Child mortality rate
    Other age specific mortality rates
    Mortality by cause of death

Life expectancy
    at birth
    at other ages

Measures of medical facilities
Population per hospital bed ratios
Number of hospital beds

Number of
    hospitals by type of hospital
    health centres
    other health facilities

Number of
    medical schools
    nursing schools
    dental schools

Population per
    physician ratios
    nurse
    dentist
    midwife etc.

Number of medical personnel trained per annum by type of personnel

Measures of public health and nutrition
Proportion of children vaccinated against common diseases

Proportion of population with access to safe drinking water
Proportion of dwellings with sanitary facilities by type of facility

Calorie consumption per capita
Animal protein consumption per capita

Measures of health expenditure
Private and public health expenditure as a proportion of GNP
Public health expenditure as a proportion of GNP
Public health expenditure as a proportion of total public expenditure
Per capita public health expenditure

Table 2.5   Commonly used social indicators of housing

Measures of housing conditions
Occupancy rates
Average number of rooms per dwelling

Number of dwellings by type (housing stock)

Proportion of dwellings with
  piped water
  electricity
  flush toilets
  indoor baths, etc.

Proportion of dwellings declared unfit for habitation

Proportion of the urban population living in slums and squatter settlements

Measures of housing facilities
Residential construction rate

Public residential construction rate
Public housing stock

Measures of housing expenditure
Residential construction as a proportion of GNP
Public housing expenditure as a proportion of GNP
Public housing expenditure as a proportion of public expenditure
Per capita public housing expenditure

---

monitored and its success is evaluated at the completion of the plan period. Indicators can be used at different stages of this process and are helpful because they operationalise and quantify different elements in the planning field.

Information indicators are useful at the outset of the planning sequence because they describe the social system in general terms and provide social planners with a broad understanding of the community in which they are working. The demographic and poverty indicators shown in the tables are just two examples of this type of descriptive social indicator but there are many others which enlighten social planners and give them valuable insights into prevailing social and economic conditions.

Planning problem indicators are also descriptive but they provide specific information about the nature and extent of the immediate problem with which the social planner is concerned. As Brand (1978) suggested, it would be very difficult to formulate a housing policy if there were no statistical information about existing housing conditions. Indicators such as occupancy rates, waiting lists for public housing and the number of homes without basic amenities are some examples of planning problem indicators which are used in formulating housing policies. When used in conjunction with information indicators, they permit a better understanding and relatively more precise formulation of the problem.

Resource indicators provide information about the resources which are used in the planning process. As Carley (1981) observed, they are also known as input measures and provide information about monetary as well as personnel resources. Data about budgetary allocations and expenditure are needed at both the plan formulation and the implementation stages and are also used to evaluate the effectiveness of a plan. Personnel statistics such as population per physician or pupil–teacher ratios are also used in these ways.

Performance indicators refer to particular programme achievements such as the number of vaccinations undertaken by paramedical staff or the number of home visits made by social workers. They are also sometimes referred to as throughput measures. They may, in certain cases, be used as *target indicators* or measures of the achievement of a plan when the plan has been designed from the outset to achieve a defined improvement in performance. For example, measures of improvements in school enrolment or the number of public dwellings constructed may be used as indicators of the attainment of targets if these were defined as the objectives of the plan. On the other hand, improvements in performance may not have a significant impact on the problem the planners are seeking to remedy. For example, improvements in the frequency of visits made by a mobile child health team in a developing country may not reduce infant mortality if nutritional standards do not improve at the same time. In this case it is misleading to use performance indicators as a measure of achievement. Resource indicators are sometimes also used as target indicators because it is assumed that the allocation of more money and personnel to a programme will improve results. But this is not always the case and most authorities insist that quite separate measures of achievement be employed.

Target indicators are also known as output measures and are actual measures of the achievement of a plan. Since they are often used to measure changes in the conditions originally defined as the planning problem, the same indicators are often employed. Typically they measure changes in literacy or the prevalence of a contagious disease or a decline in the fertility rate brought about, respectively by an educational, health and family planning programme. Target indicators are sometimes used in conjunction with *impact indicators* which, as Brand (1978) pointed out, are employed to assess the total impact of social plans on the community and not only their intended consequences.

As may be seen, these different indicators can be used interchangeably at different stages of the planning process. This is particularly relevant at the outset of the plan when various indicators are used to define problems, set targets and link particular inputs and outputs within the framework of a predictive model adopted for policy formulation purposes. When used in this way, they should be known, as Carlisle (1972) suggested, as *predictive indicators* since they help planners to assess causal relationships, anticipate future events and predict the consequences of using particular resources in a particular way. It is for this reason that they play an important role in applying planning techniques such as cost-benefit analysis and planning budgeting systems.

The following case study material is not intended to describe all the applications of social indicators to social planning and policy-making but will, hopefully, provide some insights into their use in practical situations. Firstly, several illustrative examples are provided to show how social indicators have been used in Britain; these deal, for example, with the role of social indicators in the designation of educational priority areas, the allocation of central government grants to local authorities and the distribution of health resources between different regions. Secondly, an example is given of the use of social indicators in national health service planning in India.

The use of social indicators in Britain
We may consider as an example a hypothetical social planning process, namely, the planning of a programme designed to reduce poverty in Britain. Such a programme would need to be planned in relation to the extent and nature of poverty. The first need would therefore be for *information indicators* on the distribution of the population in terms of economic circumstances and incomes. The Census collects information on economic status (employed, unemployed, retired and on occupation and industry), but it may be several years out of date, and in Britain no income information is collected. Sample surveys carried out by the government (such as the Family Expenditure Survey and the General Household Survey) collect income information to provide an overall description of the distribution of incomes. For an anti-poverty programme more specific *planning problem indicators* are needed which provide a measure or indication of the extent of poverty: this requires a definition of 'poverty' and a source of data; while general sample surveys may provide such data, the number of very low income respondents may be small so that sampling errors may be large; to improve the accuracy of the estimate the sample may be stratified to over-represent low income households or a special survey only for low income households may be carried out (such as the Family Finances Survey). *Resource indicators* which show the resources currently

devoted to social security and income maintenance are obtainable from operational statistics or budgeting documents (Social Security Statistics or Public Expenditure White Papers). Alternatively, the resources available for the programme may be specified and budgeted separately so that the resource indicator need not be based on existing resources. In planning a new programme it is clearly necessary to assess the performance of existing programmes. *Performance indicators* might be of several types. They might show the number benefiting under existing programmes, which can be derived from operational statistics; or they might show the proportion of this total who are eligible for benefiting from an existing programme organised in a certain way, which might be based on the analysis of survey data. When the new programme is planned, it will be desirable to monitor its effectiveness by devising *target* or *impact indicators*. In order to plan the programme into the future, *predictive indicators* may be used to estimate the changing extent of the planning problem. Demographic changes, such as an increase in elderly people, may *ceteris paribus* increase poverty; forecasts of demographic changes are prepared by the Office of Population Censuses and Surveys. Changes in the economy, such as in the level of unemployment, are another major influence on poverty; forecasts of future unemployment are produced by the Treasury and may, with caution, be used as a predictive indicator.

Having considered a hypothetical example, we may turn to some practical applications of the use of social indicators in Britain for social planning; these examples involve decision-making and resource allocation in the fields of education, local government and health.

The first example concerns Educational Priority Areas. A review of primary education recommended positive educational discrimination in favour of areas 'where educational hardships are reinforced by social handicaps' (Plowden, 1967). The Inner London Education Authority attempted to develop appropriate objective criteria; these included:

1. Occupation: the proportion of occupied males in skilled or semi-skilled jobs;
2. Supplements in cash from the State: the proportion of children receiving free meals;
3. Overcrowding of houses;
4. Lack of basic housing amenities;
5. Poor attendance at school;
6. Proportion of handicapped pupils;
7. Proportion of immigrant children;
8. Teacher turnover;
9. Pupil turnover.

These measures were combined using a complex scaling procedure to identify which schools should be given educational priority (see Little and Mabey, 1972).

The second example concerns the allocation of central government funds to local authorities through the rate support grant. This grant has been modified many times for many reasons, most recently to try and control local authorities' expenditure. Under the system operative in the 1970s part of the grant was determined according to a 'needs element': among other factors the following social indicators were used to assess variation in need (Jackson and Sellars, 1977):

1. Number of primary school pupils;
2. Number of secondary or special school pupils, aged under 16 years;
3. Number of secondary or special school pupils, aged over 16 years;
4. Number attending direct grant grammar schools, aged under 16 years;
5. Number attending direct grant grammar schools, aged over 16 years;
6. Number of students, full-time or full-time equivalent, attending establishments of further education;
7. Number of pensionable age living alone;
8. Number of persons aged 65 years or over;
9. Number of lone-parent families with dependent children;
10. Number of persons unemployed and registered for employment;
11. Number living in permanent households, where density of occupation is greater than $1\frac{1}{2}$ persons per room;
12. Number living in households, without exclusive use of basic amenities;
13. Number of new permanent dwellings (public and private);
14. Number living in shared households in permanent buildings.

A third illustrative application comes from the health field. In an attempt to provide a fairer distribution of resources between health regions, social indicators were used to assess the relative needs of each region. The estimates of need took account of:

1. Population, taking account of age and sex;
2. Variations in the incidence of particular health conditions;
3. Differences in the use of health service for treating particular conditions;
4. Movements of patients across regional boundaries.

In this way, through a complex formula, the relative needs of each health region were estimated (United Kingdom, 1976a).

All these three practical applications may be – and have been – criticised. But they are attempts to use social indicators as objective criteria to assist in social planning.

Social indicators and health planning in India

Although procedures for statistical record keeping have now been established in most developing countries, considerably more data are available to social planners in India than in many other Third World nations. Censuses have been undertaken for many years and routine data collection has become increasingly sophisticated and reliable. Indian planners believe that statistical information is of great importance in their work: because of the immensity of the country's social problems, its huge population of about 700 million people and heterogeneity, accurate data are a necessary element in the planning process.

Centralised economic and social planning has been a major function of the Indian government since independence from Britain. Impressed by central economic planning in the Soviet Union, where it was introduced in the 1920s, India's first Prime Minister, Nehru, actively promoted central planning. The Planning Commission, which was established to prepare national development plans was given a considerable degree of authority and since 1951 it has formulated a succession of five-year development plans dealing both with economic and social questions.

India's Sixth Five Year Plan came into effect in 1980 and will guide the nation's economic and social development efforts until 1985. Among the many issues dealt with in the plan is health. The government's health service policies are described and these are linked to policies for the provision of clean drinking water, sanitation, nutrition and family planning as well as broader social and economic policies designed to deal with poverty. As the plan (India, 1980, p. 368) pointed out: 'An attack on diseases cannot be entirely successful unless it is accompanied by an attack on poverty itself.' Although these policies are described in the plan, it is not possible because of limitations of space to review them in this chapter; instead, the use of indicators in the provision of direct medical services will be described.

Social statistics are freely employed in the plan's account of the government's health service policies. However, it notes that the government's health information system is still inadequate and that one of the plan's targets is to strengthen health care data collection procedures. *Information* and *planning problem indicators* are used at the outset to review the country's health conditions and facilities; these consist of demographic data as well as statistics about existing services and morbidity. The plan reports that life expectancy at birth for men and women was 52 and 53 years respectively, that the crude death rate was 14.2 per 1000 and that infant mortality was 129 per 1000. A considerable amount of statistical information about existing services is provided. The country has 106 medical schools and teaching hospitals, about 500,000 hospital beds, 55,000 primary health centres or clinics and a population per physician ratio which varied from 1400 per doctor in New Delhi to 8300 per doctor in one of the country's predominantly rural and poorest states. Morbidity data are provided for certain diseases such as leprosy and tuberculosis and these reveal that there were some 3.2 million and 7 million people affected with these diseases respectively in the late 1970s.

Although there have been considerable improvements since the 1950s, the plan noted that these conditions and facilities are far from satisfactory and that further efforts will be made during the plan period to deal with them. Its major health service strategy is to expand health facilities in the rural areas where health problems have long been neglected even though they are the most pressing. Together with water supply, sanitation, nutrition, family planning and other policies and programmes, this strategy will, it is hoped, facilitate the attainment of the plan's objective which is to improve health conditions among the population and to provide better access to health care facilities.

Indicators are used explicitly to formulate targets for the attainment of these objectives. Firstly, the plan employs certain *performance indicators* as *target indicators*. It reveals, for example, that the number of health centres which are located chiefly in the rural areas will be increased to 96,000 and that these will cover 74 per cent of the population. *Resource indicators* are occasionally also used as *target indicators* in the plan; it reveals, for example, that one of its objectives is to increase the number of primary health workers from 140,000 in 1980 to 360,000 in 1985. Independent *target indicators* are also used although cautiously. Although the plan anticipates that its policies will lead to a reduction in mortality and an increase in life expectancy, no targets are set for the end of the plan period but rather for the year 2000 when, it is hoped, infant mortality will have fallen to 60 per 1000 and the crude death rate to 9 per 1000; it is also hoped that life expectancy will have increased to 64 years for both men and women.

Indicators about the *resources* to be used to achieve these targets deal with both money and personnel. Statistics concerning the use of primary health workers have been given already and reveal the plan's intention to make as much use as possible of locally recruited personnel and community involvement. In addition to training local health workers, villagers will be organised to participate actively in health programmes and particularly in those which are of a preventive nature. The country's 106 medical schools, which train approximately 11,000 doctors per year, will not be expanded and instead, more emphasis will be placed on improving the quality of medical education and encouraging a greater concern with rural health problems in the curriculum. The plan also provides detailed health budgetary allocation figures which show how much will be spent on rural health services, hospitals, medical education and the control of infectious diseases.

As this brief account has attempted to show, social indicators form an integral part of health service planning in India. A variety of indicators ranging from *information* and *planning problem indicators* to *target indicators* have been used. Also, it may be seen how certain indicators are used interchangeably; in addition to the use of *performance* and *resource indicators* as *target indicators*, measures such as infant mortality and life expectancy have been used both to identify health conditions at the outset of the plan and to define its objectives. Although imperfect, these social statistics have made a useful contribution to the social planning process in India.

The limitations of social indicators

Although social statistics and indicators play an important role in social planning, there are several difficulties associated with their use. Some of these need to be discussed so that the limitations of indicators in social planning can be taken into account. Some have been mentioned already when the conceptual and methodological characteristics of social indicators were described. Apart from the fact that there is no standardised definition of the term indicators, the methodological problems of measuring social phenomena are considerable. This problem is exacerbated by an inadequate body of knowledge which will supply a suitable theoretical framework for the use of these measures. Although, as Moser (1978) pointed out, statistical measures are more meaningful if applied within a suitable theoretical model which links different measures to each other in a coherent system, models for the use of social indicators are poorly developed.

The use of social indicators is seriously handicapped in many countries by problems of data collection. Although most developing countries have enacted legislation establishing population registration procedures, it is widely recognised that they grossly under-report the number of births and deaths. Census results are also suspect, especially in countries where populations are widely dispersed and levels of literacy are low. Routine data collection procedures in government departments are frequently neglected or inaccurate. Problems of unreliable data are, however, not to be found only in the Third World but in the industrial countries as well. Just one example is the problem of measuring income which, as most authorities recognise, is exceedingly difficult since many respondents in household income studies do not provide accurate information either because they do not know exactly what their incomes are or because they are reluctant to disclose them. Problems of this kind are often overlooked by social planners who are excessively enthusiastic about using statistical data in their work.

A similar problem is the unnecessary collection of statistical data. From the vast quantities of statistics that are eagerly amassed by some social planners it would appear that statistical information is required for its own sake. Many government organisations collect large amounts of data or readily commission expensive surveys or other studies even though adequate information is already available. Also, the results of these studies are frequently not used in decision-making. Often the same problem is researched by different investigators who make little use of each other's findings or of other existing data. Over-surveying of deprived communities is counterproductive and wastes resources which could be more usefully employed to establish much needed services.

Another problem with the application of social statistics in social planning is that they are often used to draw the wrong conclusions. Contrary to popular belief, facts do not always speak for themselves and usually need to be interpreted by the research worker. Although the actual data may be accurate, they may be presented or interpreted in ways which are misleading. A good example of this problem comes from the United Nations (1979a) which used housing occupancy rates to reveal that the countries with the highest rates of overcrowding in the world were El Salvador, Morocco and Sri Lanka. However, the report failed to point out that only a small number of countries in the world have published housing statistics and that of these, the highest occupancy rates were found in the countries mentioned. Obviously, there may be others which have higher rates of overcrowding but have not published statistical information on this subject.

Coupled with this is the problem of the deliberate disortion or manipulation of data to provide support for a particular point of view or to defend a particular policy. As Brand (1978) observed, indicators may be presented in such a way as to justify a policy decision or they may be concealed to prevent information about 'difficult' social problems becoming widely known. An example of this is the suppression of census results by governments of several Third World countries because they reveal sensitive information about the relative numerical strengths of different ethnic groups. Similarly, in Glasgow, as Brand (1976) revealed, public officials resisted the disclosure of statistical information about the city's social problems. The use of social indicators thus requires more than a knowledge of statistical bookkeeping and data analysis but calls for integrity and a commitment to broader social ideals among social planners.

3   Social Surveys and Social Planning
Margaret Hardiman

Surveys are frequently used to collect information for planning purposes, and as social planning has gained increasing recognition, so the social survey has become an essential tool in the process. There are many different reasons for undertaking social surveys; they may be used to discover the existing situation, to assess need, or to evaluate the success or failure of a project or programme. They may also be used as a means of consulting users and educating the public. The methods are flexible and can be adapted to cover a wide variety of circumstances in which inferences about populations are required. Surveys may be descriptive, explanatory or analytical, predictive or evaluative. In most cases a survey will cover several of these aspects, and in all cases a certain amount of descriptive material forms a necessary basis. But the distinction is important when considering the main aims of a particular survey.

Although in theory a survey can amount to a complete enumeration this coverage is usually referred to as a census, and the main feature of most surveys is the use of sampling. This means that only a small proportion of the population needs to be covered. Not only is this more economical; it is also more appropriate to in-depth enquiries conducted by trained interviewers, particularly where questions of opinions and attitudes are being investigated. Because a survey can be tailored to fit a specific need it can, if appropriately designed, prove an accurate tool for planners. That this has not always been the case is sadly true, and some of the reasons for this will be discussed in this chapter. First, however, we shall look briefly at the historical development of survey methods before going on to examine the essential characteristics of the survey process. In this section we shall particularly consider the use of these methods in different socio-economic and cultural settings. The two case studies, one from a developing and one from an industrialised society, will further illustrate these points. A final section will assess social survey methods, their uses and limitations for social planners.

The historical development of survey methods
Although records of the study of society are as old as history, the use of a scientific approach is relatively recent. In Britain during the nineteenth century, the fundamental social changes associated with industrialisa-

tion and the rapid growth of towns stimulated an increasing number of empirical studies. The condition of life in towns, particularly for the urban poor, was a matter of concern. One of the best known accounts of this period is Mayhew's *London Life and the London Poor*, and is a work of considerable literary merit. It makes fascinating reading today, as do other surveys of working-class life. They may not possess the methodological sophistication of later surveys, but they offer a wealth of illuminative material and a graphic quality of description often lacking in later studies.

Mayhew's study can be described as pre-scientific; the first researcher in Britain to use a scientific approach was Booth who began his monumental study of poverty in London in 1886. Booth, deeply distressed by the apparent poverty of the working class, set out to discover the nature of their living conditions and asked the questions, 'Who are the poor and why are they poor?' To find answers to these questions, he decided to use school attendance officers to collect information by the method of 'wholesale interviewing'. Although the study was mainly descriptive, he did seek to 'show the numerical relation which poverty, misery and depravity bear to regular earnings and comparative comfort and to describe the general conditions under which each class lives'. From his analysis of the wealth of data collected he constructed eight classes, four of which he designated as being above the poverty line and four below. Although his description lacked precision and was limited by only covering families with children of school age, it did introduce a new technique which was further developed by Rowntree in his first survey of York at the turn of the century.

Booth and Rowntree carried out their surveys before the development of sampling techniques. Their surveys covered all families in the categories studied. It was some years later, in 1912, that Bowley used systematic sampling in Reading in the first of his Five Towns surveys. Based on the analysis of the normal distribution and its relation to the 'law of errors', Bowley showed that a standard deviation calculated from only the sample information can provide a measure of the sample average. This was a major breakthrough in methodology and the greater economy which it allowed led to a further stimulus to the use of surveys, although for many years there was scepticism about the reliability of sampling techniques.

The early surveys mainly concerned working-class life and were carried out by people interested in social reform. They certainly succeeded in raising social consciousness about the deplorable conditions in which the majority of the population lived and in this way they influenced social policy, but they were not especially commissioned for planning purposes. The first field in which this occurred was in town planning in the 1930s, an early example being the survey initiated in

1935 by the Bourneville Village Trust which studied the housing situation in and around Birmingham. A later example was the use by Max Lock, a town planner, of a sociologist, Ruth Glass, when he was commissioned to prepare a master plan for Middlesbrough (Glass, 1948), the particular methodological interest here lying in the sociological concept of neighbourhoods.

The Second World War gave rise to new demands for information and the establishment of the Government Social Survey in Britain in 1941 marked a landmark in the development of survey methods. The range of subjects commissioned by government departments and other official bodies had been extremely wide and has resulted in the refinement of methodologies to cover the many different types of survey required to collect data for policy-making and administration.

In the United States, as in Britain, social surveys developed from studies of social conditions carried out by people concerned with social reform, such as Jacob Riis, who in 1890 published *How the Other Half Lives*, a study of tenement housing conditions in New York. Although much of what these social reformers discovered was vigorously exposed by the press, the influence on social policy was probably less than in Britain because of the prevailing philosophy of rugged individualism (Young, 1956).

The establishment of the Russell Sage Foundation in 1907 marked a new stage in the development of the social survey in the United States. The Foundation shared the concern of earlier practitioners with social conditions, but it also aimed to develop scientific methods of data collection and analysis. Its work stimulated the growth of a new generation of studies. An early example, in which systematic methods were used for the first time in the United States, was the Pittsburgh Survey which was started in 1909. The survey, which was financed and published by the Russell Sage Foundation, studied the effects of urbanisation. Surveys were increasingly accepted as a realistic method of studying American society and by 1928 when a major bibliographic review of social surveys in America was published, no fewer than 2775 titles of projects were listed as having been completed (Young, 1956).

Survey methods have become increasingly popular not only for governments' policy and planning purposes, but also in the fields of market research, political forecasting and public opinion polls and audience research, such as that carried out by the BBC. They are also extensively used in academic research both on an institutional and on an individual basis. All these developments have contributed towards the refinement of methods. Another important advance has been in the improvement of methods of tabulation, culminating in highly sophisticated computer technology, which has served to enlarge the scope of surveys and extend their analytical possibilities.

So far this brief historical outline has concentrated on the development of survey methods in Britain and the United States which has been paralleled in other industrialised countries. To what extent have surveys been used in the Third World, and with what success? Since most developing countries have gone in for comprehensive planning to a greater degree than many of the older industrialised countries, it would seem that their need for the type of information surveys can provide is self-evident. The creation of national statistics offices, moreover, would appear to provide the necessary framework for the use of sampling techniques, and these techniques should have the advantage of being economical in time, labour and cost.

In practice, however, there are few countries which have so far made a coherent use of surveys for planning purposes. The main exception to this is the National Sample Survey which was set up in India in 1951. There are many reasons for this, and given the problems facing the transfer of this particular technology it is perhaps fortunate that progress has not been more rapid. So many of the surveys that have been undertaken, either by individuals or by international agencies, have not sufficiently considered the ethnocentric nature of the questions asked. Even such apparently simple concepts as marital status may be seen very differently in another cultural perspective. This is not to deny the need for more information about conditions in developing countries. It is merely to introduce a word of caution about the methods used and the interpretation of results.

Essential characteristics of the survey process
The planning of a survey demands attention to a series of methodological questions. In this section we consider the essential steps that must be taken, whatever the type of survey and whatever the nature of the individual or team responsible for it. Although the steps are arranged more or less in the order in which they must be considered, some of them take place at the same time or need to be repeated.

The objectives of the survey
The choice of objectives is an obvious start to any exercise, but what is important is that the statement should be clear and precise. What exactly is it that the survey intends to study? A vague intention, for example, to investigate 'poverty in rural areas' does not give sufficient guidance. We need to know what for the purposes of this survey is meant by poverty, and how rural areas are to be defined. If the survey is commissioned by a government department, or voluntary agency, it is essential for the client and the surveyor to have full discussions at this stage about the objectives of the survey and the uses to which it will be put. These discussions should include consideration of whether the

information sought is really necessary, and if so whether a survey is the best means of obtaining it. Casley and Lury (1981) suggest three characteristics which should lead to the rejection of a survey at an early stage, namely the unnecessary survey, where nothing of value to the society is likely to be revealed; the trivial survey, which does little more than confirm well-established knowledge, and the worthy but excessively expensive survey. And there are others. As surveys gain in popularity there is an increasing temptation to rush into them without sufficient thought, and this danger is particularly great in developing countries (Chambers, 1981).

Resources

Alongside the determination of objectives consideration must be given to the resources available. If there is a fixed budget it may be advisable to reduce the amount of information collected rather than extend the survey beyond the limits in which it can operate efficiently. A limited budget can be an advantage as it concentrates the minds of the planners on what is really essential. Far too many surveys ask far too many questions of far too many people. The result is that a mass of data is collected which on the one hand may be poor in quality due to over-lengthy, tiresome or ambiguous questionnaires, or on the other hand is rarely fully or properly analysed.

But there are real and important financial constraints which most planners of surveys have to face. Ideal coverage of the population may be unduly expensive, so that difficult decisions have to be made about how far the survey can aim at reflecting the situation of the people as a whole. Detailed aspects of these decisions are made at a later stage, but even at the outset it is important to look realistically at cost factors and to attempt a rough budget.

As well as money there are resources of time and labour to be considered. An estimate must be made of how long the survey should take and what is the best time of year to conduct it. Where demographic data is being collected there may be variations in the composition of the population at different seasons, for example during holidays, or at the time of seasonal migration. In tropical countries it is often impossible to reach villages during the rainy season; in mountain areas roads may be impassable during the winter. There are times of the year when people are so busy that they are reluctant to be interviewed, such as during planting and harvesting.

The availability of suitable personnel is a critical factor, as so much of the success or failure of the survey will depend on it. If the work is being carried out by a permanent survey body its team will already exist; but even in this case thought should be given to the particular requirements of the exercise in question. It may, for example, be more appropriate to use women interviewers when family planning questions are being asked of women. In developing countries, especially, the sex of the interviewer has to be carefully considered. Another factor is what educational level is thought to be necessary. Where team members are engaged in analysis as well as data collection some numerical expertise will be required. And even for interviewing, literacy is necessary, except perhaps in the simplest possible type of survey where illustrations can be used for recording information.

With *ad hoc* surveys university students are commonly used, and in developing countries much use is also made of secondary school children. Providing they are properly trained and supervised they have proved effective workers. But in rural areas experience has shown that locally recruited personnel can often be more effective. They know the area and the people, and they are less likely to invent answers or put them into the mouths of respondents. They are also more economical to employ.

At this stage, then, the overall decision has to be made about what results can be achieved given the resources available, and a rough time schedule has to be constructed.

Collection of background information: public relations
Before starting to design the survey as much information as possible should be collected about the area of study. Public records offices and libraries are a starting point. Civil servants, local government officials, and voluntary agencies can provide much information in their particular fields. In addition planners of surveys should themselves make a preliminary reconnaissance of the field. They should, for example, spend time walking around the town or visiting villages, observing what is happening and talking to as many people as possible. They should also make sure, at this stage, that the public is informed about the objects of the survey and how and when it is being conducted. These are steps that are not taken in the market research or opinion poll type of survey; but for social surveys for planning purposes the understanding and cooperation of the public is an essential feature, particularly in developing countries. Many instances can be quoted of the success of surveys being jeopardised by interviewers moving into an area without paying attention to public relations. For example, a survey was made of villages in Ghana which it was intended to flood in order to build a reservoir, without the villagers being aware that this proposal existed; the shock and resentment experienced by the people can be imagined, and they were naturally not very willing respondents.

Formulation of the research problem
Having done the preliminary work outlined above, the survey leader

and the team are now in a position to formulate the problem more precisely. This may or may not involve the setting up of hypotheses to be tested. Some studies, for example, set out with certain theories in mind about the existence of relationships, such as, low-income families have on average higher mortality rates; other studies use an entirely empirical approach, the main purpose being to estimate the frequency of certain population characteristics, allowing the subsequent data to reveal relationships. The practical differences between these in terms of formulating the problem are not great, as even where no hypothesis is explicit certain assumptions about relationships are implied in the definition of the problem. Most social surveys for planning purposes are concerned with estimation rather than testing specific hypotheses.

At this stage the detailed information required must be listed. This will consist firstly of variables to be measured, a variable being a characteristic such as age or sex which varies between different members surveyed. Decisions must be made about the form the recording of variables should take; for example, in measuring age is this to be recorded in broad bands such as under 1 year, 1 to 5, 5 to 15, and so forth, or is each year to be recorded separately? If the survey aims at comparisons with other data already collected, such as a census or labour office return, care should be taken at this stage to ensure that the information will be comparable. If there is doubt about how data is to be used it is safer to disaggregate than aggregate; data can always be grouped at a later stage, it cannot easily be separated. For example in collecting data about school enrolment even although total figures may be required it is advisable to break them down by sex in the first instance, or by other variables if these are thought likely to be significant.

Variables can also cover differences in attitudes or opinions. These are notably more difficult to collect and a great deal of thought needs to be given to the meaning of the concepts involved. The problem is complicated when the surveyor comes from a different culture or sub-culture than the respondent. For example in a family planning survey in India, the question 'What do you think is the ideal family size?' was asked, and found incomprehensible by respondents who tended to answer 'It is not for me to judge for other people.' And many opinions regarding whether conditions or services are 'better' or 'worse' are so subjective or abstract as to be meaningless.

This problem leads on to the general consideration of operational definitions. What exactly do we mean by the terms we use, such as household, unemployment, marital status or working class? There are often many different ways in which these concepts can be interpreted and the surveyor must decide which one is most appropriate. Is the household, for example, to be defined in terms of all those sleeping under one roof, or is eating together to be taken into account? Or again, should all those acknowledging a common household head be the criterion? If these decisions are not made before interviewers go into the field they may well follow different definitions, and this will seriously bias the results.

Although questions of processing and analysis are dealt with at a later stage it is important to consider them when the research problem is formulated and before the survey design is undertaken. If another individual or organisation is involved, as is often the case where computers are used, consultation should take place at this stage. It is frustrating to find after data has been collected that it is impossible to process or analyse it adequately because of the form in which it is presented.

Survey design and implementation
It is at this stage that the technical aspects of survey methods using sampling are important. They will be referred to here, but no attempt will be made to cover the theories themselves, and for these the reader is referred to the extensive literature that exists. (See, for example, the bibliographies in Peil, 1982 and Moser and Kalton, 1977.) The basic idea underlying sampling is that we can infer the characteristics of a population by selecting only a proportion of the total. The result cannot be regarded as a statement of fact, as with a census, but as an estimate of probability. Sampling theory deals with the likely accuracy, bias and precision of a sample, how it can be estimated and how the significance of the results can be tested.

(a) The area of operation   The first step is to define the *population* to be covered. Population in this sense means all the units to be studied; it may consist of all the people in a geographical area, or all the people in a particular age or occupational group. The population, or as it is sometimes called, the universe, can also be used to describe livestock or motor cars or other inanimate objects, but in social surveys the human element will always be central.

Having defined the population, *the sampling unit* has to be decided. Is it for example to be the family, the household or the individual? This will depend on the objects of the survey. If it is individual responses which are required then it will not be economical to collect data on the whole household. It may be necessary to use the household as a means of selection in a multi-stage model (see below), but this should not be confused with the sampling unit itself.

The task of defining the population is never as easy as it sounds. In a national survey decisions have to be made as to whether some areas are deliberately excluded because of inaccessibility or sparsity of population. A frequent problem concerns the inclusion, or otherwise, of those living in institutions, such as hospitals, prisons or army barracks. A decision will often have to be made on grounds of convenience as it is on the definition of population that the sampling frame is constructed.

(b) The sampling frame   This is a complete list of all the units of the population to be covered and is the critical tool on which random sampling is based, as the underlying principle of this method is that each unit of the population should have an equal chance of inclusion. If the coverage is not complete or accurate, bias will enter into the sample selection. Even in developed countries which keep up-to-date statistics, and in which street lists and electoral rolls are available, the construction of an adequate sampling frame is difficult. But in developing countries there is often a complete lack of the data necessary to construct a frame. Most frames start from records compiled for other purposes, such as taxation or land registration. They may therefore leave out units that are relevant to a survey being done for another purpose. Social surveys characteristically seek information from households, and the relationship between these and other lists or between dwellings and households is not always clear. In small surveys it may be possible for the team to make their own lists and where this can be done accuracy is more likely. But in extreme cases so little information exists that it may be necessary to abandon random sampling and use quota or purposive sampling instead, that is where once the general breakdown of the sample has been decided the choice of actual sample units is left to the interviewer. Another solution, used mainly in developing countries, is to mark a map of the area with grids and choose, by random methods, a determined number of intersections for selecting the units to be interviewed. For purposes of economy it is usual to cluster the sample by interviewing several units round each of the chosen intersections. Although estimates of the parameter (that is the existence of the characteristic being measured in the entire population) is possible it is likely to be less reliable than with the more usual processes of random sampling.

(c) The type of sample   As is indicated above the selection of the type of sample is to some extent dependent on the available sampling frame. It may not, for example, be possible to choose random methods. Assuming that we have come to a satisfactory solution of this problem and that randomness is possible, there are still several questions to ask. The main ones concern size, whether the sample should be stratified, and whether it should be single or multi-stage.

Common sense suggests that one will get more accurate results from a large sample than from a small one. This is true, but the formula for measuring the standard error of a sample of a population shows that as the size of the sample increases, there is a diminishing return in terms of accuracy. The precision of a sample estimate depends on the spread of the sampling distribution and this can be conveniently measured by its own standard deviation. The appropriate size of a sample also depends on the variability of the units. If for example all the units of population were identical the standard deviation would be zero. The presence of a high degree of heterogeneity therefore suggests the need for a larger sample.

Stratification is another way of increasing the precision of a sample. As with size, decisions depend on prior knowledge of the population's characteristics. If, for example, a national survey is being conducted it is necessary to ensure that different types of area are covered. In this case, before a random sample is taken the country is divided into strata and selection of the sample takes place within each stratum. Other types of stratification may be by sex, age group, occupation and so forth. What is important to consider is the relevance of stratification to the subject of the survey; but even where it is considered relevant there may not be sufficient data available to make use of it in practice. For example, if in a study of women in the labour force it is considered relevant to stratify by type of occupation, this can only be done if data on the distribution of women between occupations exists.

Multi-stage sampling is where the process of selection is carried out in two or more steps. This is a common and useful practice, not least because it leads to greater economy in interviewing as it concentrates efforts on more limited areas. The method involves regarding the population as a whole as being composed of a number of first-stage units, for example regions; each of these may be composed of a number of second-stage units, for example districts. One can proceed to third-stage units, which in this case would be villages and fourth-stage units of households. A sample is then taken of the first-stage units, with or without stratification; then of the second-stage units, again with or without stratification and so on, according to the number of stages used.

Multi-stage sampling has great advantages besides economy where sampling frames are lacking at the unit level. Regions and towns can always be identified, and most countries have lists of sub-divisions of towns or districts. Once the lowest level is reached it is a simpler matter for the surveyor to make his own sampling frame for the final stage of selection.

The next decision is how exactly the random sample is to be taken. The main criterion is that selection must be independent of human judgement. Two basic procedures can be used to ensure randomness; one is the 'lottery method' where all units in the population are represented by a disc, mixed up in a container and drawn, as from a bran tub; the other is the use of specially prepared random tables. Both these are simple random sampling, which ensure that every unit in the population has an equal chance of selection. In practice, however, many surveyors find it more convenient to sample from lists. All the units on the list are numbered and the desired sampling percentage is calculated. The first unit is chosen by random methods and thereafter every *n*th unit is selected. This is not simple random sampling because the systematic selection of units means that not all have an equal chance of being included. It is sometimes called systematic sampling but this meaning can be misleading. It suggests explicit ordering and it is better described as *quasi-random* sampling (Moser and Kalton, 1977). It is generally justified in terms of the list being arranged fairly randomly, and is often reasonably acceptable as equivalent to random sampling. But the surveyor must use this method with caution, noting for example whether the arrangement of houses in an area is such that the selected unit is always at the end of a block, or on the top floor of a building. Such a situation would obviously introduce bias.

(*d*) *The questionnaire*   This is sometimes referred to as a schedule, the term questionnaire being restricted to where the respondents fill in the answer themselves. For our purposes here, however, we shall use questionnaire to cover both types, although the differences between the two are important for design purposes. Although in developed countries questionnaires filled in by respondents are frequently used, including mail questionnaires, this is far less possible in developing countries because of lower levels of literacy and less familiarity with form filling.

A great many difficult decisions have to be made at this stage, even if the question of items to be covered and operational definitions have already been decided. The nature of the respondents will have to be considered. How can questions be phrased so that they will understand the intended meaning? Are they likely to be able to give accurate answers, for example about age? Are some of the questions about sensitive areas which are likely to upset the respondents, thus prejudicing their response to other questions as well? Will respondents know the language in which the questionnaire is written? If not, then it will have to be translated into one or more local languages or an interpreter will have to be employed. If this is done translation is still necessary if standardisation between interviewers is to be achieved. Above all, in this respect, surveyors should put themselves as far as possible in the respondent's shoes, and ask whether they could or would answer the questions proposed.

Other decisions concern whether questions should be open-ended or limited to specific choices, and whether or not answers should be pre-coded. Wherever pre-coding is possible it saves time in analysis, but if the system is unduly complicated it can lead to inaccuracies by the interviewer which are unlikely to be detected at a later stage.

It is tempting when constructing a questionnaire to include questions on everything one would like to know. This temptation must be resisted. Throughout this chapter we have stressed the importance of clarifying objectives, of deciding on priorities and of defining variables and concepts as simply as possible. These principles apply particularly to questionnaire design where we must continually ask ourselves 'Is this question really necessary? What use are we going to make of the answers? An interview ideally should not take more than 30–40 minutes; after this the respondent will tire and the quality of answers will suffer accordingly. For example, one survey for a broadcasting corporation in a developing country had a questionnaire which was taking three hours to administer, and in which all the really important questions came at the end.

We cannot deal here with all the details of design, but there is finally one point that is often neglected and that is the lay-out of the questionnaire. It is worth spending time and money on this as interviewers cannot be expected to work well with scruffy pieces of paper, badly arranged and with inadequate space to fill in the answers. The same applies to the lay-out of instructions for interviewers.

(e) Training of interviewers However good the preparation has been up to this point the quality of the survey depends ultimately on those who collect the information. The selection of interviewers has already been mentioned. Equal care has to be taken in selecting other members of the team at all levels, such as supervisors, data processors, secretaries, typists, clerks, office messengers and drivers. Whoever is in charge of the survey must be continually available in the field; in a big survey delegation of day-to-day work is necessary, but whoever is ultimately responsible must get around as much as possible, not rely on issuing orders from a central office. Surveys are hard, tiring work and if the morale of those in the field is to be sustained, constant support is needed. The lack of this close contact between the centre and the field is the reason why so many large-scale surveys produce such questionable results.

The efficient training of interviewers takes longer than is often imagined. The actual time required will depend on the complexity of the survey and the number of different forms to be used. But in all cases at least two days at the outset should be allowed for introducing the objectives and background of the survey, explaining the duties and responsibilities of different team members, and describing interviewing techniques and methods of form filling. Another day should be devoted to going over the individual questions, discussing the reasons for asking them, what it is expected to find out, and what problems are likely to be encountered in responses. Team members should be encouraged to comment on the questions and suggest alternative formats. (In some surveys, where standardized forms are sent down from above, this may not be feasible, but where it can be done it adds enormously to the interest and enthusiasm of the interviewers.) Where questions have to be translated into local languages additional time will be required. Otherwise the afternoon of the third day can be used for interviewers trying out the questionnaire on each other, and this exercise can be continued on the fourth day. The next step is to try out the questionnaire in the field. This serves several purposes; it is part of the training exercise, it tests the questionnaire, and it can also be used as a pilot survey for purposes of deciding on the size of sample. On returning from the field the team should then discuss the revision of the questionnaire, analyse their findings and consider their significance. A minimum of a week is needed for this training. Where team members are very inexperienced obviously longer will be required. It is easy to overestimate the interviewer's initial understanding of all that he or she is expected to grasp, as ideas familiar to the survey leader may be completely new to the team members. Even when clear and detailed 'Instructions to Interviewers' are provided, they need time thoroughly to absorb their contents.

(f) Survey implementation   If the groundwork has been sound this can go ahead with confidence. The main point to stress here is the importance of supervision. The supervisor must be continuously in the field, being present at some interviews of all team members and checking and editing forms on a day-to-day basis. It is no use collecting forms and setting them aside. By the time they are checked it will be too late for the interviewer to recall what happened, and in the meantime similar errors may be perpetrated.

Even where processing is to be done by computer it is an advantage to analyse some of the data by hand in the first place. This acts as a check on the reliability of the survey, and also helps to sustain the interest of the team when they can see some tangible results of their efforts.

(g) Analysis of the data   Decisions about the sort of analysis to be used will have been taken at an earlier stage. The task now is to process the raw material by whatever system has been determined. If a computer is to be used the questionnaires must first be edited and coded, and a sample must be taken for initial examination. If this is satisfactory the next stage is to punch the computer cards, and this may well not be the

responsibility of the survey team. The output required from the computer will already have been discussed, but an examination of the sample may suggest further fruitful cross-tabulations. After the material has been processed the main analysis can be made in preparation for writing the report. This will include the calculation of sampling errors.

Hand tabulation may be a more appropriate method for small surveys or in countries where computers are not readily available, unreliable, or expensive to use. In this case the data is extracted from the forms and put on summary sheets in order to obtain frequency distributions, totals and simple cross-tabulations. If properly designed this method can be very effective. An intermediate form of technology is the card sorter, or other comparable equipment. The data is punched on special cards which when run through the machine fall into the appropriate boxes. Although an analysis as sophisticated as by a computer is not possible this is a relatively quick means of getting frequency distributions and cross-tabulations, and it is easy to build up tables as one goes along. In tropical countries, particularly where humidity is high, such equipment has to be kept in air-conditioned rooms if it is to perform efficiently. This should be borne in mind in planning a survey as the breakdown of equipment can dislocate the whole time schedule and lead to great frustration. It is sometimes better to use hand analysis for this reason, although it may be cumbersome. At least it provides employment and the fascination of the data unfolding its secrets as the operation proceeds.

(h) Report writing   It is not necessary to say much about this stage of the survey. It is self-evident that a report should be well presented and clear to its prospective readers, who may not have much knowledge of the survey. Diagrams, maps, and tables should be carefully selected; if there are too many and they are too complicated it may only confuse the reader, instead of clarifying the issue. Attention to such details as rounding the numbers and percentages makes a great difference to clarity. It is meaningless, for example, to express a percentage as 88.235% when the margin of error on the estimate is at least 10%.

In some cases it is useful to write two reports. A full report for those immediately involved with the results of the survey, and for the purposes of recording the data in detail and describing the methodology used, and a brief summary for general publication. The survey may be of great significance to a wider public, but it is unlikely to be read unless it is presented in a brief, palatable form.

Finally we must consider the question of the surveyor's responsibility to examine critically the implications of the data, including its limitations. The sampling and non-sampling errors affecting its reliability should be discussed and the results examined in this light. A comparison should be made with previous knowledge of the subject, new findings should be highlighted and implications for policy-making indicated.

It is easy to emphasise these requirements of report writing, and no doubt most surveyors bear them in mind. But in the stress of completing the task, often behind schedule, it is too easy to neglect the importance of this final stage. This is probably one reason why so many survey reports end in oblivion.

Concluding remarks

Throughout this section references have been made to some of the differences between conducting surveys in developed and developing countries. The term 'developing countries' covers a wide range of situations so that generalisations about the differences have to be made with caution. The main issue is the degree to which methods developed in the west can be successfully transferred to very different cultural settings. This is the question which requires much thought if the survey is not to fall into the trap of ethnocentricity. Experience has shown that however well intentioned the surveyor may be, because he is collecting data in an essentially quantitative way he or she tends to be carried away by techniques, overlooking the more qualitative aspects of the problem. This can be equally true of surveys in developed countries, which may be by no means as appropriate as is generally considered: the gap between predominantly middle-class team members and predominantly working-class respondents may lead to as great misunderstandings as Europeans or Americans asking questions of African villagers. In some ways it can be worse, as the differences in Africa are more apparent and a greater effort may therefore be made to accommodate them.

But this does raise the more fundamental issue of whether there are not equally useful ways of getting information than the standard sample survey. The techniques of enquiry developed by social anthropologists have yielded a wealth of ethnographic material which is of great value to the social planner. The anthropologist focuses on the social field as relationships between people rather than units of population (Leach, 1967). The method is connected in peoples' minds with long-term isolation in the field, with knowledge of the local language and the technique of participant observation. All these preclude quick results and much of what is learnt cannot be expressed quantitatively. What is less often appreciated is the perspective that the anthropological approach brings to the study of society (Wallman, 1977; Wallman *et al.*, 1980). For example some anthropologists have recently attempted 'to devise research strategies that are feasible in a dense urban setting – as participant observation is not – and yet do not distort the realities of ordinary life by dealing with people as "units of population", classified only by characteristics which can readily be seen and counted by outsiders in the way that conventional social survey tends to do' (Wallman *et al.*, 1980, p. 6). The survey carried out by Wallman and her team in Battersea, London, to study the ways in which people of different ethnic origin living in the same area use the resources available to them, used the questionnaire and computer analysis as part of their methodology. But this was set in a framework of gaining a thorough knowledge of the population to be studied. In order to help in gaining confidence, local people were included in the process of the survey, both as contributors to the questionnaire and as interviewers. It was found that this produced far more qualitative material than had been expected, and local participation really constituted the mainstream of the research activity. Many months before the main survey was carried out members of the team had made informal contacts in the area, and had taken part in local activities, such as the play-group.

Such long-term involvement is not possible where quick results are demanded. But these methods do suggest lines of approach that are important in all survey contexts. Stress has already been laid on the importance of thoroughly studying all the available literature and records, and of getting out in the field to meet the people before designing the survey. Where the survey and the team are alert to the limitations as well as the possibilities of survey methods, they are much more likely to produce reliable and meaningful results.

The use of survey techniques in social planning
These two case studies illustrate the way in which the processes outlined above have been used to meet particular requirements. The first, from a study made in Nigeria, was a large-scale exercise with multiple objectives; the second from London, was more limited in scope, but part of an ongoing attempt to discover the views of tenants on Greater London Council housing estates. In both instances the sub-headings used in the previous section will be used in order to give a clear picture of the processes.

The Household Survey of Maiduguri in Northern Nigeria
This survey was carried out for town planning purposes and was part of a wider study of Maiduguri which included surveys of traffic systems, building construction, drainage and refuse disposal, commerce, industry and employment. The Max Lock Group of Town Planning consultants had been commissioned by the North East State of Nigeria to draw up a master plan for the city, which had become the state capital in 1968 and was rapidly expanding. Max Lock was a

pioneer in the use of social surveys to provide information about the towns he was commissioned to plan. He believed that planning should involve the people for whom the plans were being made, and that the collection of data about their way of life was a two-way educational process, that is for the planner and the planned. The use of this method in Middlesbrough has already been mentioned (Glass, 1948) and in Nigeria the Kaduna Plan of 1967 also made use of the social survey.

The objectives of the survey
Broadly the objectives of the household survey (Hardiman, 1974) were to establish the existing situation, to assess trends, and to provide material for decision-making by the town-planning team. In terms of the data to be collected these were defined more specifically as follows:

(a) to estimate the population of Maiduguri and its distribution by age, sex, marital status, ethnic group, birthplace, occupation and education   This is census type data, and at the time of the survey in 1973 a national census was due to take place. But not only was the breakdown of census figures unlikely to be available until after the information was required by the town planners, it would also not relate to the other aspects of living about which the planners needed to know. So it was necessary to collect this data independently; in the event the 1973 Census proved to be so unreliable that it was cancelled and the 1963 Census is still used as a basis by the Nigerian government.

(b) to collect data about fertility and child mortality   The purpose of this was to assist in predicting trends of population growth. It had been suggested that fertility rates amongst some of the northern women were low, but very little information existed on this.

(c) to determine household size and composition   The traditional form of living in the north is the compound, within which is found a number of different households related to each other by blood or marriage. Much of Maiduguri is built in this way and the Survey intended to find out to what extent the traditional patterns of relationship existed. Furthermore household and compound types were to be related to the variables listed in (*a*).

(d) to study migration into Maiduguri   The Survey sought to determine the direction of migration, the reasons for coming and the duration of residence in the city. This alongside an estimate of the natural rate of increase would assist in predicting population trends.

(e) to collect data on types of occupancy, rent and services   Information

was needed about how many people owned their own houses, whether they paid an economic rent, what amenities existed, such as electricity, piped water, and whether the compound was used for commercial purposes.

(*f*) *to find out how many householders had been allocated new plots* These plots were in the outlying development areas of the town. The Survey sought to establish who was getting them, whether they intended to develop them and had the finance to do so, and for those not allocated plots whether they had aspirations to acquire them.

(*g*) *to explore peoples' views about their housing and neighbourhood* It was realised that this was a desirable objective but one not easily explored in the type of survey envisaged, which already sought a great deal of detailed factual data. As will be seen below, most of this information was gathered informally.

This list is long. It was the result of discussion with the team members, some of whom would have liked even more included. Rather than overburden the main survey further it was decided that supplementary surveys should be made on a small-scale in order to study some aspects in greater depth. An example of this is the Survey of Women carried out in 1974 (Hardiman, 1974) as men were the principal respondents in the main survey.

Resources

The budget for the survey had been worked out at an early stage of the town planning exercise as a whole. The infrastructure already existed in the consultant's office, so the main expenses were stationery and the hiring of interviewers and computer time. In order to complete the household and other surveys as quickly as possible it was decided to recruit up to 30 interviewers, mainly from Ahmadu Bello University at Zaria as students would be on vacation at that time. One of the main criteria for selection was language. Maiduguri was traditionally a Kanuri town and although most would understand Hausa, it was obviously desirable to speak to them in their native tongue. Interviewers were also needed to interview the Fulani people in the town; the other language groups could speak either Hausa or English. Another criterion was elementary statistical ability, as it was intended to use the interviewers on the preliminary analysis and processing of data. This was assessed by a simple test during selection. In addition, an attempt was made to assess the general suitability of the applicant in terms of interest, personality and a general knowledge of the town.

Collection of background information: public relations

This had been proceeding ever since the Max Lock Group came to Maiduguri in 1972. One of the senior partners was already well known in the town and his previous work in Kaduna had given him experience in how to seek out information. Elite circles in Maiduguri are restricted and most of those included meet regularly at the Club; this proved an excellent place to get and give information. At the same time a land use survey was being carried out by permanent members of the Max Lock Group; this was a complete count of every building in the town and was being used to fill in and up-date the aerial maps. This exercise meant that the general public was well aware of the presence of the Group and opportunities were taken to explain what it was all about.

Immediately prior to the household survey a final public relations exercise was mounted. Broadcasts were made in the main language by several of the interviewers, local papers carried articles, and loud-speaker vans toured the town. These measures were intended to ensure that the public would appreciate that it was in their own interests to cooperate and give the information sought. By the time of the survey the team was well known in the back streets of Maiduguri, and members were frequently stopped by local inhabitants asking whether they intended to visit their compound; they were disappointed when it was explained that the sampling process had not drawn them in the 'lottery'.

Formulation of the research problem

This stage had largely been completed when the specific objectives were defined. The survey was mainly descriptive in nature, but it was hoped to analyse certain relationships. For example it was intended to test the hypothesis that in the older parts of the town surrounding the Shehu's palace, compound patterns would be more traditional, that the proportion of Kanuri would be higher, that more of them would have been born in Maiduguri or migrated many years previously. The intention was to define divisions between different types of area in order to plan them appropriately. The other matter for decision at this stage was the operational definitions to be used. What exactly, for example, was meant by compound or household? How were occupations to be recorded? Should questions be asked about incomes? In the last mentioned case it was decided after much discussion not to attempt to get information on incomes, partly because to do so might have created suspicion. Different areas of the town were entered under the auspices of the ward heads and therefore inevitably were associated with them, and these ward heads were the tax collectors. Professor M.G. Smith had warned that this might lead to an under-enumeration of adult men. The other reason was that most of the people were self-employed, and many had more than one occupation and derived income from a wide variety of sources, such as other members of the family, or farms elsewhere. They would have difficulty in assessing their annual income, which fluctuated seasonally and varied from year to year.

Survey design and implementation
The *population* or *universe* of the survey was taken as all those living within the boundaries of Maiduguri, with the exception of those living in institutions such as hospitals, prisons, or those without a fixed abode (it was reckoned that the number living in the open was very small). The *sampling unit* was the compound and it was decided to collect information about all the householders and their members in the sample compounds. The *sampling frame*, therefore, was the list of all the compounds in Maiduguri, just over 25,600. This list was available as a result of the land-use survey already made. Without this, other methods of selecting the sample would have had to be used.

As little was known about the demographic and other characteristics of the town and through observation and informants it was apparent that it had increased in heterogeneity it was decided to take a large sample in order to ensure that the survey adequately covered all the areas of the town. As it was decided to *sample from lists* at agreed intervals, all areas of the town would be proportionately represented, so that a multi-stage design was not necessary. Detailed decisions on the actual percentage of the sample were left until after the pilot survey. The questionnaire or interview schedule was also being prepared at this time. Most of the essential information required was straightforward census type data, but even with the collection of such data, many problems arose and required a thorough knowledge of the culture to avoid pitfalls. Much thought was given to this and the draft questionnaire was discussed with the interviewers who made valuable suggestions about how questions might be put. Decisions were also made on which answers could be precoded, as this not only saved space on the form but allowed for easy processing. The revised draft was supported by instructions for interviewers and the next stage consisted of training the interviewers, testing it out between themselves and finally by a pilot survey. On return from the field the interviewers themselves analysed the results and discussed problems in the questionnaire. These were incorporated into the final questionnaire which is shown in Figure 3.1. The size of the sample was then decided on the basis of the time taken on the pilot survey and the average number of households in the compounds; in the main survey, every thirteenth compound was to form the sample.

During this time a member of the Ahmadu Bello University

Fig. 3.1 Interview questionnaire for household survey of Maiduguri

1. MAP NO. 14 STREET BLOCK 1 COMPOUND NO. 12C **FORM A. HOUSEHOLD INFORMATION**

2. SAMPLE 1 1 5 5 HOUSEHOLD NO. 0 1

Reason for no interview.

Interviewer's No. 12
Time of Interview 4:10 pm
Date of Interview 15/8/7..
Serial No. of Form A. ..

Informant	Line	Household Positn	Sex	Age	Marital Status	Place of Birth	Tribe	Years lived in Maiduguri.	Reason for coming.	Main Occupation	type of occupation	Secondary Occupation	Education.	Reason Absent.	Form of Transpt.	WOMEN HOUSEHOLD MEMBERS ONLY: How many children born alive? (18) M	F	How many children died since? (19) M	F	Date of last live birth (20) Yr	Mth	Is last child still alive? (21)
1	3	4	5	6	7	8	9	10	11	12	13	14	15	16	17							
	1	0	1	45	2	Kumshe 06	Shewa 03	01	1	Sn. C. S. 11	5	x	3	3	1							
✓	2	0	2	30	2	Ngala 06	Shiwa 03	01	5	Housewife 01	x	x	0	0	0	0	0	0	0	x	x	x
	3	1	2	16	2	Bama 06	Kanuri 00	01	5	Housewife 01	x	x	0	0	0	1	0	0	0	0	6	1
	4	2	2	14	1	Bama 06	Shiwa 03	01	5	Student 02	x	x	3	0	0							
	5	2	2	13	1	Bama 06	Shiwa 03	01	5	Student 02	x	x	3	0	0							
	6	2	1	09	1	Bama 06	Shiwa 03	01	5	Student 02	x	x	1	0	0							
	7	2	1	09	1	Bama 06	Shiwa 03	01	5	Student 02	x	x	1	0	0							
	8	2	1	04	1	Bama 06	Shiwa 03	01	5	child not at school 03	x	x	0	0	0							
	9	5	1	02	1	Bama 06	~~Shiwa~~ Kanuri 00	01	5	child not at school 03	x	x	0	0	0							
	10	5	1	02	1	Bama 06	Shiwa 03	01	5	child not at school 03	x	x	0	0	0							
	11	2	1	01	1	Bama 06	Shiwa 03	01	5	child not at school 03	x	x	0	0	0							
	12	2	1	00	1	Bama 06	Shiwa 03	00	5	child not at school 03	x	x	0	0	0							
	13																					
	14																					

Form B: Household heads only

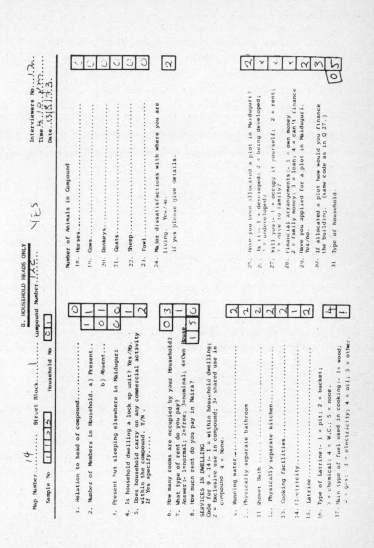

B. HOUSEHOLD HEADS ONLY

Map Number....14........   Street Block....1......   Compound Number.I.X.C...

Sample No [1][1][1][>][5]   Household No [0][1]

Interviewers No....1.2....
Time.4..1.0..p.m......
Date.13.8.7.3.

YES

1. Relation to head of compound............. [0]

2. Number of Members in Household. a) Present.. [1][1]
                            b) Absent... [0][0]

4. Present hut sleeping elsewhere in Maiduguri [1]

5. Does household carry on any commercial activity
   within the compound. Y/N . [2]
   If Yes specify......

6. How many rooms are occupied by your Household? [0][3]

7. What type of rent do you pay?
   Answer:- 1=normal; 2=free; 3=nominal; 4=Own house [1]

8. How much rent do you pay in Naira? [1][5][0]

SERVICES IN DWELLING
Code for 9 - 14:- 1 = within household dwelling;
2 = Exclusive use in compound; 3= shared use in
compound 4 = None.

9. Running water....... [2]

10. Physically separate bathroom [2]

11. Shower Bath .... [2]

12. Physically separate kitchen....... [2]

13. Cooking facilities....... [1]

14. Electricity....... [2]

15. Latrine....... [4]

16. Type of Latrine: 1 = pit; 2 = bucket;
   3 = chemical; 4 = W.C. 5 = none. [1]

17. Main type of fuel used in cooking:- 1= wood;
   2 = gas; 3 =electricity; 4 = oil; 5 = other.

Number of Animals in Compound

18. Horses....... [0][0][0][0]

19. Cows....... [0]

20. Donkeys.......

21. Goats.......

22. Sheep.......

23. Fowl....... [2]

24. Major dissatisfactions with where you are
   living. Yes/no.
   If yes please give details.

25. Have you been allocated a plot in Maiduguri? [2]

26. Is it:- 1 = developed; 2 = being developed; [Y]
   3 = undeveloped?

27. Will you:- 1 = occupy it yourself; 2 = rent; [Y]
   3 = give to family?

28. Financial arrangements:- 1 = own money [Y]
   2 = family money; 3 = loan; 4 = can't finance

29. Have you applied for a plot in Maiduguri. [2]
   Yes/no.

30. If allocated a plot how would you finance [3]
   the building. (same code as in Q 27.)

31. Type of household. [0][5]

computer unit who was going to process the data visited Maiduguri to discuss problems of processing the completed questionnaire and estimates were made of the time it would take to complete the analysis. His observations were taken into account in preparing the final form of the questionnaire.

The main survey was carried out ward by ward so that at any one time interviewers were concentrated in a particular area. This made the task of supervision easier. The team leader who was mainly responsible for the survey took interviewers into the field to meet the ward heads and was herself constantly walking around the area. Every morning interviewers brought their completed questionnaires back to the office and these were all checked by the team leader before the following morning so that queries could be raised while they were still fresh in the interviewer's mind. If necessary they were sent back for checking in the field, but this was avoided as much as possible.

There is no space here to go into the interesting conceptual problems that arose over such questions as marital status and the recording of children of any women of the household (some men insisted their children should be credited to them!). Fortunately most of the questions were not problematic, nor did they prove sensitive. The *response rate* of 96 per cent or 1936 compounds out of 2016 in the sample, was exceptionally high.

The *analysis of data* took place continuously as the survey progressed in order to extract basic information on numbers in compounds and households, age distribution, migration and a few other variables, so that decisions about the division of the town into area types could be made before the computer results were available. In the event, the computer program gave a lot of trouble and it was necessary subsequently to return to further hand analysis. When another six towns in the North East State were surveyed, it was decided in 1974 to rely entirely on hand analysis and this in the circumstances proved much more satisfactory.

The report on the survey findings was written initially by the team leader and finally incorporated in the Max Lock Group consultants' survey and plan for Maiduguri which was presented to the North East State Government in 1974.

The Housing Appraisal Survey of Friday Hill Estate, Chingford
This survey was carried out as part of a programme of housing appraisal surveys by the Central Services Division of the Housing Branch of the Greater London Council or GLC. The purpose of these surveys was to find out in the light of tenants' opinion how far the spatial solution

adopted and its management satisfied the tenants' requirements and aspirations. The final aim was to use such information for future briefs and design (GLC, 1978).

The basis used to select the estates to be surveyed was that they should (i) have some characteristics worthy of investigation which could help to improve design; (ii) comply with the Housing Appraisal Kit requirements, i.e. to have been occupied for at least one year and to have over 50 dwellings; and (iii) have different environmental and social conditions which may affect the levels of tenants' satisfaction.

Friday Hill estate was completed in December 1976 on a site adjacent to the Greater London Council's existing Chingford estate. The main characteristics which made it worthy of investigation were that it was a medium-sized estate built to test Consortium methods, which the GLC was using for the first time. The Consortium, consisting of a group of Local Authorities, had been formed to purchase materials and building components on a larger scale than was possible for a single authority, and to share the services of architects, engineers and surveyors. Rationalised traditional building systems were used, and no buildings were more than three storeys high. Particular attention was paid to both soft and hard landscaping in order to create an intimate domestic atmosphere, about 80 per cent of the estate consisting of open space, allocated partly as private gardens and partly as small amenity spaces between blocks. Social facilities included a tenants' clubroom and old people's club.

The objectives of the survey
These followed the general objectives outlined in the introduction. More specifically the aim was to assess tenants' reactions to the particular design aspects of the dwellings and environment on the estate, in the construction of which Consortium procedures had been used. These methods had considerably speeded up the time taken to complete the estate, but some compromises had had to be made with the requirements deemed necessary by the Director of Housing, such as the number of built-in cupboards, electrical points, and old people's alarm systems.

Resources
All the work involved in the survey was carried out by staff of the Greater London Council. The Central Services Division of the Housing Branch had a budget allocated for surveys, and three officers of the

Council, including the organiser of the survey, undertook the field work. As they had little previous experience of surveys they were given briefing by the team leader.

Collection of background information and public relations

All the required information was available at the Greater London Council, such as the rationale of the design, plans of the estate layout and internal arrangement of housing units. The report did not mention any attempt to give advance warning to the residents of the estate about the survey and its aims; an introductory letter was delivered to the sampled dwellings along with the questionnaire, and it was not anticipated that the nature of the enquiry would be particularly sensitive.

Survey design and implementation

The survey of Friday Hill estate used the Housing Appraisal Kit (HAK) developed jointly by the Greater London Council and the Department of the Environment. It was intended for use by people with little or no experience of surveys, so that those concerned with housing design could themselves carry out the fieldwork. The method devised consisted of questionnaires sent by post to a sample of residents, and later collected by local authority staff. This involved checking the questionnaire, asking any questions that had been missed, helping respondents with unclear questions, and asking a few additional questions about household composition. In some cases this help amounted to a full interview, as several respondents were quite unable to fill in the form. In any case the task of collection gave staff of the Council the opportunity to hear the reactions of tenants at first hand, and to observe generally what happened in a housing estate some years after it had been completed.

The Housing Appraisal Kit deals mainly with the dwelling and the estate, but also includes some questions on the surrounding area. It makes provision in the computer program for extra questions to be added to the standard questionnaire, and in this case two additional questions were included about living room/dining/kitchen arrangement preference and satisfaction with the tenants' and old people's club rooms. Both closed and open questions are included, the latter allowing for the free expression of opinions.

Friday Hill Estate had 175 dwellings, and these provided the *sampling frame*; the *sampling unit* consisting of the dwelling. It was decided to take a 50 per cent *stratified random sample* of the Estate in order to cover different dwelling types. The whole estate was therefore divided into two zones with two sub-sections in each zone:

Zone A   (i) terraced houses facing an access road
        (ii) terraced houses fronting a walkway and backing an access road

Zone B   (i) blocks of flats surrounding an amenity open space and facing an access road
        (ii) blocks of flats surrounded by amenity open space and access road

In November 1978, one week before collection started, 87 question-naires were delivered, and 73 of these were successfully collected over a period of three weeks, thus totalling an 84 per cent response rate. The questionnaire had 25 questions, many of which were subdivided into several parts. For most of them the respondents were asked to tick one of a series of boxes to indicate their views; but space was provided for alternative answers or for general comments, as is shown in the example in Figure 3.2.

A number of the questions asked respondents to rate feelings about certain aspects on a five-point scale, ranging from, for example, very satisfied to very dissatisfied, or like it very much to dislike it very much.

The staff who collected the questionnaires found most tenants cooperative and able to complete the majority of questions. Some of them had had difficulty in either understanding or seeing the point of questions such as 'Do you think that any rooms in your house or flat are badly placed?', or 'Do you have enough room indoors generally?'. Both these questions were followed by a series of boxes in which the re-spondent was asked to tick those which were appropriate. And some found tedious the constant repetition of questions about likes and dislikes, firstly about the house or flat, and subsequently on points such as the outlook from the kitchen, the living room, the estate as a whole and its appearance. They had not really thought about it in this way and found it difficult to express their feelings at all, let alone on a five-point scale. It did seem that the standardised HAK questionnaire, despite the great care with which it had been drawn up and tested, did not alto-gether take into account the likely reactions of respondents, who tend to view things very differently from architects and planners, or even sociologists.

Many of the old people were totally baffled by the questionnaire and had to be fully interviewed. Even then they found it difficult to answer many of the questions and the interviewer tended to suggest answers to them, as much as anything in order to make them feel happy. They were anxious to cooperate, but embarrassed at their lack of under-standing.

These problems were not mentioned in the report (GLC, 1978), but were gathered from one of the fieldwork team. He felt that the survey was superficial, and that he was not at all happy with the questionnaire. This is often a problem where interviewers have to use a standardised questionnaire. Nevertheless certain important problems did come out in the survey. Where people felt strongly about something they were able to express their views clearly. For example, 64 per cent of the respondents said that they had problems with noise disturbance and those suffering most were living in terraced houses or old people's flats, on the ground and first floors of blocks fronting the external road. Visual privacy affected fewer respondents (36 per cent), but this proportion is sufficient to constitute a real problem. Of the households with children 50 per cent had some sort of problems with children playing, and those without children also expressed difficulties, particularly the old people; overall 62 per cent of elderly households complained about children playing and this rose to 88 per cent for those living in flats in the blocks referred to above.

When the team collected the questionnaires they asked a few additional questions about household composition and also completed zone, block, and estate questionnaires for the whole estate. The data was then transcribed, punched onto cards and computed by using a specially designed programme, which was part of the Housing Appraisal Kit. This Kit prints out results in two forms: as a set of edited tables incorporating symbols and intended for direct inclusion in the survey report; and as a set of full statistical tables.

The final report (GLC, 1978) was prepared by the organiser of the survey and included plans, photographs, pie charts, tables and bar charts. As well as the full report, a summary of conclusions was printed on yellow pages and bound in at the front of the report. The use of a standardised format of presentation meant that this survey could be easily compared with others in the series.

Assessment of social survey methods

These two case studies are examples of the survey approach, and illustrate only some of the wide range of possible uses of surveys, and the methodologies that can be employed but they can be used to examine the main issues in the design of appropriate methodologies for particular purposes.

All social surveys are concerned with finding out about people. It is therefore essential to know as much as possible about the groups to be studied. The collection of reliable data depends upon winning the

Fig. 3.2 Question 23 in the Housing Appraisal Kit questionnaire

23. Would you say that this is a convenient place to live generally?

Tick a box   YES ☐   NO ☐

Tick the boxes to show the ways you find it inconvenient, if any:

	Tick if INCONVENIENT	Write in the REASONS below
For getting to:		
local shops	☐	....
nearest main shopping centre	☐	....
chemist shop	☐	....
Post Office	☐	....
clinics	☐	....
a doctor	☐	....
launderette	☐	....
public house	☐	....
For:-		
primary school	☐	....
parks	☐	....
public telephone	☐	....
public transport	☐	....
For getting to:		
work	☐	....
friends and relatives	☐	....
entertainment	☐	....

For getting to other places. Write in below.

confidence of respondents; if this is to be obtained they must be informed about the nature of the survey, and understand its purpose. Ideally this information should reach the population as a whole, and not only those in the sample. Where there is a high level of interest and respondents feel that they can make a positive contribution they are much more likely to take trouble in answering questions. In Maiduguri a great deal of effort went into this part of the exercise. At the Friday Hill estate it appears that it was not felt necessary to involve any but the sample, and these only in a cursory manner; the survey team first went into the estate when the questionnaires were collected, and apart from that had no real contact with residents. Although the questions may not have appeared particularly sensitive, there was probably some suspicion surrounding the fact that the team was from the Greater London Council and might be using the survey as a cover to snoop around, finding out about such things as overoccupancy. For example it was thought that 'the relatively low number of responses to questions about repairs and getting complaints attended to might be attributed to the fact that some tenants feared they would have difficulties with the housing management of the estate if they criticised the service provided' (GLC, 1978, p. 68).

This leads to the point about framing the questionnaire in conceptual terms that will be meaningful to respondents. The Maiduguri survey tried to take this into account, not only by testing the questionnaire in a pilot survey, but by involving interviewers who were themselves familiar with the society in formulating the questions. The Friday Hill survey used a standardised questionnaire, which had already been tested in a pilot survey elsewhere. This has many advantages, particularly where computer analysis is used. It is economical to operate, and it means that data collected in many different locations can be compared. The Housing Appraisal Kit was designed specifically for Council Housing Estates and it may have been assumed that sufficient homogeneity existed in the cultural backgrounds of tenants. In a class based and ethnically plural society this is a dangerous assumption. But it could be overcome, at least to some extent, by a more sensitive application of a standardised Kit. Much more attention could be given to preliminary investigations and to contacting residents. For example a meeting might have been convened at the tenants' clubroom to explain the purposes of the survey; perhaps not many would have attended, but people on estates talk to each other, so the general level of interest could have been raised. The team members also might have spent more time on the estate before the questionnaires were posted to the sample, chatting to the people and observing how they used facilities. All these, admittedly, add to the cost of the survey but not to a great extent; if they result in better data they are well worthwhile. A good example of how this was done is the survey undertaken by Wallman and her team in Battersea (Wallman *et al.*, 1980). This survey had different objectives and was designed specifically for the area in question; it collected a much wider range of information. The methods therefore would not be directly transferable to the sort of exercise envisaged for users of the Housing Appraisal Kit, as they depended on a qualified and trained team of investigators. But they do emphasise the importance of involving the people and taking account of their points of view and life style (Oppong and Church, 1980).

The question of involvement is crucial, particularly for the team, and this has already been stressed. The preparation of interviewers must be allowed adequate time to be done in depth, an obvious point which is too frequently overlooked. Money thought to be saved by crash methods is all too often money wasted. Interviewers must be trained not only to administer the questionnaire but to observe what is going on. This involves a broad understanding of the cultural situation, the purposes of the particular survey and how it relates to wider objectives, such as the part it plays in social planning as a whole.

It is essential to ensure that the technical aspects of the exercise are correct, that due attention has been paid to the methodological requirements of sampling, analysis, and all the other matters outlined above. Moreover these should be clearly laid out in the report so that a proper evaluation can be made of the results. The limitations should be spelt out, as much can be covered over by the use of statistics which mislead rather than inform, particularly where percentages are used to express very small sample numbers.

Finally we return to where we started, that is with the objectives. These should not only be clearly stated at the outset, but continually borne in mind. It is easy to get so immersed in the technicalities of quantitative data collection and analysis that the main purpose of the enquiry is neglected. The exercise of carrying out a survey enables those involved, by working with people in a defined area, to get to know the community. A great deal can be gained by building in this opportunity to the survey design. Qualitative records lack the precision of statistical data, but they add meaning, and if used aright contribute to the interest and usefulness of the findings. They help to enliven the report in ways exemplified by some of the early writings of people such as Mayhew and Booth. In Maiduguri we asked interviewers to write essays about neighbourhoods in which they were particularly interested; many of their remarks were illuminating and were incorporated in the report.

In conclusion, it can be said that social surveys are a valuable method of improving decision-making for social planners providing that sufficient attention is paid to designing appropriate methodologies, and using them in a manner sensitive to the cultural situation. This applies as much in the industrial countries as in the Third World.

4 Cost-Benefit Techniques and Social Planning
David Piachaud

Cost-benefit techniques are methods of assessing the desirability of projects taking a broad view in the sense of looking at all those affected by the project and a long view in the sense of looking at the effects of the project into the future. In theory cost-benefit analysis could scarcely be simpler: the purpose is to measure the cost and the benefits of a particular project. If the costs exceed the benefits then the project is not worth doing; if the benefits exceed the costs then the project is in principle attractive and may be worth doing if it is more attractive than any alternative project. Related to cost-benefit analysis is cost effectiveness analysis which has the more limited objective of assessing the outcome of a project in relation to its cost. While these techniques are in principle straightforward, in practice they give rise to great problems of measuring costs and benefits and of comparing projects which affect different groups in the population.

Cost-benefit techniques developed as a method of evaluating public works and government programmes where neither purely commercial nor purely political criteria were adequate on which to base decisions. Some early work took place in the last century and early in this century, but the attempt to evaluate public programmes and to make systematic resource allocation decisions has burgeoned in the last quarter of a century. This development has largely drawn on traditional sections of economic analysis, notably welfare economics and public finance. A major survey of cost-benefit analysis was published by Prest and Turvey (1965) Since then there has been a proliferation of studies largely or solely devoted to cost-benefit techniques (see Mishan, 1971; Layard, 1972; Dasgupta *et al.*, 1972; Little and Mirrlees, 1974; Williams and Anderson, 1975; Sugden and Williams, 1978).

The purpose of the technique
Any project may be considered in terms of four interrelated aspects which are illustrated in Figure 4.1. The core of any project is the relationship between certain physical inputs and the output they will produce. For example, certain quantities of cement, sand, wood and building labour – the inputs – can be turned into a house, the output. A

Figure 4.1 *Cost-benefit techniques*

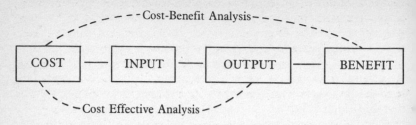

teacher equipped with certain materials can, in a certain length of time, educate a child to be able to read; literacy is an output. A certain number of health personnel equipped with transport facilities and spraying equipment – the inputs – can, in a malarial zone, produce a certain reduction in the number of cases of malaria – the output. This relationship between inputs and outputs is, in any given context, not a physical or technical relationship; it is *not* determined by decision-makers, economists or social planners. A builder or quantity surveyor is required to determine the necessary inputs to make a house, an expert on education to know how long children take to learn to read and write and an epidemiologist to assess the effects of a programme for disease reduction.

Knowledge of the input-output relationship is not enough to make any decision. It would be quite possible to estimate how many maids with how many mops were necessary to sweep up all the sand on the beaches of Britain; merely knowing this input-output relationship would not provide any indication as to whether it were a worthwhile project. In order to judge the desirability, or not, of a project further information of two kinds is necessary. First, what is the cost of the inputs and second what is the value, or benefits, of the output. Further the costs and benefits must be expressed in comparable terms, the most common being values expressed in terms of money.

All this may sound very obvious, and so it is. Yet it is worth recalling that many decisions are made without appraising the costs or the benefits. Often there is a kind of technological imperative that if something can be done it should be done: for example, if it is possible to assemble certain quantities of aluminium and titanium into an aircraft which will, with enormous quantities of fuel, carry passengers at more than the speed of sound then there are many who seem to regard this as sufficient justification for building a supersonic aircraft such as Concorde, regardless of the cost of the inputs or the value of the outputs. Sometimes the value of the output – or benefit – is assessed and judged to be so large that there is no point in assessing the cost of the inputs; sometimes it is assumed that the output *must* be achieved and, while inputs are costed, no assessment is made of the benefits of the output. Knowledge of the benefits from certain inputs or knowledge of the costs of certain outputs is not, however, sufficient to determine whether the project is worth doing. If the cost of producing a literate child is £100 then this only tells us whether it is worth pursuing a literacy project is we make an assumption, or have some knowledge of, the benefits of increased literacy. Thus, in principle, for any project we need to know the inputs involved and what they cost, and the outputs that will result and what is their value or benefit. This is what cost-benefit analysis attempts to provide.

There may however be circumstances in which this technique may be sensibly abbreviated. If it is clear that the output or effect – for example teaching children basic literacy – must be achieved in one way or another then there may be little point in working out the value or benefit of that output or effect. If there were only one way of achieving basic literary then there would be no decision to be made. If, however, there is a choice of method of achieving the desired effect, then it may be useful to compare the inputs required for each of those methods and the costs attached to each set of inputs. Such a comparison of cost and output is what is involved in cost effectiveness analysis. This technique can answer one of two questions. What is the lowest cost way of achieving a given output? Or, for a given cost, what is the most output that can be produced? It must be borne in mind with cost effectiveness analysis that an overriding assumption is being made – namely that the benefits of some method of producing the output justify the cost. Since cost-benefit analysis is more comprehensive as a decision-making technique than cost-effectiveness analysis it is the former that will be discussed in this section.

The first task is the definition of the project. Often this is straightforward but it may involve complexities where a certain organisation is pursuing many different programmes with different objectives. As far as possible, such programmes should be divided into separable components: for example, if an irrigation project is being appraised which involves three dams which could be built separately then it is desirable to appraise each of them separately and consider combinations of them. What must *not* be separated are the different outputs from the same project. Anyone who considered the dam solely from the point of view of its effect on irrigation, and the value of that output, and disregarded other effects on, for example, health, transport and housing would be defeating the very objective of cost-benefit analysis, which is to consider all the effects together.

Having defined the project or set of alternatives to be considered, the next question is what inputs would be required for each of them and what outputs they would produce. Clearly the information necessary is entirely different for health projects from education projects from transport projects. All that can be said in general is that the purpose of this is to list systematically all the necessary inputs and all the expected consequences. Major problems may arise in assessing the output arising from specified inputs. If a swamp is sprayed how far will this in practice reduce the number of cases of malaria? If a new underground is built how many people will use it and what effect will this have on other transport systems? Often the problem of predicting the input-output relationship is extremely complex; experience of similar projects in other places and at other times may be a useful guide but if the project is highly innovative then there may be little precedent on which to build. Whatever the difficulties it is essential to describe and list as systematically as possible all the expected inputs and outputs. Beware of people who say a project is so complicated that this cannot be done and then go on to argue that a project should, or should not, be carried out; such people are making implicit judgements about some of the inputs or outputs which would, from a decision-making point of view, be much better spelt out.

The next stage is to value the cost of the inputs. Most projects will require a variety of inputs – typically, personnel, materials, equipment and buildings. The purpose of estimating the cost is to express these inputs in terms of a common denominator – namely, money. For most purposes the cost of the inputs can be estimated quite straightforwardly from estimating what will have to be paid for those inputs. If the inputs required in terms of hours of labour of certain grades of workers are known then it is relatively simple to combine this information with the prevailing rates of pay for those grades of workers to estimate the total labour cost. Materials and equipment can be assessed in terms of what will have to be paid for them. Buildings are more problematic since the building may last longer than the project; methods of dealing with costs which are non-recurrent will be considered further below.

Two principal problems may arise in relation to costing inputs. First there is the crucial distinction between average and marginal costs. The average cost is the total cost divided by the units of output whereas the marginal cost is the extra cost (or saving) if one more (or less) unit of output is produced. The average cost may be very different from the marginal cost. For example if alternative sizes of hospitals are being compared the estimated cost for a 100-bed hospital may be £1 million per annum with an average cost of £10,000 per bed. With 110 beds the cost may rise as illustrated in Table 4.1 where three alternatives are shown. In other words, the extension by ten more beds may be viewed as a separate investment and evaluated as such.

Even though the average costs are not very different on the alternatives A, B and C, the marginal cost of the extra ten beds differs

Table 4.1 Average and marginal costs

Beds	Total cost	Average cost	Marginal cost
100	1,000,000	10,000	—
110	A 1,050,000	9,545	5,000
	B 1,100,000	10,000	10,000
	C 1,200,000	10,909	20,000

greatly. In deciding whether to provide 110 beds rather than 100, it is the marginal cost of the extra ten beds that is relevant (and of course their marginal benefit).

A second, quite different, problem in relation to costs arises where the market valuation of inputs is not a reliable guide to their opportunity cost, that is what has to be given up if the resources are used in a particular way. This may best be illustrated with a number of examples. If unemployed people are hired on a project they may be paid the going wage but, from a national point of view, there may be little loss of other output because the workers were previously unemployed. Therefore to use what they are paid in wages as an indicator of the cost of employing them may be to overstate the cost to the economy as measured by lost output. In a quite different context, countries which ration imports by systems of licensing may have import prices which do not reflect the scarcity of foreign currency; thus the market valuation of the imports, assuming a licence is granted, may not indicate the true value that is put upon a given quantity of imports, because some other valuable import may not be purchased as a result. A third example may be drawn from a situation in which inputs are not paid, such as voluntary labour. It is tempting to say that voluntary labour is free and therefore can be used in any quantity at zero cost. However, this is clearly not the case since there is not an unlimited supply of voluntary workers. Thus if a volunteer now working on, say, visiting old people is transferred to other voluntary work in, say, a hospital, then there may be no financial payment from the hospital to the volunteer but there is nevertheless a cost in the form of the loss of voluntary work visiting the old people. Thus it may be a mistake to plan as though volunteers were 'free' since their use on one activity has an opportunity cost, namely, the loss of their services on some other activity. In all these cases where the market evaluation of certain inputs does not provide a reliable indication of the cost of the input then adjustments can be made. For example 'shadow prices' can be used to indicate the scarcity or opportunity cost of using certain inputs.

The use of shadow prices – for example treating volunteers who do not have to be paid as though they had a price – may seem to be a marvellous example of 'cooking the books'. Certainly there are dangers of doing just that, but it is important to remember that cost-benefit analysis is not an accounting exercise. Rather it is a planning exercise designed to improve decision-making. What is therefore important is to use the most relevant information; this may or may not be the same as the financial information necessary when drawing up a detailed budget for implementing whatever projects are decided upon.

Evaluating benefits
Measuring benefits is often the most difficult part of cost-benefit analysis. The complexity may be seen if we consider the outputs of three projects.

A disease prevention programme may serve to reduce the demand for medical treatment for the disease. It may also reduce the loss of production caused by the disease because fewer people will be off work or die as a result of the disease. And it may reduce the pain and suffering that the disease inflicts. The first of these affects the health service, the loss of production affects the economy and the individual, whereas the pain and suffering affects the individual and relatives and friends.

A second project may be to reduce air pollution. One benefit of this may lie in improved health, with similar effects to a disease prevention programme. It may also result in a reduction in costs of washing and costs of deterioration of clothing and building fabrics. Finally it may provide an environment which is generally more pleasant to live in. Again each of these benefits is very different in its nature.

A third project may be to build a motorway. This may reduce travelling time, cut fuel bills and reduce accidents. On the other hand some people living close to the motorway may suffer increased noise and environmental damage. While the saving on petrol may be quite easy to calculate, the valuation of time saved, partly by people going about their business and partly by people enjoying more leisurely holidays, raises further problems.

The diversity of the outputs of different programmes makes it impossible to have one straightforward method of assessing benefits. We may however categorise certain types of effect:

(a) *Direct savings to other programmes*   The first example given – a disease prevention programme – might reduce the costs of medical care for sufferers from the disease. This is a direct benefit and its value can be estimated based on the existing costs of caring for sufferers from that disease. It is important to note that this saving is of benefit whether or not the health service decides to cut the budget by this amount. If, after the disease prevention programme, the government decides to maintain the health budget this does not mean that there has not been a saving in health care as a result of reducing the number of cases of the disease; rather it means that the healthy authority has decided to use those resources for some other purpose to improve health elsewhere.

(b) Direct effects on production If a project increases production either through increasing productivity, for example by reducing transport time of lorry drivers, or by reducing lost time, for example by reducing the incidence of a disease, then these have a direct benefit to the economy. This is measurable in terms of the value of the extra output gained.

(c) Potentially marketable outputs Many projects result in output which is directly sold. The benefit of putting fertilisers on fields may be measured in terms of the value of the increased yield of the crop. In other cases the output may be potentially marketable but may not actually be sold. For example, if a ferry across a river which charges a toll is replaced by a bridge then the former users of the ferry would presumably be prepared to pay for the use of the bridge (although in practice to get the maximum utilisation of the bridge it may be decided not to charge any toll for crossing the bridge). In determining how much people value a service what is important is what people would be prepared to pay for it. This is not the same as the price at which the service would be provided if it were organised commercially. Most consumers value what they buy more highly than the price, the difference being 'consumer surplus'. The relevant concern is with the sum of individuals' valuations of the service.

(d) Non-marketed time Some of the savings from a motorway are in terms of time that is marketed, that is to say paid time, for example of bus and lorry drivers. However many projects may affect the use of time that is not paid for but is nevertheless of value. A motorway reduces the time taken by people going on holiday which is of value to them. If a health clinic is re-sited closer to people's homes then this reduces the time spent travelling to it. This time is of value because it might be used to earn income or because it allows more time for doing other more pleasurable activities.

The question then arises of how much time is worth. If people choose to take leisure time rather than stay in paid work then this might suggest that they value this time at least as much or more highly than the amount they would have gained at work in post-tax pay. Alternatively the value of time spent on housework could be based on the cost of providing a substitute housekeeper. Where the time saved involves people when they are in paid work then their wage rate is in most cases a suitable valuation on their time. For unpaid time outside the labour market, then there is no clear-cut answer as to how such time should be valued. Nevertheless it is clearly wrong to value such time as being of no account.

(e) Other intangible outputs Projects that affect levels of noise or other environmental characteristics or that affect individuals' pain and suffering present formidable problems in terms of valuing the output. On noise, for example, attempts have been made in relation to the siting of airports to estimate the cost of reducing noise levels through double-glazing and other techniques, to estimate how much people would need to be paid to compensate them for additional noise, and to estimate the effects that noise levels have on property values. In the case of pain, even methods such as these are not available. On the other hand the reduction of pain through the prevention of a disease or improved dentistry or improved analgesics is clearly of benefit – but how much?

(f) The value of life Many social projects have a direct effect on life expectancy. With crash barriers along motorways this is obvious but it equally applies to the projects to reduce air pollution or extend immunisation. One of the benefits of reduced premature mortality is increased production since the individual's productive life is not cut short by premature death. However society does not value people's lives solely in terms of their productive potential; if it did all pensioners whose consumption exceeds their output would be considered as having lives which were worthless. Therefore lives have an intrinsic value – but how much? To those who recoil and say that such questions are unduly mercenary and that life is of infinite value, it must be said that society does not, and could not, operate on that basis. We do not devote all possible resources to reducing the loss of life. When decisions are made to limit health programmes or street lighting then this is implicitly stating that the lives that would quite indubitably be saved are of less value than the cost of the programme. Yet to state that we do put a value on life provides no answer to the question of what that value should be.

Decisions over time
If the costs and benefits of a project occur simultaneously or over a limited period of time there is no need to take account of the time dimension. However, in projects which last a number of years the time dimension cannot be ignored. It is not enough simply to add up all the costs and benefits whenever they occur. This may best be illustrated by comparing two projects which have the same cost, one of which yields the benefits in one year's time whereas the other yields the same benefits in one hundred years' time; clearly there is a major difference

between the two projects. It may also be seen that even if the latter project yielded twice the benefit of the former, it might still be far less attractive. Some technique is therefore necessary to take account of the time at which costs and benefits arise.

Such a technique is available in the form of 'discounting'. This technique is essentially quite straightforward but it needs some explanation to avoid an undue sense of mystery. The purpose of discounting is to test the rate of return on a project. By rate of return is meant what accrues on the investment in the project. If we have two projects each costing £100 and project A yielding £15 per annum evermore and project B yielding £20 per annum evermore, then it is clear that the rate of return on A is 15 per cent and on B is 20 per cent. If the choice is between A and B, then B yields a higher rate of return. In practice most projects do not have a steady and indefinite yield of this nature. This poses an arithmetical problem of calculating the rate of return which can be overcome by discounting.

There is however a more fundamental economic justification for discounting. This can be illustrated by considering what takes place when a private saver lends to a private investor. The private saver defers present consumption in return for the prospect of higher consumption in the future. The investor, on the other hand, incurs the liability in the hope of investing in some form of capital which will accumulate in the future so that even after paying the saver for the use of the money there will be a profit for the investor. In the public sector the position is not very different. A future return must be offered to people in order to encourage them to defer present consumption; this return is known as the social time preference rate. Depending on the projects that are available in the economy, there will be a sacrifice involved in using resources for a particular project in that those resources cannot be used in any other way. Thus there is a cost of capital, known as the social opportunity cost of capital, which is the rate of return offered by the best project which could proceed if we were not using the capital in the present scheme. If the market for savings and investment is functioning efficiently then the social time preference rate will come to equal the social opportunity cost and we may call this rate the discount rate. If we assume this rate is, for illustration, 10 per cent, what does this mean?

From the saver's point of view it means that in order to give up £100 now the marginal saver would have to be offered £110 in a year's time or £121 in two years' time or £161 in five years' time. From the point of view of public investment, if there is a project available yielding 10 per cent, then £100 would have increased to £110 in one year, or £121 in two years, or £161 in five years. Now if £100 is equivalent to £161 in five years' time, we may then ask what is the present equivalent of £100 five years hence; the answer is £62.1. Thus we may state that the *present value* of £100 in five years' time is £62.1. We are in effect discounting future values back to present values. The discount factor for year 5 is 0.621. For year 1 it is 0.909 and for year 2, 0.826 (110 × 0.909 = 100; 121 × 0.826 = 100). This is illustrated in Table 4.2.

Table 4.2   Growth and discount factors

Year	Growth at 10% p.a.		Discount factor
0	100	62.1	1.0
1	110		0.909
2	121		0.826
3	133.1		0.751
4	146.4		0.683
5	161.1	100	0.621

The technique of discounting in effect allows costs and benefits accruing at different points in time to be added together to produce a *net present value* of the project. If this net present value is positive it indicates that the rate of return on the project is greater than the discount rate. If the net present value is negative the rate of return is less than the discount rate. Therefore what the technique of discounting makes possible is a testing of any project to see whether the rate of return is better or worse than that of a hypothetical project which yields a return at the discount rate. We assume that projects are available yielding 10 per cent return: does the project in question do better or worse than this? A simple illustration of discounting is shown in Table 4.3.

Table 4.3   Cash flow and present values

Year	Cash flow	Discount factor 10%	Present value
0	−1500	1.0	−1500.0
1	+ 400	0.909	+ 363.6
2	+ 400	0.826	+ 330.6
3	+ 400	0.751	+ 300.5
4	+ 400	0.638	+ 273.2
5	+ 400	0.621	+ 248.4
		Net Present Value	+ 16.3

The question inevitably arises of what is the appropriate discount rate. Discounting factors using three different rates are shown in Table

4.4. It will be seen that using a high discount rate (e.g. 20 per cent) the discount factor for year 20 is 0.026, a very small factor; what this means is that if we have projects available yielding 20 per cent per annum return then what happens twenty years hence is of very little importance compared to what happens in the early years of the project. By contrast, with a 5 per cent discount rate the discounting factor is 0.377 for year 20. The appropriate rate depends on many factors – the availability of capital, market rates of interest, government objectives in relation to social investment for examples.

In appraising any project the dimension of time must be taken into account, the testing of the rate of return on a project by discounting offers a systematic method of doing so.

Table 4.4 Discount factors

	Discount rate			
Year	5%	10%	15%	20%
1	0.952	0.909	0.870	0.833
2	0.907	0.826	0.756	0.694
3	0.864	0.751	0.658	0.579
4	0.823	0.683	0.572	0.482
5	0.784	0.621	0.497	0.402
10	0.614	0.386	0.247	0.162
15	0.481	0.239	0.123	0.065
20	0.377	0.149	0.061	0.026
50	0.087	0.009	0.001	0.0001

Decisions affecting the distribution of incomes

Just as costs and benefits do not occur at the same time, they do not always affect the same individuals. If a road is built through a poor neighbourhood then poor people will lose and better-off people with cars will gain. The cost to the losers may, if measured in money, be less than the benefit to the gainers; however if measured in terms of social welfare – by weighting the gains or losses according to the importance attached to the incomes of each group (i.e. their marginal social values) – the losses of social welfare may exceed the gains. Put simply, the loss of a pound to a poor person means a greater loss of social welfare than the gain from an extra pound (or perhaps even ten pounds) to a better-off person.

In evaluating gains and losses it may be desirable to take account of the income level of the gainers and the losers. One way of doing this is to weight the gains and losses so that a change to a low-income person counts for more than the same money-value change for a high-income person. The question then is how can these weights be determined. Weisbrod (1968) has suggested that the appropriate weights should be inferred from the government's previous decisions on whether to adopt various projects or not. This approach stresses that government decisions *should* embody some consistent set of distributional weights but it is doubtful how far governments actually do so. Another approach (Marglin, 1967) is to maximise the benefits subject to some minimum being secured by specified disadvantaged groups. A third approach is simply to show the costs and benefits to different groups and leave policy-makers to decide on their own weights (Roskill, 1970).

A project may affect rich and poor differently. Similarly, men and women may be very differently affected. In all such cases what is important is to be explicit about the differential effects.

Criteria for decision-making

There are many aspects of valuing costs and benefits that have not been discussed here – the treatment of risk and uncertainty, dealing with transfer payments, and the problem of second-best, for example. Let us, however, make the heroic assumption that we have been able to measure all the costs and benefits of a particular project and when they occur. How then do we decide whether the project should be carried out or not?

At the simplest level we may examine whether the benefits exceed the costs. If they do then it is worth doing. If they do not we should be better off not doing the project. Such a simple approach must be complicated to take account of compensation and of choice between projects.

To take account of compensation two possible criteria have been proposed. The *Pareto* criterion is that a project should be undertaken if as a result no one is worse off and someone is better off; in effect there must be gainers but no losers. This does not mean no one will suffer any adverse effects from the project but it does mean that if they do they will be fully compensated. The *Hicks–Kaldor* criterion is much less restrictive: a project should be undertaken if the gainers *could* in theory compensate the losers and there still be a net gain *whether or not* that compensation actually takes place. On this criterion the question of compensation is a separate issue of redistribution to be considered after examining whether the project increases the total resources available. In practice because of the difficulty of compensating all losers by the amount of their losses the strict Pareto criterion can never be used. For example, in building a new school the cost in terms of extra noise would have to be assessed by taking into account individuals' hearing and sensitivity to children's cries, and each individual would have to be compensated accordingly; on this basis no new schools would ever get built. It is, nevertheless, important to recognise the important difference between the two criteria.

Second, in relation to choice, the question arises of what are the available options. If the benefit of a project exceeds the costs then in theory it is a 'good project' and should be carried out. If, however, there is a budget constraint and only a limited amount can be spent at any one time then what must be selected are the *best* projects (not just *good* projects). Thus if only £1000 can be spent and one project would have benefits of £2000 and the other of £3000 then clearly the latter is preferable. It is therefore important to set out all the available options (including doing nothing, or waiting) rather than pick the first project for which benefits exceed costs.

In choosing the best project, various criteria are possible which have slightly different properties. One is to discount all costs and benefits to their present values and select the project with the highest benefit:cost ratio. Another is to calculate the internal rate of return to each project. Whatever the method used, the most important practical requirement is to set out the options with their costs and benefits as realistically and fairly as possible.

Cost-benefit in social planning

The three examples of cost-benefit techniques presented here are different in nature. The first is a simplified exercise designed to illustrate the application of the general approach, and discounting over time in particular. The second is a relatively simple cost effectiveness study designed to illustrate some practical problems of estimation and method. The third is a brief account of a major study designed to indicate the considerations and complexity involved in appraising a major public investment.

A low-cost housing scheme

A temporary low-cost housing scheme was under consideration as part of a rural resettlement scheme in a developing country. Each unit would cost £50 to build and would last five years. The total maintenance cost over the life of the housing was estimated at £10 and administration would cost £1 per year per unit. Because the Government wished to encourage rural resettlement it was prepared to give a housing subsidy of £10 per year to anyone moving to the area. The maximum rent that potential occupants could and would pay was £10 per year.

The problem was to decide whether it was worth undertaking this project, taking into account that the Government had other alternative projects which would yield a 10 per cent rate of return and required this project to do the same.

The first step was to work out the time-flow of costs and benefits. It was assumed that the maintenance cost would be spread evenly over the five years' life of the housing. Thus there would be a cost of construction of £50 at the start and £3 per year thereafter (£2 maintenance + £1 administration). On the benefit side it was assumed that the rent that occupants would pay indicated their valuation of the housing and that the subsidy the Government would pay indicated the additional value that the society (as represented by the Government) put on achieving the rural resettlement. Thus the benefits amounted to £20 per year. The time-flow of costs and benefits are shown in Table 4.5 as are the discount factors at 10 per cent and the present discounted value of the net flows. The net present value (the sum of all the present discounted values) is positive. This shows that the rate of return is greater than 10 per cent. The project was therefore worth undertaking.

Table 4.5   **Low-cost housing scheme**

Year	Costs	Benefits	Net flow	Discount factor 10%	Present discounted value
0	50	—	−50	1.0	−50.0
1	3	20	+17	0.909	+15.5
2	3	20	+17	0.826	+14.0
3	3	20	+17	0.751	+12.8
4	3	20	+17	0.683	+11.6
5	3	20	+17	0.621	+10.6
				Net Present Value	+14.5

The cost effectiveness of treating varicose veins

The next example of cost-benefit techniques is not a full cost-benefit study but a comparison of the cost effectiveness of two methods of treating varicose veins (Piachaud and Weddell, 1972). The purpose was to compare treatment by means of surgery with treatment by injecting a substance into the veins and then bandaging them – injection-compression sclerotherapy. To make the comparison a randomised controlled trial was carried out with patients randomly assigned to one of the two treatments. After three years the patients were re-examined and the effectiveness of the two treatments was compared.

It was found that the success of the two treatments did not differ significantly – they appeared to be equally effective. It was therefore decided to compare the costs of the two forms of treatment. These costs were divided into costs to the National Health Service and costs to patients. Surgery involved a stay in hospital averaging about four days. Injection-compression treatment was carried out at an out-patient clinic and required an average of seven attendances. It was not feasible to estimate the capital costs of the facilities; the limitation to running costs only is likely to understate the costs of surgery relative to injection-compression treatment. For out-patient treatment estimating costs presented no great problems. The salaries for each of the staff taking part in a typical clinic were assessed; cleaning, building maintenance and heating were all costed and the secretarial costs covered the costs of medical records. The average cost of an out-patient session was £41.50. The average number of patients treated per session was 31; the average number of clinic attendances per patient was 7.3. Thus the average total cost per patient of out-patient injection-compression treatment was £9.77 (all figures in 1967/8 prices).

For surgery many more problems arose because the construction of a complete system to cost the surgical treatment of varicose veins would, if it were to cover the full range of hospital costs, be a vast undertaking. Existing information was, however, quite adequate to estimate most of the costs. The Hospital Costing Return provided average costs per in-patient week for each of a number of categories of expenditure and unit costs for most of the major departments. A number of categories of expenditure were assumed to be 'shared' equally by all in-patients (domestic staff, catering, staff residence, laundry, power, light and heat, building and engineering maintenance, general administration, general portering, general cleaning, maintenance of grounds, transport, other services and equipment). The inclusion on a shared basis of equipment needs some explanation: while certain items of equipment may rarely, or never, be used on varicose vein patients, it was virtually impossible to say which were essential and which were not, given the countless contingencies for which a hospital must be prepared. Further, the use of an operating theatre for varicose vein surgery precluded its use for other operations and therefore any equipment primarily for other types of surgery necessarily lay idle.

The sum of these 'shared costs' was £29.09 per in-patient week or £15.38 for the average varicose vein patient's stay of 3.7 days.

The cost of nursing and medical staff could not be assumed to be shared equally by all patients. On the basis of a small survey it was estimated that one-quarter of all nursing time was spent on 'general' activities. The time spent on particular nursing activities associated with varicose vein patients averaged $1\frac{1}{2}$ hours during the in-patient stay and in addition approximately half an hour was required for the out-patient attendances subsequent to discharge, thus making a total nursing cost of £2.02 per patient. A similar method was used to estimate medical staff costs which added up to £2.01 per patient.

The average cost per operation for the use of the operating theatre (drugs, dressings, equipment and staff employed on theatre duties, etc.) was £13.71 which was a reasonable approximation to the cost of varicose vein operations.

Pathology tests, X-rays, drugs and dressings were specially recorded and costed, in all £8.33 per patient. Medical record costs were taken to be the average per case, namely £2.76, giving a total of £44.22 for the hospital costs of surgery for varicose veins.

Thus, even allowing for a substantial margin of error, the cost to the health service of surgery (£44.22 per case) was higher than that of injection-compression treatment (£9.77 per case).

The second part of the costing involved estimating costs to patients. Not all of these costs were studied, only costs in terms of lost production. It was found that the mean number of days taken off work at the time of treatment and for convalescence was 6.4 days for those treated by injection-compression and 31.3 days for those treated surgically. Thus the average loss of earnings of those in full-time employment receiving surgical treatment was £118 and of those receiving injection-compression treatment was £29.

Since injection-compression treatment had a lower cost to both the health service and to patients and did not differ significantly in effectiveness from surgery, it appeared to be a preferable method of treatment.

This finding was disturbed by the five-year follow-up of patients (Beresford *et al.*, 1978). It was found that after five years significantly more of those who had first had injection-compression treatment needed re-treatment. Thus effectiveness of the two forms of treatment was not the same – this finding was in direct contrast to what had been found at the three-year follow-up. This later finding illustrates the problems of doing an appraisal with limited data. It also shows the limitations of a cost effectiveness study. On the earlier results with effectiveness apparently equal the less costly technique appeared preferable. With the later results it appeared that surgery cost more and produced better results. But the study shed no light on whether the benefit of the better results justified the extra cost. There would have been no difficulty if surgery cost more and yielded *worse* results. But re-treatment was less common in patients treated initially with surgery. One in nine patients given injection-compression treatment might have avoided re-treatment if the initial treatment had been surgery. Yet for every nine patients treated surgically, instead of by injection-compression, the additional cost to the National Health Service was £1500, and the cost to society in terms of lost output was £2480. The issue was therefore whether the benefit of avoiding one case needing re-treatment justified the costs and also whether this benefit exceeded the potential benefit available from using the same health service resources in another way.

The Victoria Line
The Victoria Line is a part of the London Underground railway which was opened in 1968. Before its construction was authorised a cost-benefit study was carried out by Beesley and Foster (1963).

The cost side was relatively straightforward. Estimates could be made of the costs of tunnelling, construction, rolling stock and manpower to run the service. The benefit side was much more complex. Three main types of benefits were distinguished: (i) time savings, (ii) cost savings, and (iii) increased comfort and convenience.

The most obvious time saving was to those who would use the proposed line and make their journeys faster than before. Some of the journeys on the Victoria Line would not otherwise have been made; but many would be diverted from other modes or routes. Thus the new line would reduce congestion and speed up traffic on other underground lines and on the roads, so that buses and cars would travel faster. Estimates were made of all these time savings.

The proposed line would provide many people with a more direct route at lower cost. This is a social benefit. In addition reduced congestion will lower costs for other underground services and on the bus services; other road users would save in vehicle operating costs.

While journeys may be faster and cost less, they may also be more comfortable with more chance of sitting rather than standing. This too is a benefit.

All these benefits were considered in relation to those who would travel on the new line rather than some other way, those who would continue to travel some other way, and those who would travel only because of the new line – generated traffic.

Only the main elements of this study have been mentioned; there is no space to describe how each of the elements was estimated. The main results are shown in Table 4.6. It will be clear that a study of this kind not only involves a large amount of complex data analysis but also requires a clear head to avoid terrible confusion about different effects.

The costs and benefits of cost-benefit techniques
Cost-benefit techniques require the enumeration, estimation and aggregation of the costs and benefits of a particular project. Some of the difficulties involved in carrying this out have been described but it is important to be aware of some of the dangers and limitations.

First, there is a danger of false precision. Many estimates of costs and

Table 4.6   Social costs and benefits of the Victoria Line

		Annual amount (£m)	*Present Discounted Value (rate of interest 6%; £m)*
A.	Costs (other than interest charges)		
	Annual working expenses	1.413	16.16
	Benefits		
B.	Traffic diverted to Victoria Line		
	1. Underground		
	time savings	0.378	4.32
	comfort and convenience	0.347	3.96
	2. British Rail: time savings	0.205	2.93
	3. Buses: time savings	0.575	6.58
	4. Motorists		
	time savings	0.153	3.25
	saving in vehicle operating costs	0.377	8.02
	5. Pedestrians: time savings	0.020	0.28
	B. Sub-total	2.055	29.34
C.	Traffic not diverted to Victoria Line		
	1. Underground		
	cost savings	0.150	1.72
	comfort and convenience	0.457	5.22
	3. Buses: cost savings	0.645	7.38
	4. Road users		
	time savings	1.883	21.54
	savings in vehicle operating costs	0.781	8.93
	C. Sub-total	3.916	44.79
D.	Generated traffic		
	Outer areas		
	time savings	0.096	1.37
	fare savings	0.063	0.90
	other benefits	0.375	5.36
	Central area		
	time savings	0.056	0.80
	fare savings	0.029	0.41
	other benefits	0.203	2.90
	D. Sub-total	0.822	11.74
E.	Terminal scrap value		0.29
F.	Total benefits (B+C+D+E)		86.16
G.	Net current benefit (F−A)		70.00
H.	Value of capital expenditure		38.81
I.	Net benefit (G−H)		31.19
J.	Social surplus rate of return		11.3 per cent

Source: Beesley and Foster (1963)

benefits can, at best, be approximate: for example, the reliability of equipment and the number of people who would use a social service may be very hard to estimate. There is a common tendency to treat estimates – once they have been made on a very approximate basis – as though they are absolutely precise. Houses built on sand tend to fall down; similarly false precision may lead to mistaken conclusions. This does *not* mean that vast resources must be devoted to trying to achieve greater precision on *all* estimates: in planning schools an error of 50, 500 or even 5000 per cent in estimating the price of blackboard chalk probably makes little difference. It *does* mean that the sensitivity or robustness of the results should be tested by comparing the results of making different assumptions about the key elements in the costs and benefits. It has to be remembered that the resources used in project appraisal have their own cost; these resources – principally the time of the social planner, economist or other decision-maker – should clearly be concentrated on those elements of a cost-benefit analysis that are most significant in terms of how they affect the conclusions of the project appraisal.

A second danger arises because of the difficulty of valuing certain intangible effects. As has been stated, even if no quantitative value can be put on, for example, reduced pain or a quieter environment, the effects should at least be described. There is a tendency, however, to mention such effects once (often in a footnote) and then ignore them thereafter; only the quantified costs and benefits get added up. If there are important intangible costs or benefits which cannot be quantified then they must not be forgotten in the final analysis.

A third danger is an extension of the second. In deciding on a set of alternative projects to compare there is a danger that projects which are harder to quantify will get excluded or given less favourable treatment. A project which looks (perhaps falsely) 'cut and dried' with everything certain and quantified may appear more attractive than another project about which there is a lot of uncertainty and for which estimates are more difficult. Thus projects which are similar to past developments have an advantage in that estimates can be made based on past performance; in part this is appropriate because alternative novel and untried projects do have a greater degree of uncertainty than tried and tested methods. But it may cause new methods to be rejected simply because the existing method can be explained with more impressive looking figures.

A fourth danger is that cost-benefit techniques may bias decisions towards those that reinforce the existing distribution of incomes. If a benefit goes to a rich man it is easy to value this more highly than the same benefit to a poor man if the rich man would be prepared to pay more to enjoy the benefit. As discussed above, it is possible to 'weight' effects to avoid this and wherever possible this should be done. But the danger remains that in aggregating costs and benefits the question of which social groups gain and lose will be obscured and only 'net' effects will be seen. Many decision-makers may on being presented with a project appraisal turn to the last page to see what the overall rate of return is and ignore the intermediate steps. It is, nevertheless, important that it be spelled out very clearly *who* would gain and lose, and by how much.

A fifth limitation, rather than a danger, is that no cost-benefit techniques serve much purpose in comparing projects which are entirely different. A project to build a school cannot usefully be compared with a project to build a dam. Two projects designed to improve literacy may usefully be compared; or two projects to improve agricultural output. But the more distinct the projects are, the less comparable they become.

Many of these dangers are symptomatic of a general problem – namely the power of the technician who carries out the cost-benefit techniques. If this power is abused this can mean, at the extreme, that the social planner, or whoever carries out the cost-benefit analysis, decides which projects to appraise, goes away and comes back and announces which alternative should be carried out. If the results are questioned the impudent questioner is overwhelmed with jargon, tables and often computer print-out which is beyond comprehension. Such an approach, which is not unknown in practice, negates the entire purpose of making the appraisal of projects more systematic and open to scrutiny with clearly stated assumptions and comprehensible methods. Inevitably the technician who has studied a project for weeks, months or years will know more about a project as a whole than anyone else. But the technician should remember that on particular aspects others may be far more expert; for example villagers whose village is threatened with submersion in a hydroelectric scheme are not likely to be pleased if a brash social planner with a calculator tells them their village is worth £x without even consulting them about their views. The responsibility of the technician is to be as public as possible so that the assumptions, methods and estimates are entirely open and there can be no suspicion of a technical (or political) 'fix'. Cost-benefit techniques should never be mysterious 'black-box' techniques with the social planner cast in the role of magician.

Some dangers and limitations of cost-benefit techniques have been described. But the benefits of such techniques should not be ignored. Overwhelmingly the most important is that cost-benefit techniques require *clarity*. The effects of a project have to be enumerated and their quantitative importance estimated. Assumptions must be made explicit. Thus cost-benefit techniques can and should illuminate the choices to be made.

5 Programme Budgets and Social Planning
Howard Glennerster

Plans can only be translated into practice through the budgetary process. Social plans must get off the planner's desk and into the finance officer's budget. The budget *process* is the drive shaft which links social policies and plans to service delivery, and it is, of course, a political process. It is political in two senses. First, it is party political. The budget will embody the ruling party's priorities and aspirations, its judgement about what the electorate is prepared to pay in taxes. In a congressional system like that of the United States, with responsibilities divided between a legislative and an executive branch, the budget is the outcome of an intense round of politicing between the administration and the various spending committees in both Houses. The budget is political in another sense. Each agency or department's bid for funds is also an outcome of organisational politics. To quote one of the leading and illuminating writers in this field, Wildavsky (1975, p. 4): 'If organisations are seen as political coalitions, budgets are mechanisms through which sub units bargain over conflicting goals, make side payments, and try to motivate one another to accomplish their objectives.'

The budgeting process has traditionally been brief, hectic, and conducted in negotiations with finance officers who are the only ones who understand the complex accounts. Long established budget routines edge forward existing expenditures – increments added on, or subtracted from, the base budget. Yet if social policies are aiming to introduce some kind of spending priorities, and there is not much point in them unless they do, social planners have to seek to change the nature of the *budget process* so that it reflects these longer-term considerations. They also have to seek to change the nature of the *budget structure*. Until recently budget accounts were designed by accountants to prevent the misuse of funds. Headings on a traditional functional 'line item' budget refer to salaries, wages, superannuation costs, expenditure on building maintenance, supplies of materials, equipment and many more. These derive from the actual bills paid out and it is crucial for the accountant to be able to check them back to ensure no one has absconded with the funds. Yet these categories are useless to the planner. He or she is interested in the purpose of the spending, on whom it is spent and where it is spent and with what results.

Programme budgets were designed to transform the *budget structure* into a planner's tool, and programming, planning and budgeting systems were designed to transform the *budget process* into a planning process.

The origins of programme budgeting

It is possible to trace the intellectual origins of programme budgeting to three sources (Schick, 1966; Williams, 1967): (i) the scientific management school of writers in America and the impact they had on methods of public and business administration; (ii) the development of cost-benefit analysis and project appraisal, again notably in the US Federal Government; and (iii) the acceptance of a Keynesian view of government's need to plan the size of the public sector of the economy as part of its macroeconomic budget strategy.

While critical of earlier attempts to apply scientific measurement techniques to human organisations, Herbert Simon (1957), the influential American writer on public administration, did claim that organisations were capable of operating in more rational ways than they usually did. To do so senior administrators must be clear about the objectives of the organisation, agency or service. They must distinguish between the means (resources, employees) and the ends – the outcomes of their activity. Moreover, Simon argued that the purposes of the organisation should be reflected in the structure of its budget.

Cost-benefit analysis is discussed elsewhere in this volume but the particular contribution made by the RAND Corporation economists who had been working on such studies for the US Federal Government in the 1950s and 1960s was to see that all three strands of thought could be fused to make the Federal Budget process the vehicle for forward planning, and the budget structure the means to enable cost-benefit choices to be made between different programmes or activities of Government (Novick, 1965; Hitch and McKean, 1961; McKean, 1958).

The pure theory of programme budgeting (Novick, 1965) stated that each government department or agency should clarify and define its objectives. This could be done initially in broad terms, for example, preventing illness, curing illness, long-term care, maternity. These broad purposes could then be subdivided more elaborately, for example into the type of illness to be cured, and then into the alternative means available for treatment or care. At each stage the budget could be structured accordingly. It would show how much was spent on each kind of treatment. Ministers would then be able to decide whether to increase that part of the budget devoted to long term care or acute curative medicine or to prevention. At lower levels it would be possible to undertake cost-benefit or cost effectiveness analysis to see which form of treatment was most effective and allocate money within the acute sector accordingly.

Then, it was argued, the length of the budget process should be extended to give time for such analyses to be undertaken and digested by senior management and put before ministers prior to the time final budget decisions had to be made. This meant extending the budget *process* backwards in time, perhaps to begin work on next year's budget a year or more in advance. Since policy commitments to new activities or new buildings may often cost very little at first but then build up into very large expenditures, in say five years' time, it was also necessary to extend the time-scale of the budget forward to produce a multi year budget. This would set out in constant prices the forecast spending the department required to meet present policies and any new ones. These could then be matched against revenue projections to see if the plans would entail raising taxes.

Finally, the budget process should involve the ongoing monitoring and evaluation of departments' activities, the results of which would be fed back into the budget process in the next preliminary phase. The budget process was therefore to be the focal point at which many of the techniques discussed in this book would be deployed. Similar arguments had convinced the British government in 1961 to introduce a four or five-year public expenditure planning cycle (PESC), and the two approaches intermingled in the mid-1960s and early 1970s (Glennerster, 1975). The idea spread through the world, not least to the developing countries, like a bush fire.

There have been other fashionable reforms to budgeting practice which have similarly come and gone. Performance budgets were one predecessor (Schick, 1966). They involved attaching a measure of output to each group of expenditure items. Zero-based budgeting was another. This preceded and followed Planning, Programming and Budgeting or PPB. It was tried in the US Department of Agriculture in the early 1960s (Wildavsky, 1975). President Carter reintroduced it in the 1970s. It too faded away (Draper and Pitsvada, 1981). Programme budgeting remains the most comprehensive reform that has been attempted and has had by far the most influence.

Planning, Programme and Budgeting Systems (PPBS) were first used in the US Defense Department in the early 1960s. Then in 1965 they were spread by Presidential decree to the whole of the US Federal Government (Novick, 1965). In fact, there could scarcely have been a less propitious place to begin. The US Budget process is an extraordinarily complex one involving not merely a myriad of diverse agencies and a relatively weak central controller – the Office of

Management and Budget – but, most importantly, the real decisions lie in the interplay of political interests in Congress and between Congress and the White House. Moreover, the inherent weaknesses of the original concept became apparent when they were applied to social service programmes (Glennerster, 1975). How do you define the objectives of the health service or social work or education in measurable and agreed terms? When planners tried, they soon found the objectives were disputed, they were multiple, often confused and subtly changing and above all were interpreted and carried out by professional workers in the field who were guaranteed a large measure of professional or 'clinical' freedom. The activities of a single professional, like a general practitioner, covered the whole range of objectives – prevention, cure, care, he did them all, possibly all at the same time. The failure of the original, more visionary attempts at budget reform, which political scientists rightly condemned as unrealistic (Wildavsky, 1975), should not blind us to the fact that important and lasting changes have taken place not only in budget processes but in the way budget figures are presented – even in the United States.

The notion of a longer time-scale, both for pre-budget analysis and for estimating the long-term consequences of present policy changes, are now widely accepted, at least as ideals. Less readily accepted, but just as important, was the stress the original reformers laid on the way the budget was analysed and structured. It is on this more technical aspect of programme budgeting that we concentrate in the rest of the chapter. We take as one example the attempt by the Department of Health and Social Security (DHSS) in Britain to apply the approach to the health and personal social services budget between 1971 and 1978. In many ways it was successful and continues to form the basis of the Department's forward planning. An account by one of those responsible for much of the work, Mrs Banks, is to be found in Booth (1979). We shall also look at an example from Nepal and some other developing countries. First, however, we spell out the essential steps needed to undertake a programme budget analysis of a limited but practical kind.

The original ideal modified – a practical approach
The DHSS economists, like those in the British Education Department before them (United Kingdom, 1970), decided to modify the original conception of a multilayer budget to more realistic proportions. In their final published account (United Kingdom, 1976b, p. 78) they summarised in a very down to earth way what they thought the technique was aiming to do:

The programme budget is not a complex technical tool but a crude method of costing policies based on past expenditure. Its central purpose is to enable the Department to cost policies for service development across the board, so that priorities can be considered within realistic financial constraints. The programme budget is neither a forecast nor a plan: it is a way of exploring possible future strategies for development . . . it attempts to group expenditure into programmes which are more meaningful in considering options and priorities than the public expenditure survey breakdown or the traditional estimates and accounts. In health and personal social services a complete breakdown of expenditure by objectives (e.g. treatment of specific medical conditions) would be extremely detailed and complex, and far too cumbersome for an across-the-board review; the necessary data is in any case not available. The programme budget does not therefore contain the kind of information needed for evaluating options in detail (e.g. by a cost-benefit analysis of one kind of treatment versus another). However, there are certain major groups of services cutting across administrative boundaries, which provide complementary and alternative forms of care for certain important groups of users, in particular the elderly, physically and mentally handicapped, mentally ill and children. These 'client groups' are also the subject of special policies and priorities, and their numbers are changing in very different ways with the changing age structure of the population.

This statement contains the essence of the approach and the kind of questions planners must ask in setting up a programme budget. We spell them out below.

What should the scope of the budget be?
In general the principle should be to include in the same programme services which are complementary to or alternative to one another. For example, in the case of the elderly, this would include geriatric wards, nursing homes, residential homes, sheltered housing and home care services (see Table 5.1). Changes in the age structure of the elderly population and its dependancy will shift the balance of demand for care from one kind of institution to another. Planners will want to show the effects of changes in the size and dependency of the population on the expenditure for this range of services, assuming standards are to be maintained. Hence they will want them all in the scope of a single budget. Planners may also wish to show the consequences of improving or reducing staffing levels or other inputs.

On the other hand the budget must reflect administrative and organisational reality. If these interrelated services are administered by separate departments or authorities which are not financed out of the same budget and have no means of coordination, such a combination of expenditures would be no more than an academic exercise. The budget must relate to some decision-making unit capable of making budget allocations across its entire scope.

What should the sub-programme categories be?
Here there are at least six considerations to bear in mind. First, the categories must reflect the political priorities of ministers. There may

be groups they feel should be given priority. In that case spending on those groups must be disaggregated and shown separately. Priorities of politicians will clearly change, but budget categories cannot that frequently. This is where the political judgement of the planner becomes important. What are the continuing priority choices that all ministers or committee members will need to consider? This task is critical. If a budget is presented to a committee in terms of staff costs and expenditure on travel and equipment, this is how the political debate and choices will develop. If issues of social equity between groups or areas are to be discussed, they must be reflected in the budget structure.

Second, the categories chosen must reflect the underlying and changing trends in demands for the service. If one part of the service is being affected by a rapid decline in the number of users – the maternity service or primary schools, for example – this should show up clearly in the expenditure consequences. Thus the programme structure must reflect demography and the institutional structure of the services that are provided for these different groups in the population.

Thirdly, the programme structure must be capable of reflecting changes that are occurring in technology and costs, i.e. the supply side. Politicians will want to know how much money it will cost to go on doing what we are doing now, given increasing or decreasing demands and costs.

Fourth, categories must translate easily into the existing accounting structure of the department or agency. Thus, in the case of local authority residential homes for the elderly there is a clearly recognisable account and budget holder responsible for that expenditure. They can usefully appear as a sub-category. On the other hand it may be illuminating to estimate how much money is spent on the elderly who occupy acute beds in a district hospital. It may help estimate likely trends in spending on such wards. But for a long-term budget category it is unhelpful because elderly people are merely one amongst many occupants of the beds in a surgical ward. There is no separate account from which their care can be financed.

Fifth, the sub-categories must reflect the basic economic distinction between current and capital expenditure, spending on transfer items and current goods and services. The latter must distinguish between salaries and other forms of spending.

Sixth, the costs should be in gross *and* net terms. There are charges for many services. Payments made by residents of old people's homes are an example. The scale of charges is a major policy issue and must be included. Politicians and planners should be interested *both* in the scale of service provided, i.e. the gross cost, and in the cost to taxpayers or ratepayers – the net cost.

In brief, then, there are no simple technical rules to be applied in devising budget categories. They will differ depending on the kind of agency, service and political priorities for whom the planner is working. Table 5.1 summarises the points made in this section. Level three contains the basic building blocks from which the higher level programme categories can be built up. These basic building blocks must be compatible with the statutory authority's or agency accounts. This enables the programme budget to be translated back readily into finance officers language and, if their accounts are computerised, to link the two financial data systems. Ideally, the two should be fused into a single accounting framework.

ble 5.1   A programme structure

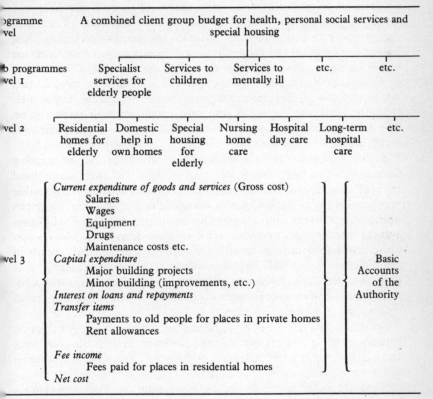

ɔgramme vel	A combined client group budget for health, personal social services and special housing						
b programmes vel 1	Specialist services for elderly people	Services to children	Services to mentally ill	etc.		etc.	
vel 2	Residential homes for elderly	Domestic help in own homes	Special housing for elderly	Nursing home care	Hospital day care	Long-term hospital care	etc.

vel 3

Current expenditure of goods and services (Gross cost)
　　Salaries
　　Wages
　　Equipment
　　Drugs
　　Maintenance costs etc.
Capital expenditure
　　Major building projects
　　Minor building (improvements, etc.)
Interest on loans and repayments
Transfer items
　　Payments to old people for places in private homes
　　Rent allowances

Fee income
　　Fees paid for places in residential homes
Net cost

Basic Accounts of the Authority

What time period?

In order to illustrate the importance of recent trends, it is important to show past expenditure figures. At least five past years are necessary to do this. A budget is an attempt not merely to plan future priorities but to monitor how past priority decisions have worked out in practice. If the elderly or the mentally ill have been designated a 'priority group', have they in fact been receiving a larger share of the service budget? If the aim is to achieve a shift from hospital to community care or small institutional care, do the expenditure trends show this has been happening? If not a major planning task will be to find out why and what could be done to change the situation.

How far forward the budget goes will depend on a range of economic, political and technical matters. If the economic, fiscal and political climate is very volatile it makes little sense to draw up plans let alone detailed budgets far ahead – perhaps no further than the next financial year. Yet, in any moderately stable economy, the case for an extended budget time span is strong, especially if there is any significant capital expenditure. New buildings usually generate increased current expenditure – more sophisticated equipment, more heating. They also generate new staffing requirements unless they are replacements of old buildings. If the capital expenditure is financed from a loan there are also loan repayments and interest. All these constitute 'the future revenue consequences' of capital expenditure. One of the most important features of social service budget planning is to ensure that capital expenditure is not increased unless the revenue consequences have been faced and planned for. Not to do so will mean a completed hospital lying idle for lack of money to appoint new staff or pay the fuel bills. This has happened even in an advanced economy like the United Kingdom. Since complex capital projects like a new hospital may take ten years from initial decision to build to full use, indeed often longer if things go wrong, a budget should in outline seek to include the consequences of present and past capital spending decisions on future current spending. That means an outline budget up to ten years ahead. More detailed 'filling out' is useful up to four years ahead. The timespan should reflect the period in office of a majority party. More detailed estimates for two years ahead and full budget estimates for the next financial year will be necessary.

What price basis?
It is essential to present figures on a constant price basis. Past cash prices which include the effects of inflation as well as 'real' spending changes are meaningless to politicians or managers. The British government (United Kingdom, 1982), having for many years published constant price figures, recently reverted to actual cash figures for past years and some guess about inflation for future years – 'unreal spending' one may call it. One can only assume this is a deliberate attempt to confuse and hide the effects of real reductions in expenditure. In fact, it illustrates a conflict between the planning function of a budget and its control function. Planners wish to gain a secure, or at

least a reasonably predictable, future for the service. They wish to know how much real money the service will have to pay its employees next year. Those who are trying to control or reduce the budget would like to hold the cash constant and let the service and its users take the consequences of any price increase. For planning purposes, and a programme budget is a planning tool, it is essential that all figures are in constant prices and, moreover, on a price basis which reflects the price changes specific to that service. Medical costs, for example, have tended to rise much faster than other prices. When it comes to arguing about next year's estimates attempts will have to be made to estimate inflation, and bargain for funds to meet it. The finance department or the Treasury may impose a real cut by keeping the service to the same cash limit while prices are increasing. That is what the control function is all about, but planners must not seek to confuse decision-takers or the public about *real* trends in spending on their services. Hence accounts of past spending and alternative scenarios for the future must be expressed in real or volume terms. What politicians then do about that spending level is another matter. They should know the consequences.

Is a budget a one shot exercise?
No! The whole point of a programme budget is to use it as a 'what if' tool, to simulate different consequences which would flow from meeting alternative estimates of demand for the service, or different policies and priorities politicians may wish to test. The published exercise may have the appearance of a single clear target but it will be the outcome of many trials. Indeed it will help public discussion to publish various scenarios.

What to do about performance measures?
In the original literature each element or activity in the budget was to be accompanied by a measure of output. In practice these came to be routine statements of the number of people visited or the number of patients treated – the nearest that could be got to output. In most cases even that relevance was difficult and input measures like the number of staff employed appeared. Real output measures – whether people were cured or whether their educational performance improved – involved complex studies. The best answer is for planners to be highly selective and undertake a rigorous evaluation of a very few areas of spending at any one time. They may be politically important ones or areas where preliminary work suggests efficiency could be improved. Perhaps the programme itself should be reconsidered entirely. This was broadly the strategy followed in the Department of Health, Education and Welfare in Washington and by the British government in the early 1970s in its Programme Analysis and Review system (PAR) (Glennerster, 1975).

This is not to say that some useful regular indicators, for example, of demand for services, 'throughput', length of waiting lists or waiting times cannot be added with appropriate caveats and commentary.

The UK Department of Health's programme budget

In 1971 a small team of economists was appointed to consider whether it was practical and helpful to produce a programme budget for the National Health Service in England. In an interim report they concluded that it was. Eventually the work was extended to cover the services provided by local personal social service departments – residential care, domiciliary care and social work. The DHSS had national responsibility for these departments though they did not fund them directly. The primary purpose of the budget was to provide a basis on which the central department could make a sound case to the Treasury for funds, and to help ministers and the senior staff in the department reach a conclusion about feasible options and priorities for future development within the resources the Treasury and the cabinet were prepared to agree to. Secondly, it could be used to guide the lower tiers in the NHS and local authorities to persuade them to follow national guidelines and priorities. This was the purpose of the eventual publication of a four-year version of the budget together with the rationale that lay behind it (United Kingdom, 1976b; see Table 5.2).

Having clarified the purpose of the budget, the group next considered the basis on which to categorise expenditure. Since hospitals accounted for over half the budget with which they were concerned, they began by discussing ways of dividing up that spending. They considered five distinctions: disease, diagnostic groups, specialities, age-banding and dependency. The disease category was nearest to the original ideal. Cost-benefit comparisons were most readily adapted to that structure. But few such studies existed. Moreover, there are several thousand diseases. It was rejected as an impractical basis. Groups of diseases or conditions – diagnostic groups – offered a simplified category but they had little significance for policy and were useless for cost-benefit analysis. Specialities within hospitals however seemed to offer a real opportunity. Hospitals are organised on such a basis, with a clear consultant 'command structure' to match. Moreover, basic statistical material on patients' beds and workload are collected on such a basis. By using regression analysis between hospitals with a different speciality mix some estimate of costs per patient by speciality was possible. In the long run it seemed technically possible to create accounts for hospitals on a speciality basis. Experiments on these lines have since been undertaken (Magee and Osmolski, 1979).

However, central government had no policy for allocating more resources to particular specialities, nor would the medical profession

ble 5.2 DHSS programme budget for health and personal social services, 1976
Summary table by programme (£m, November 1974 prices)

	Average current growth p.a. 1970/1– 1973/4 per cent	1973/4 Out-turn		1975/6 provisional estimate		1979/80 illustrative projection		Illustrative average current growth p.a. 1975/6– 1979/80 per cent
		Capital £m	Current £m	Capital £m	Current £m	Capital £m	Current £m	
nd total	4.3	528	3630	424	3992	304	4332	2.1
mary care sub-total	1.7	23	648	24	718	18	833	3.8
General medical services	1.9		209		223		249	2.8
General dental services	– 1.9		120		129		139	1.9
General ophthalmic services	– 8.5		19		24		27	3
Pharmaceutical services	3.3		276		312		382	5.2
Health centres[a]	25.2	23	2	24	3	18	5	11
Prevention	5.5		15		15		17	3
Family planning	66.6		7		12		14	4
eral and acute hospital nd maternity services sub-total	3.7	300	1572	233	1670	155	1733	0.9
Acute IP and OP	3.0	·	1161		1225		}	
Ambulances	4.0	} 300	75	} 233	79	} 155	} 1574	1.2
Miscellaneous hospital[b]	9.2		174		197			
Obstetric IP and OP	3.9		136		143		133	– 1.8
Midwives	– 1.1		26		26		26	0
vices mainly for elderly nd physically handicapped sub-total	9.0	96	512	76	593	44	673	3.2
Geriatric IP and OP[c]	5.2	34	195	31	212	28	243	3.5
Non-psychiatric DP	15.4		6		7		9	5
Home nursing	5.6		52		59		75	6
Chiropody	9.9		8		9		10	3
Residential care	9.1	54	117	35	142	15	154	2.0
Home help	14.8		80		91		98	2
Meals	18.9		8		14		15	2
Day care	—	8	12	9	17	1	20	4
ids, adaptations, phones, etc.	—		9		12		17	9
ervices for the disabled	8.9		25	1	30		32	1.5
ices for the mentally handicapped sub-total	8.0	32	167	29	189	25	211	2.8
Mental handicap IP and OP	6.6	14	136	12	146	9	156	1.6
esidential care	17.0	9	10	9	15	10	20	7
Day care	—	9	21	8	28	6	36	6.5
ices for the mentally ill sub-total	3.6	28	303	23	320	36	344	1.8
ental illness IP and OP	3.0	23	280	17	291	25	306	1.3
sychiatric DP	14.5		10		13		16	5
esidential care	12.6	2	3	2	4	3	5	7
Day care	—	1	3	2	4	4	7	15
pecial hospitals	5.6	2	7	2	8	4	10	6
ices mainly for children sub-total	0.5	16	232	22	266	13	290	2.2
inics	2.9		25		26		26	0

Table 5.2   (*cont.*)

	Average current growth p.a. 1970/1– 1973/4 per cent	1973/4 Out-turn		1975/6 provisional estimate		1979/80 illustrative projection		Illustr… aver… curr… growt… 1975… 1979… per c…
		Capital £m	Current £m	Capital £m	Current £m	Capital £m	Current £m	
Health visiting	2.5		33		34		43	6
School health	7.3		48		51		51	0
Welfare food	−44.6		8		8		8	0
Residential care	16.7	12	84	18	110	10	121	2
Boarding out	8.4		12		14		15	2
Day nurseries	7.2	3	17	3	20	1	22	2
Central grants and YTCs	−18.2	1	5	1	3	1	4	6
Other services sub-total	11.0	33	196	17	236	13	248	1
Social work	11.0		88		105		114	2
Additional social services training	—	—			—		6	—
Other LA services^d	—	24	18	14	23	9	23	0
Miscellaneous centrally financed services^e	17.3	9	90	3	108	4	105	−0

Rounding: Illustrative growth rates 1975/6 to 1979/80 are generally rounded to the nearest 1 per cent except where expenditure exceeds £100m. All figures are approximate. Discrepancies due to rounding
  Abbreviations: IP, OP, DP, YTCs – in-patients, out-patients, day patients, youth treatment centres
  ^{a} Capital figures include expenditure on clinics and other community health.
  ^{b} Includes extra costs of teaching hospitals, RHB and FP administration (pre-reorganisation), r radiography, blood transfusion services, income and accounting adjustments.
  ^{c} Includes units for the younger disabled.
  ^{d} Includes capital expenditure on land, vehicles, etc.
  ^{e} Includes other health expenditure, departmental administration and research.

take kindly to attempts to determine such allocations. Moreover, for the most part there was little information about long-term or underlying trends in expenditure by speciality. There were some exceptions to that rule. Both geriatric care and maternity care were specialities directly affected by demographic trends. Moreover, the mentally ill, the mentally handicapped as well as the elderly were groups in which government had declared a special interest and were paralleled by community based services. This last point also held true for dentistry.

Age made little sense on its own, but where it coincided with speciality provision for certain groups such as geriatrics, paediatrics and maternity, it reinforced the conclusion that these would be worth treating separately. Dependency also seemed a fruitful measure for some purposes. It was the basis of hospitalisation for the long-term care groups, and distinguished individuals who might be capable of being cared for in nursing homes or other establishments from those cared for in their own homes. Dependency therefore provided a logical link with services in the community. On the other hand, few established dependency measures existed.

When the team moved on to consider community health services their most difficult task was to decide how to treat primary care – the work of the general practitioner, dentist and optician. The last two formed discrete enough activities which were separately funded, but the local doctor was a real problem. They considered allocating expenditure by workload. Categories could be chosen comparable to the hospital and other community services – work with the elderly, maternity cases and so on. The time doctors spent on each could be used to allocate spending. Yet this would have meant an enormous work/time study. To repeat it regularly would have been costly. Moreover, the whole exercise would certainly be opposed by the medical profession. Rough and ready estimates might have been obtained from the General Household Survey in which informants are asked to record attendance at the GP and periods of ill health but that would not distinguish the reason for their attendance. In the end there seemed nothing that could be done but to treat general medical primary care as a speciality on its own.

Local community services fell into discrete categories – home nursing, health visitors, clinics, school health. These community workers like GPs catered for a wide range of age groups and types of client. Yet there did seem a rough and ready way to categorise them. Health visitors mainly worked with families with children under 5. They might be considered as a service 'mainly for children'. Similarly home nurses might be considered to be a service 'mainly for the elderly'.

When the discussion was extended to the personal social services the team were dependent on the kind of returns local authorities made to the department. They were also guided by the nature of the statutory requirements laid upon local authorities. Here central government had a legitimate concern with the way authorities allocated their resources. If central government lays a duty on a local authority to provide for a particular group it should be able to ensure authorities have funds to meet those duties and monitor spending on those groups. Finally, central government was responsible for providing complementary services to those provided by local authorities to the elderly, handicapped and others. These considerations led the group to choose the following categories. They drew out groups where *both* the NHS and personal social services were involved.

- Children needing help other than those falling in other specialist groups like the disabled, the mentally handicapped;
- The mentally ill;

- The younger physically handicapped;
- The elderly including the physically handicapped.

The categories were really a mixture of age and dependency characteristics.

Table 5.3 Budget categories

Dependency	Children	Age Adults	Elderly
Social handicap	[ ]	*	[ ]
Physical handicap	[ ]		[ ]
Mental handicap	[ ]		
Mental illness	*	[ ]	

* negligible expenditure

Field social work presented exactly the same difficulties as general practice and had to be left on its own. It had originally been thought useful to distinguish 'prevention' as a programme on its own, but it proved difficult to distinguish many separate activities which went under that heading which were distinctly accounted for. Health education, fluoridation, vaccination, immunisation were eventually included. There were also other fairly small items – family planning, training and research.

The eventual structure of the whole programme budget reflected the accounting limitations and practical data problems we have described on the one hand and, on the other, the primary concern of ministers with emphasising the need to shift resources from the acute specialities to the 'priority' long-stay care groups and their concern to see a shift in the balance of care for those groups from hospitals to the local authority services. Services for these groups were therefore shown separately within single sub-programmes: services mainly for the children; services mainly for the elderly and physically handicapped; services for the mentally ill; and services for the mentally handicapped (see Table 5.2). The whole of the acute hospital specialities were lumped under one heading, acute in and out-patients.

Some of the practical problems that arise in calculating expenditure under each heading can be illustrated by the example of hospital care for the elderly. In practice many old people are essentially queueing up in 'acute' beds waiting for a place in a geriatric ward, and the kind of care they receive is not very different. The dividing line between acute and elderly specialities is thus not that clear. Indeed informal arrangements between consultants make nonsense of the formal categorisation of beds. Even if the number of geriatric beds is clear, spending on them is not. Hospital costing returns do show separately the costs of wholly geriatric hospitals, but they do not show separately the costs of geriatric beds in 'mixed' hospitals. These had to be estimated from the unit costs derived from the geriatric hospitals and the number of old people in such hospitals multiplied by the average cost of caring for old people in hospitals wholly for old people. Yet these average costs were known to be a poor guide to the costs in geriatric wards in local district hospitals where the length of stay is shorter and the extent of rehabilitation and medical attention is greater and more costly. Recently the original method has therefore been refined to distinguish long-stay and short-stay unit costs for the elderly.

The method of calculating expenditure under each heading in Table 5.2 involved deriving unit costs (per bed day) for each of the specialist hospitals for the mentally ill, handicapped, etc. and then using this average costs figure to calculate the costs of patients of that kind in mixed speciality hospitals. (The returns called SH3 returns provide the patient bed data.) Similar average costing calculations based on attendances rather than bed days were used for out-patients and day patients (a full account is to be found in a DHSS publication *The 1978 Programme Budget. A Description of Methodology*; see United Kingdom, 1978). The figures under each heading are thus no more than broad estimates.

Overall, then, it is possible to see that the broad programme structure was a considerable compromise with the ideal notion derived from the original literature and from the more cautious objectives of the team in 1971. But it did provide, for the first time, some broad indication of where the NHS resources were devoted, especially between acute care and the long-term care categories. That in itself was enough to provoke a more informed public and professional discussion and to enable the Government to give guidance to local areas about the priorities they wished them to follow. It also proved its value in the debates that took place in Whitehall in 1976 and till 1981 about the scale of public spending (Booth, 1979). The NHS and the personal social services came off relatively well and in part because they could show in that debate the consequences of an ageing population on total expenditure. This should not, however, be taken as a general argument that programme budgets win more cash. The Education Department's programme budget, faced with a decline in the school population, helped document the case for a reduction in education funding.

The one major weakness of the new DHSS programme budget was

that it remained a national device. The basic NHS budgets at local level did not reflect it. They were based instead on a functional analysis – categories related to spending on medical salaries, nurses' salaries, equipment. The result was that it proved difficult for local management teams and authorities to move from planned spending derived from the national budget to their actual budgets and to monitor spending in relation to priorities. A study in Scotland (Mooney *et al*., 1980) produced a local programme budget for a regional health authority which proved valuable in doing just that. Local social service departments' budgets are separate again. In a study of services in two local areas the author produced a client group budget for the various groups for which *both* authorities were responsible. One of these for the elderly is produced in Table 5.4. This would make *joint* planning possible.

Programme budgeting in developing countries
The problems faced by planners and budget-makers in western industrialised countries are compounded many times over in developing countries. Most of all uncertainty and fluctuating economic fortunes mean that long term budgets are relatively worthless except as propaganda. In their study of budgeting in poor countries, Caiden and Wildavsky (1974) argued that poor countries consequently adopt what they called a system of 'repetitive budgeting'. To gain approval for next year's budget is not enough. New budget submissions must be made at frequent intervals and the budget remade and reapproved. Moreover, as items of expenditure come forward, the finance ministry may simply refuse to approve it because of the new economic situation. Inflation may be very high. In that case the original budget, even if not formally cut, will be reduced in real terms. This is the only way finance ministries can contain budgets when their own revenue is so insecure. The phenomenon may once have been confined to developing countries but the practice has spread for similar reasons to Britain in recent years.

Even so, budget reform may have its value. One example, quoted by Caiden and Wildavsky (1974) from Peru, illustrates the point. One agency had thirty different kinds of salary and a vast complexity of budget categories. A programme budget enabled the agency to sweep many of these away and with them many old practices of payment which were a considerable administrative cost. Yet in many places outside experts with complicated theoretical programme structures drawn from the textbook and not from experience have formulated budget systems for developing countries which they could not use. What the British experience suggests is that the task is a long-term one and must be simple in outcome if it is to succeed. Even apparent simplicity in the eventual result will mask a considerable amount of work on actual accounting and service data available, a process which took five years in Britain with a sophisticated central department and with that country's pool of qualified economists in the government service.

Detailed accounts of programme budgeting in the developing countries are few. Most are essentially descriptions of how to do it drawn from United States literature. There are some accounts of India's attempt to use performance budgeting (Gupta, 1967; Honda, 1979; Sastry, 1979). Visvanathan (1973) concludes in his survey of Indian experience:

The efforts of Central Government and State Governments so far have been directed mainly to the preparation of performance budget documents by conversion of the figures in existing demands for grants into a new format as a post budget exercise. They supplement traditional budgets. Apart from the inadequacies of data regarding targets, achievement, norms and other relevant performance indicators, the question is whether in the departments and agencies covered so far performance budgeting has been *really introduced*. The answer is a definite no.

Gupta's (1967) comment gives a genuine Indian flavour to the enterprise: 'Performance budgeting in Government is not a destination but a pilgrimage.'

By far the best detailed account of a single attempt at programme budgeting in a developing country is that by Beyer (1973) describing the experience in Nepal. In contrast to the highly readable and critical account by Caiden and Wildavsky (1974) we have referred to already, which deals more broadly with development planning, Beyer's account is much more sympathetic to budget planning and more constructive. It gives an account of the practical and political problems involved. He begins by analysing the weaknesses of traditional budgets in developing countries as they were exemplified in Nepal's national budget.

1. Like all traditional budgets it was concerned only with the immediate purposes of expenditure such as salaries, and was for one year ahead only.
2. It was incomplete. It contained only part of the whole range of government activity, a large part of which was accounted for separately in agency accounts which were separately funded by assigned revenues or were funded by the UN Development Programme, or the World Trade Programme, UNICEF, UNESCO, and the World Bank. No clear picture emerged about the overall use of resources in the country.
3. It was divided. Similar activities were undertaken by different agencies and departments.
4. There were no measures of outcomes or any attempt to measure them.

Table 5.4 Expenditure on the elderly in a London Borough 1975/6 – 1980/81

(1975 prices, CSO basis)

	1975/6	1976/7	1977/8	1978/9	1979/80	1980/81
REVENUE EXPENDITURE						
In-patient hospital care						
Geriatric hospitals long-stay	2,143,327	1,897,200	1,957,100	1,992,100	2,065,100	2,014,900
Medium-stay	—	—	—	—	—	735,600
Inpatient assessment unit	—	1,900	41,100	68,000	69,200	193,200
Total hospital in-patient care	2,143,327	1,899,100	1,998,200	2,060,100	2,134,300	2,943,700
Psychogeriatric care unit						
In-patient	—	—	—	—	—	254,800
Day hospital	—	—	—	—	—	147,000
Total psychogeriatric care						401,800
Other hospital care						
Outpatients	33,500	27,800	24,000	32,900	34,000	84,500
Day hospital	—	—	—	3,300	32,000	52,700
Transitional care	270,236	255,500	245,700	266,900	244,900	131,500
Total other hospital care	303,736	283,300	269,700	303,100	310,900	268,700
Community health services						
Community nursing	390,000	390,000	392,600	384,900	431,400	470,600
Chiropody	87,000	87,000	87,000	76,100	85,800	77,500
Health visiting	11,900	11,900	11,900	12,500	8,600	6,400
Other (medical supplies, laundry)	130,000	130,000	137,800	56,700	29,600	61,700

	1,713,239	1,938,000	13,778,900	1,817,800	1,938,000	1,762,900
Voluntary and private homes	379,036	388,500	445,200	425,900	398,300	400,000
Total residential care (gross)	2,112,575	2,294,500	2,224,100	2,303,700	2,336,900	2,162,900
Day care and support services						
Day care	274,958	336,900	347,000	372,100	397,400	315,800
Social work	317,800	408,300	433,000	435,100	444,200	474,900
Sheltered housing wardens	49,070	43,800	53,200	48,300	69,400	84,200
Home helps (including laundry)	885,547	927,900	973,300	1,004,400	1,064,900	938,500
Meals	217,900	253,800	309,600	246,200	275,500	218,400
Aids, adaptations, TV, telephones	159,829	156,800	175,100	107,800	100,500	69,600
Holidays	178,122	166,800	201,400	185,500	107,000	52,500
Transport (conc. fares)	14,727	22,300	34,100	32,800	24,500	30,200
Voluntary community organisations	27,272	25,900	29,900	27,900	30,500	28,000
Total day care and support (gross)	2,125,225	2,342,500	2,556,600	2,460,100	2,513,900	2,212,100
TOTAL REVENUE EXPENDITURE	7,303,763	7,438,300	7,677,900	7,657,200	7,851,400	8,605,400
Elderly per cent of SSD budget (net)	36.5	34.7	34.0	33.0	32.5	31.4
CAPITAL EXPENDITURE						
Hospitals						
Regional major programme	—	2,800	200	—	71,600	60,300
Area minor programme	178,600	9,600	29,000	62,500	43,900	35,800
Residential care (including fire precautions)	280,472	276,300	148,400	83,500	63,900	148,700
Day care	97,639	38,100	36,400	112,900	187,900	
TOTAL	556,711	326,800	214,000	258,900	367,300	244,800

5. There was no prior programme analysis of what many of the programmes were there to do.
6. There was a repetitive budget process. Even after a project was approved, fresh and repeated battles had to be fought first for instalments of cash and secondly approval to appoint key personnel.

In mid-1968 the process of reform began within the Ministry of Finance after a government reorganisation. Economists occupied senior positions and knew something about the American reforms, but also knew they were not being successful and that India's experience with performance budgeting had been unsuccessful. They decided to proceed cautiously in one area of spending at a time. They were, in fact, pushed into going for a budget-wide change against their better judgement. They concentrated on improving their capacity to make broad budget allocation decisions rather than attempt output measures or categories – a very similar conclusion to their DHSS counterparts. Their constraints were much tighter. There were very few trained economists, poor information, little time for reflection or analysis, and the prime necessity was not to let the planning function weaken the tight control over spending the ministry exercised.

These considerations led them to: (i) go for a single budget rather than a separate planning and 'ordinary' budget; (ii) to minimise innovations; (iii) to institutionalise budget planning in the normal decision making process; and (iv) to try to win friends for the new process in other important centres of power. In this last respect they did not entirely succeed. The Planning Commission opposed the idea, the auditor general was lukewarm, as was the legislature and the King's secretariat in the first instance.

The aim was to seek to investigate each of the faults we have outlined earlier. This meant going for a consolidated budget, for programme categories that included similar institutions performing similar functions or complementary ones, requesting agencies to justify their bids in terms of the benefits they envisaged would result, and some agreement from those who held the purse and manpower strings that if serious consideration had been given to the budget and the resource limits, the spending should be more readily approved. In all of this only partial progress was made but, as Beyer described, some was made. The programme structure for the social services is set out for comparison in Table 5.5.

An assessment–sharpening a rusty tool
PPBS's main enemies were its own advocates. By suggesting that it virtually solved the problem of government efficiency, and by making it highly elaborate and over ambitious in its requirements for informa-

Table 5.5   Nepal's programme structure for education and health services, 1972

Education
  Primary education
  Higher education
    College
    University
    Professional
  Technical education
  Teacher training
  Adult education
  Physical education
  Other
    Curriculum development
    Research
    Student scholarships

Health
  Medical care
    Hospitals
    Health centres
    Health posts
    Mobile medical centres
  Prevention
    Malaria eradication
    TB detection
    Smallpox
    Leprosy control
    Central Public Health Laboratory
  Family planning

---

tion, it rapidly died a death in the US, at least in formal terms (Schick, 1973). However, changes were made to the Federal budget which make it a more intelligible document, and a longer planning cycle was built into preparing the budget. Under the Congressional Budget Act of 1974 the administration were obliged to put a longer time-span on their major economic and spending assumptions. Planning and evaluation sections were built into agencies. In Britain, as we have seen, the DHSS budget made possible a public debate about health service priorities and a clear government policy. That the shift of spending has not been greater is partly because of the failure to carry the reform through to its logical conclusion at local level.

The presentation of financial information is crucial to any political debate, or to any internal debate about resources within an institution. If a committee is faced with a budget which distinguishes spending on teachers' salaries, porters' wages, travel expenses, books and chalk, the discussion will centre on the respective value of porters, teachers and chalk. Those who compile the accounts have a large responsibility to focus debate on important choices. This is essentially a planner's role and planners must have a large say in the shape of the budget if they are to have any influence on the kinds of choices that are discussed. The examples we have quoted all show how difficult as well as important that task is. What is needed now is to rescue the approach from the dustbin, if that is where it has been left, and simplify and sharpen the tool so that politicians and public can more clearly see what is happening to their money and decide what they want to see happen to it.

Budget structures are only one aspect of reform. Longer-term planning of resource priorities are another. That is dependent on a rather more settled economic and financial climate. Continuous fluctuations in the availability of funds, changes in government economic policy and crises of one kind or another make long-term thinking seem a waste of time. Developing countries have longer experience of that but countries such as Britain, largely through its own self-inflicted wounds, are learning what budgeting in a less developed country is like. The final element in programme budgeting is the case for evaluating the outcome and impact of services on those they are designed to serve. Once again this has been a neglected aspect of the original ideal. To evaluate everything all the time is out of the question, especially in societies lacking large supplies of social scientists. Carefully chosen and researched studies, and the extended use of small teams of knowledgeable professionals, external assessors or inspectorates, provide a time honoured but very effective way of sustaining and improving professional standards (Glennerster, 1975). As constraints tighten on social spending, the case for getting the most from every pound of taxpayer's money increases.

6 Spatial Analysis and Social Planning*
Derek Diamond

Social planning involves locating facilities for the use of client population; governments and public agencies are continually faced with the problem of modifying existing facilities and selecting locations for new ones. To assess the opportunities for altering the spatial pattern and to forecast the likely impact of such changes on the operation of the service and on the client population requires planners to offer advice as to the relative merits of alternative locations. While intuition and professional experience often serve to defend a particular choice, a stronger case can be made if the evidence showing the advantages and disadvantages of feasible alternatives is clearly listed and if there is consensus on the appropriateness of the evidence. In the rise of social planning in most countries of the world in recent decades a number of different approaches have been used to tackle such locational issues, notably rule of thumb methods, political bargaining procedures, the application of norms or standards, and more recently, analytical techniques derived from spatial analysis.

Spatial analysis refers to that body of knowledge which seeks to understand the principles of human behaviour in space by searching for answers to the question, why is this activity, be it an agricultural region, a market town, or a department store, located where it is. The attempt by spatial analysis to understand spatial organisation (in other words the aggregate pattern of use of space by a society) has involved examining the effects of location through the use of such concepts as distance decay, gravity modelling and accessibility, little of which has yet been used in social planning, but much of which by explaining spatial behaviour is crucial to several types of planning, not least town and country planning and social planning.

A location in the above sense is an area capable of recognition and definition and in which human activities take place. Understanding how such physical space is structured, how men relate through space and consequently how society is organised in space, are among the

* This contribution would not have been completed without the generous help of my colleague, Dr Michael Hebbert.

fundamental concerns of modern geography. The most fundamental concepts used in the analysis of spatial organisation are distance, direction and connection and it is the way combinations of these properties of space vary which create the significant differences that distinguish one location from another, making for example, large differences in accessibility between different sites in a city. Operational definitions of these concepts are often difficult but the wide variety of observed patterns of location and interaction and the many theories constructed to account for these patterns and their underlying processes can be unified by common principles of behaviour in space.

Many influences constantly operate to change the significance of locations by affecting the nature of distance, direction or connection, as for example the introduction of a quicker method of travel or the discovery of a new resource. Explaining why and how changes in the spatial organisation of society have occurred has been the most fruitful avenue of development in spatial analysis and has led to the conclusion that if there is an underlying order in human geography, it is that man and society try to organise space efficiently, that is to locate activities and use land in the 'best' way (Morrill, 1970). In general terms man's goal in space can be expressed as three principles: (i) to maximise the net utility of areas and places at minimum input; (ii) to maximise the spatial interrelations at minimum cost; and (iii) to bring related activities as close together as possible.

Although it is helpful to assume that aggregate human behaviour is seeking to satisfy these three aims simultaneously, the dynamic nature of the forces of locational change coupled with locational inertia, based on the many different costs involved in a change of location, results normally in the existence of a sub-optimal pattern. As in most other branches of the social sciences, the prevalence of satisficing behaviour in the real world does not in any way reduce the spatial theorist's concern for identifying optimal arrangements and the spatial analyst's hope of devising methods which will allow him to demonstrate how improvements in spatial organisation may be achieved. It is in this search for optimal patterns of spatial organisation that spatial analysis has come to be of use to social planning. It is the attempt to answer the apparently straightforward question, what is the best location for various public facilities, which justifies a chapter on spatial analysis in a book on social planning.

The development of spatial analysis and its relationship to social planning

The spatial analysis approach which now dominates modern geography has its origins in the development of location theory beginning with what are now called the classical location theorists – von Thunen on agricultural location, Weber on industrial location, and Christaller and Losch on cities and the tertiary sector. It is from these theories, compounded almost equally of geography, economics and statistics, that the first significant research questions in spatial analysis emerged. Before the Second World War effort was mainly devoted to identifying the regularities in patterns depicted in such point distributions as revealed for example in a map of shops within a metropolitan area or of villages and hamlets in an extensive rural region, and to analysis of spatial diffusion in such quantitative subjects as plant ecology and epidemiology. A notable exception was the attempt to describe such human flow phenomena as migration or shopping trips in terms of the physical laws of gravity, thus earning the description of social physics. The basic idea is that interactions or movements between places are proportional to the product of the importance (mass) of those places and inversely related to the distance between them. Although the explanatory power of the family of gravity models now in use is acknowledged to be small, it cannot be denied that for descriptive and predictive purposes these models have proved surprisingly capable of replicating reality and as Wilson (1974) has shown, they can be adapted, through methods of statistical mechanics, to fit a very wide range of real world situations.

It was the wartime experience of operations research and the arrival of the computer which led in the late 1950s and early 1960s to the birth of 'regional science' (Isard, 1956), and a growing volume of literature that dealt with the application of linear programming and other optimising models to locational problems. In a major review and synthesis of the diverse and rapid growth of spatial analysis models and techniques, Haggett (1965) produced a framework which systematised locational models under five headings – movement (e.g. traffic flows), networks (e.g. street pattern), nodes (e.g. shopping centres), hierarchies (e.g. teaching hospital, district general hospital, cottage hospital, doctor's surgery), and surfaces (e.g. isochrone map depicting accessibility to any major facility) – each an essential element in the make-up of the nodal region. A nodal region is the area which surrounds a functional node (e.g. human settlement, hospital) and which is tied to it in terms of spatial organisation.

The concept holding these elements together is the systemic view that spatial organisation is based on a constant flow of people, goods, money and information in order to maintain itself. It has stood the test of time remarkably well and thus it was only to be expected that when the impact of quantitative social science was felt in town and country planning, location theory and spatial analysis were very prominent. In his now famous (1969) text J.B. McLoughlin entitled his third chapter, 'Location Theory: A Foundation for Planning'.

It took some time for the identification of a relationship between aspects of social planning and the now burgeoning field of spatial analysis to emerge in the literature. Hodgart in his review (1978) notes the importance of Bunge's claim in 1962 that one of geography's central questions was the problem of placing interacting objects as near to each other as possible. However, it was in 1968 that Tietze in an article entitled, 'Toward a theory of public facility location' made a plea for computable models to address the problem of public facility location in cities. He drew attention to the potentially important influence on the form of cities and the quality of life within them that the multifarious public facilities could have.

Modern man is born in a publicly financed hospital, receives his education in a publicly supported school and university, spends a good part of his life travelling on publicly built transportation facilities, communicates through the post office or the quasi-public telephone system, drinks his public water, disposes of his garbage through the public removal system, reads his public library books, picnics in his public parks, is protected by his public police, fire, and health systems; eventually he dies, again in a hospital, and may even be buried in a public cemetery.

Urban planners for all their shortcomings had recognised the practical problem of choosing locations for public facilities and in the absence of a theoretical basis, or evaluation methodology had resorted to rules of thumb. Nevertheless it was a somewhat daunting arena for the spatial analyst to enter. Public services in the hands of powerful professionals did not welcome investigation of the spatial efficiency or spatial equity of their standards of provision and often the lack of competitive pressures produced a very static system lacking both in innovation and the necessary empirical evidence for the model builder in spatial analysis. However, in 1975 Massam was able to publish *Location and Space in Social Administration* with the aim of 'introducing students to a selection of procedures for analysing the influence of space and location on the provision of public services'. This book focuses upon the rationale for dividing space into units or territories for administering social services so that the state's goals in social provision can be achieved more easily and more satisfactorily. Ease and satisfaction are defined in terms of spatial accessibility, openness in policy-making and financial viability. He provides a summary of the five factors which should be given greatest weight in determining the number and size of spatial units required (Massam, 1975), the considerations that should influence the determination of the boundaries, and finally, the items to be reviewed in locating the centres themselves. These basic principles are illustrated in numerical models which evaluate the accessibility, compactness and centrality of the spatial units and which concentrate on the location of facilities and the supply structure. Issues involving economies of scale, territorial justice, local sentiment and control are discussed in the context of the geometry of the spatial units for social provision.

The aspects identified in Massam's pioneering study have received attention over the last ten years. Substantial progress has been made on the problem of locating a given number of facilities such as clinics or public libraries, so that the population concerned enjoys the best possible access to the service (Hodgart, 1978). In these cases the interacting objects are the centres of supply, treated in the model as points, and the units of demand or need usually treated as areas or grid squares. In particular, progress has been made in formulating and solving this problem mathematically by a variety of optimisation methods (Taylor, 1975; Leonardi, 1979; Beaumont, 1980). The main thrust of this mathematical modelling of facility systems involves extending the basic distance-minimisation procedure (derived originally from the industrial location theory of Weber) by including spatial interaction concepts and more sophisticated measures of accessibility.

Leonardi stresses that many practical problems share the structure of a system of spatially interacting activities such as in a multi-node, multi-level health-care system where interactions take place among different levels of health care activity. The mathematical framework and the computational tools he presents can be applied to the optimisation of the spatial pattern of any system sharing the following general features: (i) the system possesses a set of different kinds of activities; (ii) interactions take place among activities according to a linear or input–output structure; and (iii) interactions among activities are disaggregated over space according to a product-constrained spatial-interaction model.

Alongside these modelling developments there have been a number of contributions stressing that such mathematical approaches are not free of social value judgements (Doherty, 1973; McAllister, 1976; Dear, 1979) and that models should be formulated to optimise goals of equity as well as efficiency (Koleda, 1971). Improving geographical access to public services is increasingly being seen in a wider context involving the political economy of state policies, the decision-making process among the professionals who administer social services, and the perceptions of client groups. Some recognition of this trend can be found in the broad perspective adopted in Massam's recent book on spatial planning in the public sector (Massam, 1980). He argues that in the search for the best location for each of the various facilities, account must be taken of a variety of factors including construction and operating costs, utilisation patterns, environmental costs and the distribution of social costs and benefits among individuals. In the definition of 'best', consideration must be taken of long-term and short-term effects, as well as the perceptions and preferences of individuals and groups. To demonstrate the difficulties of defining any 'best' location for a public facility he devotes major portions of the text to themes other than distance-minimising; for example the 'search for the most preferred alternative' explains a procedure for using the preferences of individuals to allocate different facilities to a set of alternative locations, and this is followed by the outlining of a new model for comparing alternative locations for a public facility using multiple criteria.

What this rapid review of spatial analysis applied to public facility location issues shows is that both the demand for social facilities and their supply have a spatial aspect which is amenable to analysis. On the demand side various spatial interaction models have been developed which study how distance, mobility, preferences and intervening opportunities affect the use made of a given set of facilities by a population. On the supply side, there are methods which take the population as given, and study how facilities may best be located to serve it. The rest of this chapter emphasises the supply side; in other words, it is concerned mainly with what is known as the location-allocation problem.

The location-allocation problem

Before discussing the methods of applying spatial analysis in social planning, a brief mention of three alternative, less analytical, approaches to the location-allocation problem is worthwhile. These approaches – rule of thumb, political bargaining, norms and standards – were all used widely before the introduction of more systematic methods in the early 1960s, in both the developing countries of the Third World and in the industrialised nations. These methods are essentially pragmatic and in practice the three methods are often used in conjunction with each other in a more, or less, explicit political process. In Scandinavia where extensive areas of low population density exist, there is a long tradition of quarrelling among localities over the location of public facilities whose significance is somehow perceived as more important than is usually the case in densely settled regions. In Norwegian politics this process is known as the 'village struggle' (*Bygda Strid*).

Understandably the use of norms and standards has become most sophisticated in Eastern Europe and the Soviet Union where 'city planning is perceived as the major vehicle for attaining government social objectives of equal geographical access for all people to employment and to the entire range of personal and public consumption goods and services' (French and Hamilton, 1979). The standards are often established by central ministries, sometimes with legal force, and relate to the scale, composition and accessibility of social facilities. For example, a norm of 30 minutes' travel-time by public transport may be set as a maximum within cities of half a million or more in population. Of course legal standards may not be fulfilled, particularly in the early years of new housing districts, but where hierarchically ordered service centres are allocated according to the planning standards, they do produce a very high level of aggregate accessibility. If this is coupled with great uniformity of the quality of provision, then the distance-minimising solution is both efficient and equitable. French and Hamilton also point out that all uniform standards of service provision throughout the Soviet Union have recently been criticised for ignoring the marked ethnic differences in service preferences which exist between some of the Soviet Republics.

In some Third World political systems, the existence of widespread need, limited resources and great internal inequality results in a policy-making process which, by American and Western European standards, is remote and inaccessible from the population. Thus individual and collective demand-making, the representation of interests and the emergence and resolution of conflict mostly occurs not at the input but at the output stage. Thus, it is in the administration of policy that clientele exert direct pressure on the officials concerned with imple-mentation rather than in the systematic evaluation of alternatives in the formulation of policy, that decisions are reached. Nothing could be more of a contrast to the British situation with its statutory central–local government relations complicated in a subtle way by powerful profes-sional opinions.

Spatial analysis methods
The methods noted above essentially involve trial and error tests in the real world and contrast with the fundamental procedure of the analy-tical methods – the explicit examination of a large set of alternatives, and the choosing of one, which in some defined manner is best. In the context of a supply-side approach, i.e. one where the location of demand is treated as given and the problem is to find the best set of locations, there are three things that can vary: (i) the number of facilities (hospitals, clinics, schools) to be assigned; (ii) their size or capacity; and (iii) the possible locations to which the facilities can be allocated. The basic objective is to minimise the total cost or effort involved in using the facilities. It is easy to see why the basis for most of these models have a strong relationship to central place theory, elabor-ated originally by Christaller for market centres, which seeks to relate the location and scale of service provision to the distribution of pur-chasing power.

The purpose of using the single criterion of distance to evaluate alternative sites or routes is based upon the notion that distance is a surrogate for cost, time, or travel effort. Since the minimum distance location is the most accessible place, it therefore has the highest utility to consumers – other things being equal, people will use the nearest shop, school or clinic. The distance criterion is also used for practical logistic reasons. Generally information on the location of potential clients, the location of available alternative sites, and the distances between the set of clients and sites can be reasonably readily obtained. Further, this information can be handled by computers and appropriate programmes which are widely available. Massam (1980) notes the considerable ingenuity which has been applied to the development of mathematical models (algorithms) to solve location problems, to take into account the number of facilities to be located, the transportation system, the size of facilities, the movement patterns of individuals, and the element of time, and as a consequence a wide variety of practical location problems have been tackled. However, common to all the variations of method are the following elements: the number of facilities, their capacity, the range of locations, the transport network, the client population, and the definition of the objective, typically distance-minimising.

Before examining the actual steps involved it is helpful to discuss the general nature of the relationships between these key variables and some of the most frequent problems of measurement or estimation. The number, location and capacity of facilities are related to each other by a transportation network which allows the client population to obtain the service being provided. This means that judgements about the nature of the data on population distribution and the transport network must be made by the investigator at an early stage in the analysis. These decisions are important for they can affect the outcome.

The distribution of population has to be generalised to be usable in a location-allocation model and this implies judgement about the degree of spatial disaggregation required to maintain the accuracy of the model. For example, some compromise has to be made between a vastly complex model incorporating each individual's actual location and a model which treats everyone in an entire city or region as being located at the same point. Also, because such a compromise results in the representation of demand or need in the form of a map depicting a pattern of cells of different weights, it is important to know if minor changes in the pattern of weights causes radical shifts in the position of supply points. If the results of such sensitivity testing reveal a stable solution, then any errors in the population distribution are of little significance. Also important is the fact that all population distributions change over time and some indication of the impact of shifts in population can be obtained by comparing the results derived from different maps.

Similar judgements have to be made about the characterisation of the transport network. To operationalise the calculation of accessibility, it is necessary to measure for each cell the physical-distance or time-distance or cost-distance to a given location. In making these measurements either straight-line distance or real-road distance can be used. Considerable differences exist between these measures in some circumstances (Wachs, 1973; Robertson, 1976). At a local level physical mobility can be influenced by a number of specific factors such as car-ownership levels or the nature of the public transport provision which can be very influential in affecting individual accessibility but which are difficult to represent in the model.

With these cautionary remarks in mind, it is now possible to outline the first step which, as always, is to establish definitions in a precise manner so that the conditions for the problems are unambiguous. The following sequence is typical:

1. Define the study area, the location of users, and, if appropriate, the number of locations to be selected. (Sometimes the objective is to find the number of viable locations.)
2. Define and state a specific objective. For example, minimise the average distance travelled, or minimise the total distance travelled, or find the minimum number of locations.
3. Define special constraints in the problem. For example, no user must travel more than 2 km., or all users must use their nearest facility.
4. Define distance between users and facilities as is appropriate and define the number of users a facility can accommodate.
5. Define feasible locations for facilities within the study area. For example, which sites of sufficient size are available.
6. Define the time period for the problem. If more than one facility is to be built can they all be constructed at the same time, or must a sequence be defined? – one now, a second next year at another location and so on.

For analytical purposes it is often necessary to simplify the methodology and hold some of the three key variables constant, the choice of which is usually determined by the nature of the problem. Often the number of facilities to be assigned is given or can be limited to a small range and if this is combined with only one possible location then it is capacity (i.e. size) which is determined by the application of the model. More commonly capacity is unlimited while location of the facilities is allowed to vary between certain pre-specified sites thus reducing the problem to one of evaluating alternative locations by assigning clients to the most accessible facility and establishing the size of each facility accordingly.

There are five basic steps undertaken in working such a methodology:

1. Choose a set of locations from the feasible set, allocate users to centres according to the decision rule (for example, all users to their nearest facility), measure the distance each user travels, and calculate total and average distance. This gives a numerical score for a particular set of sites.
2. Choose another set of locations from the feasible set and repeat the allocation and evaluation procedure.
3. Compare the evaluations, for example, the average distances.
4. Examine all possible sets of locations that are feasible and evaluate each one. Usually it is too time-consuming even with a computer to examine all feasible alternatives, and therefore a modification has to be made. The normal procedure is to evaluate an alternative and determine a score for it, then evaluate a second alternative. If this has a better score it is necessary to examine a third and so on. If the second alternative has a worse score the search ends and the first alternative is claimed to be best. This heuristic approach may miss finding the site which is the best, but experiments suggest that if the procedure is run several times using different first sites and always converges on the same best site, then it is highly likely that this is the site which would have the best score if the means to examine all alternatives were available.
5. The set of locations that has the lowest average distance is considered to be the most accessible and therefore the optimal set. These locations are offered as the best sites for the particular facility since the underlying assumption of the location-allocation model is that the choice of *location* for a public facility has a direct bearing on its utility and the distribution of costs and benefits in society.

Hospital location in Sweden and the UK

In the late 1950s the Swedish government wanted to increase the provision of hospitals with very specialised facilities. Some of these facilities already existed in six of the main hospitals, those associated with university medical schools. The government for a variety of reasons identified five possible new sites and mainly on cost grounds, stated that two more specialised hospitals should be provided. The problem was thus to select the two best locations from among the alternatives while paying heed to the six locations already in use. Thus there were several possibilities to be evaluated.

It was agreed with the government that as the cost of provision and maintenance did not vary significantly between the possible sites, the best criterion in trying to decide which pair of locations was best would be to locate the new facilities so that ideally everyone in Sweden lived within a four-hour journey to these specialised medical facilities. This would mean that a person, either patient or visitor, could attend the hospital and return to his home without staying overnight.

The method adopted was to draw lines of equal travel time (iso-chrones) for each pair of possible locations and for the existing facilities. Where an area was within four hours' travel of more than one facility, it was attributed to the nearest one in time-distance terms. These maps of hospital travel catchments were then overlaid on a detailed map of the distribution of the national population as it was expected to be in 1975, then fifteen years ahead. The number of people in each travel catchment (time-zone) were counted, and the total number of person travel hours used as a criterion for the efficiency of a particular solution. Only 76 per cent of the population was within four hours of the existing facilities and on the assumption of one visit each per year the total population would spend 3.93 million person hours travelling. Obviously the addition of new facilities would reduce travel time and increase accessibility, but which locations were best? Godlund (1961) showed that the two best solutions were quite similar. One (A) achieved 82 per cent of the population within a four-hour isochrone and needed 3.57 m.p.h. of travel time, while the other (B) achieved 83 per cent and needed 3.39 m.p.h.

The difficulty was that in the apparently more efficient solution (B), a small number of people in northern Sweden had up to ten hours' travel to reach their nearest facility, while in the slightly less efficient solution (A) there were almost no people at all beyond a seven-hour journey. The reason for this is the fact that Sweden's population is concentrated very heavily in the south and that by locating both new hospitals south of Stockholm (in Orebro and Linkoping) more travel time in aggregate was saved. The Government, when shown both schemes, chose the most efficient (B). Thus they made a political choice for which they argued that some of the savings derived from their selection of the more southerly locations could be spent on transportation assistance for those who might otherwise have had a shorter journey to hospital.

A similar problem posed by the Durham Area Health Authority in north-east England was reported by Mohan (1979). Was additional hospital capacity required in the area and if so where should it be located? There was clear evidence of substantial movements across the Durham Area boundary to hospitals outside the area from two rather peripheral localities within the area and also evidence of inward movement from a neighbouring area. The first step undertaken therefore was to redefine the study area. When 'nearness' was used to define the boundary it was found to explain the cross-boundary flows already known to the authority and thus population was allocated to the study area on the basis of relative proximity to existing facilities. Population distribution within the redefined study area was plotted by 1 km. grid squares giving about 500 spatial units (cells) within the study area.

The demand or need criterion used was the National Health Service norm of beds per thousand of the population specified by age-groupings. Since the level of health was assumed to be constant over the area, population by age was used as a proxy for need. The best location was defined as that which minimised the aggregate travel distance of the existing client population. This population was heavily concentrated in three centres and already had one large hospital and a minor one. The initial step was to calculate the best site for one hospital on the hypothetical assumption that no hospital existed; this was compared with the existing major one. This showed that the existing site involved 4.6 per cent more travel over the optimum location. This was felt to be a very minor deviation from the optimum and therefore the major existing hospital was regarded as fixed. Its existing capacity (in terms of bed norms per thousand population) together with that of the second existing hospital were then compared to the overall area need to establish if any deficit existed. This revealed a shortfall of 170 beds compared to the existing total of 446.

To discover the best location a series of alternatives were examined as shown in Table 6.1. In option (c) the minor existing facility is assumed to be closed down leaving only the existing major hospital to be taken into account when finding the optimum location for one additional facility. In this comparison option (b) produces a dramatic 50 per cent increase in accessibility over the existing situation (option (a)). The fact that this also coincided with the site of a major expanding town within the area made the choice of best location very obvious.

Finally, as a way of checking the strength of the conclusion reached by examining only developments within the study area, a further comparison was made of the effect of new facilities being established in adjacent health areas. Taking each potential site in turn it was possible to determine how many people would be closer to a facility outside the study area than to one within it and thus to obtain some indication of how future development outside the area might affect demand within it. This in fact revealed that such effects would be small.

Utilisation of health care centres in Malaysia
As has already been noted ethnic, income and other differences often mean that when an individual is given a free choice among two or more alternative locations for a particular service, while some will patronise the nearest facility, others will travel further to obtain perceived bene-

Table 6.1 **Evaluation of alternative hospital provision options**

Option	Aggregate distance (m km)	Average distance (km)
(a) Expand existing 2 facilities	1.57	7.40
(b) Keep existing 2 + open 1 new facility	0.79	3.74
(c) Keep 1 existing + open 1 new facility	1.05	4.79

fits such as better quality or treatment from an ethnically sympathetic practitioner. In Britain many people seeking schools of a particular religious denomination well illustrate this kind of behaviour. Massam and Bouchard (1977) in an examination of the utilisation of health care centres in Kuala Lumpur show how such non distance-minimising behaviour can be examined and used in the planning of future provision.

The purpose of the study was to attempt to provide a preliminary classification of the health care centres based on observed aggregate utilisation patterns in order to gain some understanding of the reasons why people choose a particular facility for a specific service. The data on which the study was based were questionnaire responses from rehoused and non-rehoused squatters. The groups were comparable on a number of household attributes and those rehoused had lived in their new housing for at least two years. It was necessary to convert the flow data to an origin-destination matrix showing the number of trips made by patients from each residential cell (housing area) to the health care clinics. Then, assuming people preferred the facility they used to any that were nearer, it was possible to establish that non-rehoused squatters tended to bypass fewer alternative sites of medical care and to travel shorter distances than the rehoused squatters. By examining the full set of alternatives assumed to have been examined by each individual, it was possible to construct an attractiveness scale for health care clinics. By and large the facilities that were most attractive to squatters before rehousing continued to remain attractive.

The choice made before rehousing (and largely maintained subsequently) appeared to include not only ease of travel but also a measure of quality (the large hospitals were most attractive) and a measure of ethnicity (distinctive Chinese and Malay travel patterns). In contrast to the suggestion by Mahadur and Rao (1974) that since the utilisation of public services in the non-Western city is primarily determined by accessibility (with distance as the critical variable) then neighbourhoods with low accessibility scores should receive priority, the Massam and Bouchard study makes it clear that such a planning strategy is appropriate only if the city is homogeneous in its social characteristics.

The uses and limitations of spatial analysis in social planning

The usefulness of this kind of study of differences among the use of existing facilities to social planning includes the fact that the results may suggest that in addition to increasing the supply of public facilities or relocating them, there are other possibilities. Perhaps by supplying more information about the current facilities, by modifying administrative procedures, or by altering staffing arrangements, the attractiveness of a centre can be improved. These strategies should complement the strategy of re-arranging the location pattern by opening new centres in the overall exercise of making the best use of investments in the public sector.

These three case studies show both the advantages and the pitfalls of spatial analysis methods applied to social planning issues. They will be discussed further in the next section. They also reveal the methodological flexibility that spatial analysis techniques possess. While flexibility is a valuable property allowing appropriate modifications of practice to suit particular circumstances, it can give rise to confusion. The basic similarity between these cases is nevertheless considerable. In the Swedish case the number of facilities was set, the number of locations highly constrained but the capacity was allowed to vary. In the British example capacity was fixed, the number of facilities highly constrained but the range of locations was unconstrained. The Malaysia study examined why distance-minimisation is not necessarily the most appropriate objective to seek, at least without careful examination of the client population.

Nonetheless, the case studies clearly show that time and resources spent overcoming the 'friction' of distance does vary and that a set of locations, all other things being equal, that minimises such effort is an efficient spatial structure. These case studies also indicate clearly just what a large collection of potential cases are covered by Leonardi's definition and are therefore relevant to this discussion. An indication of the diversity can be seen in this short list of selected case studies.

Gould *et al*.	1966	Hospital location in Guatemala
Hogg	1968	The siting of fire stations
Goodchild and Massam	1969	Least cost model of spatial administrative systems (S. Ontario)
Rushton	1969	Analysis of spatial behaviour by revealed space preferences (rural centres in S. India)
Mahadur and Rao	1974	Location of service facilities in a non-western urban environment
Dear	1978	Local planning for mental health care

Robertson	1978	Location of recreation centres in urban areas (UK)
Bowlby	1979	Accessibility, mobility and shopping provision (UK)
Curtis	1982	Surgery locations in general practice (UK)

In an appreciation of the actual and potential contribution of spatial analysis to social planning it is useful to distinguish between the more technical issues closely associated with quantitative model building in the social sciences and those questions focusing on the way in which and the extent to which a concern with space is important to effective social planning.

Quantitative model building is now a fully established methodology in almost every branch of the social sciences and the strengths and limitations associated with it are well known. In this respect there is nothing distinctive about the family of spatial-interaction models discussed in this chapter. No matter how great the technical sophistication, the value of the model is dependent on the quality of imagination applied to its construction and the integrity of the analyst in its use. At all steps in model building there are judgements to be made rather than mathematical rules to be obeyed and the extent to which these are explicit is an important measure of the model's usefulness in social planning, as much as in economic planning.

Models are simplifications of reality and in two particular aspects the models discussed here have serious limitations because of the way in which this simplification is achieved. All the models are partial and static (as are most models used in social science). They are partial in the sense that they treat only a portion of reality at one time, normally just one type of service. Although complex models encompassing hierarchically ordered service systems capable of encompassing considerable variation in service variety are being devised, the models most frequently used in spatial analysis are simpler in construction, less demanding of data, and easier to use. The attempt to advance from static models and build dynamic spatial models, which incorporate the ability to respond to change, remains a highly challenging research frontier (Isard, 1976) which on present evidence will have no impact on practice in the short term, and it is therefore important to remember the static nature of the models currently in use. Since the optimum location identified under one set of conditions may not remain the optimum under different conditions, and because social systems are genuinely dynamic, this is an important consideration not to overlook. It is of course particularly important to bear in mind in those cases involving large investments in fixed facilities.

Notwithstanding these two important reservations, which only serve to highlight the role of the analyst's judgement, there is a useful, if limited, role for spatial models. Flows of people and information (or indeed goods and services) over the landscape are a truly universal phenomena which has attracted systematic description by geographers; this has shown how significant in human society is the fact of 'distance-decay', that is reduced interaction with increasing distance. Movement behaviour of many kinds – migration, shopping, visits to the doctor – shows the effect of space and if social planning seeks ways to improve the quality of life it must therefore have regard to the nature of such a universally significant concept. Some argue that in practice the limitations of these models ensure that they are of more interest to social scientists than to social planners; they point out that in any political arena, geographical decisions about where investment goes tend to be more transparent and so more controversial than sectoral decisions about what type of investment should be made. Locational choice is therefore not an easy aspect of the social planning process to technicise, and in so far as it can be treated technically, a simple technique based upon the application of standards will, they claim, generally prove more successful than a spatial-analytic approach, being more equitable even if less efficient.

On the other side of this argument is the evidence that intuitive judgements about efficient solutions to facility location problems are notoriously difficult to compare. The advantage of systematic models is that they can evaluate locations with respect to a variety of goals and explore the effect of giving different weights to social groups according to their need, demand and mobility in a manner which facilitates comparison between alternatives.

In addition to this basic functional value there appear some issues in social planning for which spatial models and spatial-analytic methods are particularly helpful. In planning the social provision in new towns it is obviously helpful to be able to simulate facility utilisation levels under different spatial arrangements and organisational structures. More generally improvements to the social and economic environment of cities require experiments in order to identify the performance properties of alternative forms of development. So far this has not been a major role for spatial analysis. The criticism that spatial models tend to conceal distributive biases and neglect important cultural or ethnic determinants of service utilisation is more a criticism of the analyst than the inherent procedures of spatial analysis. Indeed it has been shown that distance is more of a barrier to less affluent and other disadvantaged groups (Hillman *et al.*, 1976). Walking trips are numerous, even among car-owning households, and the decline of the small shop, the trend to larger schools and general practitioner surgeries means either a longer walk or use of public transport. In current city planning an increasing priority is being given to equal accessibility to public facilities and this is precisely what the distance-minimising variety of the spatial-interaction model is designed for. Of greater long-term importance is the use of such models within much broader evaluation frameworks in many types of planning, along the lines discussed by Massam (1980).

Throughout this chapter the focus has been on the use of supply-side spatial models and methods because this reflects theory and practice in spatial analysis. However, the demand side, i.e. examining the variations in space in the need for and use of social provision and how they arise and alter, is also capable of a useful role in social planning. Indeed it is somewhat surprising given the strength of area-specific public policies in Britain and other countries in the last ten to fifteen years, designed largely to combat location-specific deprivation, that there has not been more work of this sort. Maclaren's (1981) study shows the potential of this aspect of the role of spatial analysis in social planning.

As a final comment, it is perhaps appropriate to look ahead. Following the vast expansion of social provision in recent years in many nation states of the developed world, it seems likely, as recent experience already indicates, that social planning will become an increasing preoccupation of Third World countries. This in turn will lead to attempts to transfer the methods and tools which raises the question, how feasible and desirable is this? This chapter has already noted that the political culture in many developing countries will create important differences from western experience which Grindle (1980) describes well:

. . . the factions, patron–client linkages, ethnicities, and personal coalitions that are often the basis of political activity are well suited to making individualized demands on the bureaucratic apparatus for the allocation of goods and services. This kind of participation, which may have a great impact on whether and how national policy goals are achieved, frequently occurs at the local level, far beyond the purview of national administrators charged with program or policy responsibility.

Even in developed democratic countries elected representatives have an important political role in guarding the interests of their areas and pork-barrel projects are not unknown. However, there is a price to be paid for political bargaining of this kind and spatial analysis is at the very least a method for estimating what that price is. It seems desirable therefore that spatial analysis methods in social planning should be more directly related than at present to their political contexts. In this context it is worth noting that the location of public services such as major colleges, hospitals or administrative headquarters of for example a nationally owned transportation service are increasingly being

identified as a key instrument to influence and direct the spatial consequences of national economic development strategies.

7 Operational Research and Social Planning*
Jonathan Rosenhead

Operational research is a problem-solving activity carried out for the management of large enterprises by staff specialists, usually with a science-based training. From seemingly accidental military origins in Britain in the late 1930s it has spread round the world and become part of the standard fixtures and fittings of virtually all substantial industrial, commercial and financial undertakings in the developed world, and increasingly of local and national government also. Areas of application in government have included health, transport, financial control and civil service manpower planning, as well as work for the military and the police. Local government has carried out a host of cost reduction exercises in specific areas, as well as studies of how to improve the delivery of particular urban services. Developing countries too have been making appreciable use of operational research for state planning, especially since the 1970s.

Operational research (often abbreviated as OR) has also had effects beyond its own boundaries. It has served as a model of formal 'scientific' decision-making which has been widely imitated, for example by the rational comprehensive planning tendency within urban planning, and through the invention of 'policy sciences' to continue the same thrust at a more strategic level. Manpower planning (in Britain a virtual spinoff from OR) and cost-benefit analysis have extensive overlap and shared personnel with operational research; and OR is also one of the strands intertwined in the influential 'systems approach'. Though not without its external detractors and internal critics, OR is evidently a significant element in the way complex organisations and societies are managed and controlled today.

The history and pre-history of operational research
History can be written in more than one way, each carrying aspects of the truth. Most accounts of the origins of OR have been written by pioneer practitioners, or by latter-day OR workers content to bask in their reflected glory. The result is a received view of the history of

* I would like to thank Richard Carter, Greg Parston and my father Louis Rosenhead for their constructive comments on an earlier draft.

operational research as the history of great men (no women). This is history as anecdote. Even so, it makes a gripping yarn (see Crowther and Whiddington, 1947; Waddington, 1973; Clark, 1962).

This story (which we will summarise here before going on to other aspects of OR's history) is concerned initially with military and industrial organisations rather than the governmental agencies which practise social planning. However patience will be rewarded. The nature of these origins is relevant to the strengths and weaknesses of operational research in social fields. The historical account will also concentrate on Britain, both for simplicity, and because Britain has been the site not only of OR's birth, but also of significant developments in the governmental application of OR, paralleled to a greater or lesser extent in other developed countries.

It was the development of radar in the late 1930s which spawned the approach which came to be called operational research. A whole range of novel organisational challenges needed to be tackled – for example, how to reduce the interval between identifying incoming bombers as blips on the screen, and the take-off of intercepting fighters. Interdisciplinary groups of scientists were put to work on such problems, using in part their technical knowledge, but also what could loosely be called 'the scientific method'. Up to that time the more conventional military role of scientists had been as developers of new weapons; OR by contrast looked at how a given weapon system could be more effectively employed. It was this distinction between weapons research and research into operations which led to the coining of the term 'operational research'.

The approach was widely successful, and quickly spread during the war through the British armed services, and on to the United States military. After the war operational research in the United Kingdom made a relatively smooth transition to the industrial sector – it was increasingly realised that the problems of running a large industrial enterprise in peace-time had much in common with those of managing a branch of the armed services in war-time. Early attempts to establish OR in government were much less successful, and few vestiges survived into the 1950s. Industrial OR groups however grew in number and size, and in the mid-1960s the OR approach was transferred back to government from the private sector. By that time technical leadership in operational research had firmly passed to the United States. It was there that a range of formal mathematically-based techniques had been developed, often under military sponsorship, to find short-cut solutions for recurrent problems with particular structures. The ability of these techniques to solve ever larger and hence more complex problems has depended on the developing power of electronic computers, itself another wartime innovation.

The United States and Britain remain the countries with the most concentrated operational research activities, but other developed countries have significant OR communities. Areas of application have spread to include commercial, financial and banking undertakings as well as to government, and to both tactical (resource allocation) and strategic (resource acquisition) problems. Multinational firms and roving consultants have achieved the transfer of OR technology to developing countries; this export of 'software' has been in many cases as inappropriate as the better known transfer of the hardware of high technology processes and products. In 1981 thirty-one national organisations were members of the International Federation of Operational Research Societies, nine of them from the Third World.

That is one way of writing the history of OR. But there are other ways. Operational research happened, but it didn't *just* happen. Gifted individuals were the innovators, but they were influenced and conditioned by ideas and social movements larger than themselves, as well as by society as a whole. Looked at in this light, a striking but neglected fact comes into focus. Many of those wartime pioneers of operational research (and most of the leading figures) had been participants in the radical science movement of the 1930s, with a strong socialist and often Marxist orientation. Bernal, Blackett, Gordon, Waddington, Watson-Watt, Zuckerman – all with significant roles in the early development of OR – had previously been active in the Association of Scientific Workers, the Cambridge Scientists Anti-War Group or other more liberal organisations. A principal demand of this movement was that science should be used in the national interest, rather than for the sectional advantage of profit-making. The justification for this strategy from a Marxist position was that capitalism would then be seen as unable to harness the full beneficial potential of science; in this way the development of science would hasten the transition to socialism (see articles by Heinemann *et al.*, 1982).

Although Marxism is a materialist approach, this line can in retrospect be seen as an idealist formulation. The power of ideas, even scientific ideas, could not overcome the material forces at work in society. The initial radical thrust of operational research was soon deflected by the laws of motion of capitalist society into safer channels. Indeed already by the 1930s the development of advanced industry was presenting managerial problems which were intractable using current techniques. As industry became more capital intensive it became ever more necessary to establish tighter control, so that extra percentage points of productivity could be achieved. Yet growing scale and complexity made control harder, not easier. Industry had encountered 'managerial limits to growth' (Chandler, 1977; Rosenhead, 1982). This was fertile ground for the science-based approach to organisational problems of the early operational research – though the consequences were not what they had expected. Operational research became not a precursor of socialism, but a key element in the success of managerial capitalism.

There remained, in Britain, at least, the little problem of the bridge-heads of 'OR in the national interest' which had been established in government immediately after the war. However by 1948 the combination of a cold-war environment antipathetic to notions of central planning as totalitarian and the innate conservatism of the civil service had squeezed them out. Operational research did not re-establish a significant presence in government in Britain until the advent of a new Labour government in 1964. That government entered office with a policy of refurbishing British industry through the white-heat of the scientific and technological revolution. Effectively this was a watered-down version of the radical scientists' campaign of the 1930s – only now science was supposed to achieve not the socialist revolution, but a revitalisation of British capitalism. Much else had changed in twenty post-war years. The public sector had grown in scale and complexity to the point where its costs were of major concern to those running British industry and commerce. Private industry's massive, inflexible and interconnected projects now required government regulation of the economy if there was to be a reliable return on investment. Planning was no longer a dirty word, but a tool accepted as a necessary precondition for the survival of 'free enterprise'. Operational research could be, needed to be, readmitted to government.

In the government applications of operational research of the 1960s–1980s we can see these two opposing tendencies at work. Operational research is often genuinely conducted with an eye to the pursuit of some overall 'interest of society'. But it inherits a technocratic approach from its military/industrial ancestry, and also has to operate in an environment in which 'the interest of society' is likely to be interpreted in some very partial ways. The project of providing formal analysis to aid decisions under conditions of complexity, risk and uncertainty becomes steadily more critical as countries develop and their economic activities grow in scale and interconnectedness. But OR, as the particular form of analysis now on offer, carries sufficient compensating disadvantages that its use in particular circumstances needs to be critically assessed.

The practice of operational research
Why does operational research offer positive advantages in the planning and management of complex systems? In previous generations the people who ran businesses, hospitals, government departments, navies seemed to get by quite well without it. They were able to manage their

organisations, taking decisions about changing their operations, without leaning on such specialist advice. This style of management could work quite well, but only under certain conditions: that the nature of the organisation and what it was trying to perform did not change too precipitately; that the economic environment in which it had to operate was not over turbulent; and that those in control of the organisation had at least a good general knowledge of how the workers at the base of the organisational pyramid got the work done.

Under these circumstances decision-makers, when confronted with a problem situation, could often recognise it as one which had presented itself in very similar form in the past. There was a traditional managerial response to it, which the present manager had imbibed along with much other collective wisdom, during his (rarely if ever 'her') long apprenticeship in the organisation. When the problem was not quite in the accustomed form, the manager would use the inherited 'wisdom', plus his working understanding of how the organisation ticked, to adapt the traditional response. By observing the success or otherwise of this innovation, the collective wisdom was enriched.

Such decision-making, by rule of thumb plus hunch, should not be scorned. Where it is feasible, it provides a very sound basis for the gradual acquisition of new understanding, tested in practice. Unfortunately in our major organisations it rarely is feasible these days. Certainly in developed capitalist countries (Japan excepted) it is now exceptional for managers to make their lifetime's career within one organisation, or even within one type of organisation. Job mobility means that the manager's conceptual tool-box is packed with knowledge about 'management' in the abstract rather than with the particulars of the organisation she or he is working within. It also often means that the manager won't be around to observe and judge the outcome of any innovatory decisions – so short-circuiting the feedback of experience to understanding.

Others of the conditions of successful 'on-the-job' learning for managers are also absent. Changes in technology, in market structure, in social organisation, in politically derived policies are continuously and dynamically transforming the way organisations operate internally, the problems they confront and the environment in which they must function. To take just one example, the National Health Service in Britain operates in an area in which technology and theories about treatment are in constant flux; where its activities are politically highly contentious; and where a marketing-oriented private sector is posing a variety of threats and challenges. In addition the entire system has been subjected to virtually complete organisational reconstruction in 1974, and again in 1982.

The National Health Service, like other major organisations in both the public and the private sector, is a vast bureaucracy. Top management is remote from the shopfloor workers, the ward-nurses, the miners at the coal-face. Top managers deal in budgets, financial forecasts, strategic investments, negotiations with other top managers and senior civil servants. Their expertise, and usually their experience, does not permit them to take decisions about how the actual work of production, or of healing, should be changed. (Lower level managers may have a good deal of relevant knowledge; but they do not – indeed are not allowed to – have an adequate perspective on the functioning of the organisation as a whole.) If higher management is to remain in control, taking informed decisions which guide overall strategy, it needs to augment its understanding of the processes which it in principle commands, and of their interaction with the external environment. And it must find ways of learning which are less lengthy and potentially ruinous than trial-and-error.

This is what operational research tries to provide. Its key contribution is the 'model'. This is a formal representation of the chief factors affecting the outcome of a decision. The factors and the outcome are usually represented in ways which can be measured; and the model purports to give predictions of the form 'if you do *this* and *this*, the result will be *that*'. For example, the problem may be that of deciding how low stocks should be allowed to fall before a reorder is made, and also how much to reorder. Then the model consists of mathematical statements expressing the total cost of the stock system in terms of the probability distribution of demand, the reorder level and the reorder quantity, and the costs of issuing an order, running out, and of holding a unit in stock. If the data on costs and on demand for the item are good, this model enables us to predict what the system running cost will be for any given combination of reorder level and reorder quantity.

With a model like this it is tempting to go one step further, and try to use mathematics to find that setting of the variables which management can control (in this case, reorder level and quantity) which minimises cost, or maximises some performance measure. Indeed the models are specifically constructed to make this optimisation possible – using either calculus (which is what happens with the stock control model) or purpose-built computer 'algorithms', programmes which search systematically and efficiently over the feasible values of the control variables to find 'the best'. And once such a computer package has been constructed, often after the investment of many person-years of work by systems analysts and computer programmers, it is tempting to use it repeatedly rather than to try and think out from scratch in each problem situation what particular factors and relationships between them are in fact appropriate. In this way it is easy for the model, which should be a key instrument for clear-thinking about complex problems, to become instead a mental straitjacket.

Nevertheless there are in principle a number of advantages to the modelling of complex problem situations. A formal model can handle far more dimensions and factors simultaneously than the informal mental models with which managers otherwise operate, especially if some of the factors are probabilistic. By being explicit, it can expose to critical debate the underlying assumptions about the consequences of decisions, and about the desirability of particular consequences. If the model is embedded in an appropriate social decision-making process, it can educate understanding of the system under study, and partially substitute experiment on the model for the costly process of trial-and-error in the real world.

The model is the keystone of the operational research approach, and supports any claims to its status as science. Certainly the mathematical formulations and technical opacity of many OR models give them the trappings of high science. Less meretriciously, the model can be seen as at least an analogue of the scientific 'hypothesis'; to find out whether the analogy will hold up, we must see to what extent the *process* of conducting OR can be viewed as a version of the scientific method.

An operational research project is generally regarded as having the following five phases: (i) problem formulation; (ii) model construction; (iii) model testing; (iv) model solution; and (v) implementation and monitoring. In brief, problem formulation is the task of identifying the scope of the project, what factors are seen as relevant, and what aspects of the organisation's performance are likely to be affected by any decisions taken. Model construction is the process of finding operational measures of the relevant factors and performance dimensions, and using available data to specify any constraints and the cause–effect relationships among them. Model testing is the procedure of confirming that the model as a whole can reproduce the behaviour of the real world system when historical data are fed to it. Model solution is the identification of that setting of the control variables, satisfying any and all constraints, which gives the best value of performance. And implementation and monitoring is the continuing activity of ensuring that the proposed solution is accepted by management, that the improvement offered is not eroded in the process of implementing the change, and that any subsequent unpredicted system behaviour is the subject of further investigation.

This neat categorisation suggests an orderly and rational procedure, by which general statements of scope and objectives are used to deduce the actions concretely needed to achieve them. But the practice is a good deal more messy. Thus an OR project is not normally a linear progression through the five phases. Two-steps forward, one step-back is a more common experience – for example, the need to construct a complete and consistent model can throw up unresolved issues of problem formulation; or the model solution when propounded may remind managers of an undisclosed constraint which renders the proposal quite infeasible. It might be more accurate to see this as a process whereby the problem is successively redefined – indeed we only know that the problem definition is complete when the solution based on it is accepted.

Each phase of the project, if examined in detail, can reveal deviations from the assumed path of scientific rectitude. For example, the model testing phase is frequently all but omitted. Often there is not enough data, still more often there is not enough time or money. When managers are eagerly awaiting model results to assist them in key decisions, it would, after all, be an unworldly OR worker who pronounced that the validation of the model had failed, and that there was therefore nothing of value on offer. So rather than objective testing against reality, there is commonly 'social reality testing'. The model is good enough when the responsible managers say it is good enough.

Or consider the implementation phase. A report does not recommend itself. An OR group anxious to see something for their efforts must act as advocate for the model and the conclusions derived from it. To be effective, they must be aware of intra-organisational politics, presenting the conclusions in a light which will enable a supporting coalition of interested parties to be built up. That is, the operational researcher must be partial and committed, not neutral and dispassionate, as scientific stereotypes would suggest. Indeed, the need for commitment by the OR analyst arises from the very beginning of the problem formulation phase. Management will only reveal their objectives and range of strategies if convinced that their technical experts share their values and priorities. Operational researchers need to win the trust of management, but trust can only be bought with the coin of partiality and commitment.

None of this is intended to derogate from the potential importance of operational research, or at least of OR-like activity. Rather it is intended to imply that OR is a more complex social phenomenon than conventional pictures of science allow (but then, so is science).

It is worth describing in some detail a few of the formal mathematical techniques which operational research has developed. They are in many cases elegant, seductive. Each imposes a very definite problem structure; if it is accepted, then the standard technique offers a powerful means of achieving understanding and deriving solutions. The disadvantages of such pre-structuring by technique have already been touched on, and will be returned to in a later section. But some examples of techniques will give a clearer idea of the OR repertoire. The techniques chosen for illustration have been selected principally for their mathematical simplicity and ease of exposition.

Stock control

Hospitals need stocks of sterile material; local governments need stocks of street lamps. In common with industrial situations, there is a penalty attached to having either too much stock or too little. Too much, and you have expenses for storage, deterioration, capital tied up. Too little stock and there is a need for more frequent reorders, and an increased risk of running out. If the costs associated with these eventualities are known (and that is a sizeable 'if'), then the overall costs of any stocking policy can be estimated.

A simplified example of the way in which the components of stocking costs may vary is shown in Figure 7.1. The lowest point P of the total cost curve indicates the ideal stock holding policy N. If the component costs vary with stock held in ways which can be represented in explicit equations, then calculus can be used to find the 'optimal' value of N. Thus for the classical formulation of stock control theory (which neglects shortage costs) a simple formula can be derived:

$$\text{Economic reorder quantity} = \sqrt{\frac{2 \times \text{reorder cost} \times \text{demand rate}}{\text{holding cost per unit per time}}}$$

However as more realistic assumptions are brought in (e.g. the holding cost curve is less likely to be a smooth ramp than a number of upward steps) computing the formula for optimal order quantity gets more complex. More complex, but not particularly fruitful. For one can observe from the graph in Figure 7.1 that there is a considerable region

Fig. 7.1 Components of stock costs

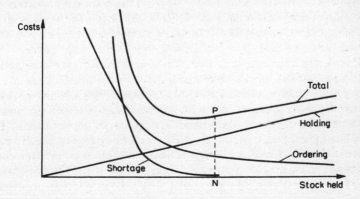

on either side of N in which the total system costs are only marginally above the supposed optimum. Further, the location of N is only known with the same dubious precision as the parameters (such as reorder cost, holding cost) which enter the formula.

Why then calculate an 'optimum' which has no guarantee of being optimal? The explanation comes in the use which is made of such formulae. They are embedded as ordering rules in computerised stock control systems. By this means a minor craft of lower management is automated, so that top management gains added control. Furthermore, costs are reduced by the elimination of jobs. None of this depends on the stock control rules being truly optimal – they only need to give a performance comparable with the earlier human control system.

Mathematical programming

Stock control deals with just one specific function of organisation. By contrast, linear programming is a quite general technique. It can handle a wide range of problems in which scarce resources are to be apportioned between competing uses.

Consider first a simplified example from the area of production. Suppose a firm makes beds, chairs and tables. The production programme for the next time period is limited by the amount of wood available, and by the potential bottleneck of a wood-planing machine. The amount of wood required per unit varies between the three products, as does the planing-time and the profit per unit.

Any production programme is defined by the numbers x_1, x_2 and x_3 of beds, chairs and tables to be made; the problem is to choose the setting of x_1, x_2 and x_3 that will maximise profit without violating resource constraints. The total profit from a programme (x_1, x_2, x_3) can be written mathematically as

$$z = c_1 x_1 + c_2 x_2 + c_3 x_3 \qquad (1)$$

where c_1, c_2 and c_3 are the unit profits from beds, chairs and tables respectively. The constraints can be written as

$$a_{11}x_1 + a_{12}x_2 + a_{13}x_3 \leqslant b_1 \qquad (2)$$

where b_1 is the total amount of wood available, and a_{11}, a_{12} and a_{13} are the amounts of wood needed to make one bed, chair or table respectively; and

$$a_{21}x_1 + a_{22}x_2 + a_{23}x_3 \leqslant b_2 \qquad (3)$$

where b_2 is the amount of time available on the planes, and a_{21}, a_{22} and

a_{23} are the times required to plane one bed, one chair and one table.

This sort of problem formulation, where the profit function (usually called the 'objective function') is a linear combination of the control variables and where the constraints also have a linear form, is one which can be handled by 'linear programming'. (Related methods, generically known as 'mathematical programming', are available when some of these assumptions need to be varied.) This is a method for systematically hunting among the feasible values of the control variables, using the results of one stage of the search to find an improved value of the objective function at the next, and continuing until no further improvement is possible. The optimum has then been found. For large-scale problems it is only practicable to carry out this search by electronic computer.

The breadth of the approach can be demonstrated by thinking of a quite different problem which fits the same formulation, and so can use the same solution method. Suppose you are in charge of diet at a hospital. Three foods are available in the market, with different unit prices and different quantities of two key vitamins per unit. (This is another simplified example.) Your objective as dietician is to meet desirable levels of vitamin input at minimum cost.

The total cost of purchasing x_1, x_2 and x_3 units of 1, 2 and 3 can be represented by equation (1), where the cs are now the unit prices of the various foods. The expressions (2) and (3) will serve to represent the dietary constraints (provided we make the inequality signs point the other way). Then the bs are the desirable quantities of the two vitamins, the a_1s are the quantities of vitamin 1 in one unit of the alternative foods, and the a_2s are the quantities of vitamin 2.

Mathematical programming, then, is a technique powerful in its versatility. It has been widely used in social planning. One such application is discussed in the next section, where some of its disadvantages will also emerge.

Simulation

Along with mathematical and especially linear programming, computer simulation is the major general purpose technique of operational research. It is a method of using the computer to act out a period of activity of the system under study. If the computer representation of reality can reproduce the historical behaviour of the system, then it can also be used to explore what effect on behaviour might result from changes in the system – for example, acquisition of new facilities, or changes in the rules for using existing facilities.

Simulation is employed when the logic of the system's operations is too complex for expression in overall formulae such as those of mathematical programming. This is especially true when the way in which the system works depends on a network of interlocking activities whose individual durations are quite variable, and when the decision-making rules of human actors are among the elements which need to be represented. For example, the study may be to determine whether the lock entrance from a tidal river into a dock would be capable of handling more ships, deeper ships or larger ships. The simulation would take the ships as units to be processed in and out of the dock – but their punctuality and the time taken for manoeuvering have wide variability. Furthermore, the sequence in which they pass through the lock is decided by the dockmaster, who has complex rules depending on the set of ships wishing to use the lock on that tide. Their depths must be matched to the tide profile, outward ships are dealt with before inward bound, ships greater than a certain length cannot enter at some stages of an ebb tide, etc. If the study can model all this adequately, then the analysts can generate sample days of activity with more and/or deeper and/or larger ships to see whether any vessels are shut out or shut in.

One widely applied version of computer simulation is 'System Dynamics' developed by J.W. Forrester. Its first guise in the early 1960s was Industrial Dynamics, designed for the analysis of production and distribution systems. Successive metamorphoses took it into Urban Dynamics and then Global Dynamics, whose most celebrated application was 'The Limits to Growth' (Meadows *et al.*, 1972). However these developments have received vigorous criticism elsewhere (Cole *et al.*, 1973; Clark and Cole, 1975) which there is no need to repeat here.

A major but less well known application of computer simulation is its use by the consultants Arthur D. Little to model the San Francisco housing market in order to assess the effects on the housing stock of alternative municipal policies and programmes (Greenberger *et al.*, 1976; Jacobs, 1976; San Francisco Department of City Planning, 1972). The policies and programmes under consideration included land-use zoning, code enforcement, redevelopment and provision of public housing. Within the simulation, for any set of policies, the city population forecast for a particular period is allocated to housing using rules by which rents and house prices respond to inbalances of supply and demand. These rents and prices in turn determine what private investments will be made in new or improved housing stock.

In principle this attempt to model the housing market would seem to be a rational approach to investigating the consequences of governmental actions when these consequences depend on a host of private and business decisions. Unfortunately the level of detail needed to bring it off was overwhelming. The city had to be divided into 4980 two-acre 'fracts' with similar dwelling units. Housing stock was subdivided by dwelling-type, condition and location – 288 categories in all.

Householders were partitioned into 114 population groups according to size, race, age of head and rent-paying ability; and for each of these groups it was necessary to specify a preference ordering of 50 housing choices. And so on. Computer runs took over two hours and cost around $2000 each, and the output of a run was some 900 pages of numerical printout. This required at least a week of highly skilled interpretation before it could be made intelligible to non-experts, who were effectively barred from active participation in the use of the model. When attempts to validate the model with newly available data demonstrated errors of prediction for particular housing types rising as high as 1600%, the City of San Francisco decided that enough was enough, and buried the model.

This cautionary tale indicates something of both the strengths and weaknesses of computer simulation. It permits asking and answering 'what if . . .' questions (whereas mathematical programming, for example, is organised to tell decision-makers what to do, not what will happen). Its loose structure – it should really be regarded as more a language than a specific technique – permits the modelling of situations so complex and irregular as to defy other approaches. But this power must be employed with extreme caution, or one is in danger of over-whelming the available data and computing capacity, as well as the comprehension of those who must understand and trust the model if they are to base decisions on its outputs.

Applications to social planning

Operational research has been used in many areas of social planning, for example in education and manpower planning, in transport planning, and in aspects of urban and regional planning. (For case studies of British local government applications of OR, see Ward (1964) and Pinkus and Dixson (1981).) Planning of health and personal social services has been one of the major fields of application, and certainly the most revealing. To avoid too confusing a diversity, the examples here will all be drawn from this single area.

The major examples will also be drawn from developed countries rather than from the Third World. The reason for this is that there is a paucity of stimulating case histories from less developed countries. Why this should be so must be a matter for speculation. One factor may well be the more highly developed state of health and social services in the developed world, leading to more challenging management prob-lems where uncertainty confounds complexity. Conversely, the less developed health services of the Third World leave such pressing and self-evident gaps of provision that formalised planning may seem an unnecessary diversion.

Another factor is the more advanced technical state of operational research in the developed world. Much of the technique applied in the developing world is a derivative version of the practice in (especially) Britain and the United States. In many cases this is inappropriate to the particular problems (including relative lack of data, computers, technically trained personnel) of less developed countries. (For the particular problems of applying OR in developing countries, see Sagasti (1974, 1976).) These problems are therefore ignored by OR, or distorted by misformulation. There are, of course, many useful studies of particular, almost technical, aspects of health services – the location of clinics, for example, or the mix of hospital beds between specialities. But these are problems whose major features are common to developed and less developed countries alike.

There is, however, one documented case of an operational research study in a less developed country which reflected in its approach the particularities of the milieu in which it took place. This was a programme initiated by British operational researchers seconded by the World Health Organisation to work at the Centre for Research and Development in Health Services, located at Surabaya in Indonesia (Luck, 1979; Hindle, 1978). The purpose of the programme was to 'grow' operational research/systems analysis (ORSA) in a way which would enable it to survive and develop with indigenous human resources once the visiting 'experts' were withdrawn.

A series of training courses were held for staff of the Indonesian Ministry of Health and provincial health service administrators, to develop the ability and skill of the participants in the ORSA approach. Gradually the courses were transformed from a more conventional format, with formal lectures and large ring-binders full of notes; they developed instead into what has been called 'barefoot ORSA'. This was a programme of field training in which the 'students' principally learned not from reports of simplified case studies (which tend to concentrate on techniques) but by going into the countryside to identify and tackle problems of rural health. Staff and students split into small groups to visit a number of villages. Their objectives in each were (i) to formulate a systems view of the rural community; (ii) to assess the factors that influence health and sickness; and (iii) to make suggestions for community development. This was followed by periods in a number of health centres, to study their operation and management and make recommendations to improve performance. Interspersed were periods back at the training centre to discuss experiences, and formulate problems for the students to tackle in their own work using the ORSA approach.

This approach of 'learning by doing' shifts the emphasis towards problem structuring and communication with people who have relevant knowledge about the health care system and environment, and away from formal analysis and model building. It encourages the teamwork important for operational research work, rather than the more individual and passive attitude generated by one-way instruction from teacher to student. In 'barefoot ORSA' there is no sharp distinction between staff and students – each contributes particular skills, knowledge and experience. In this way the students are given the best opportunity of developing both a realistic approach to the problems of health care, proposals for improvement which are feasible with available practical and technical resources, and the self-confidence to proceed without the direction of expatriate consultants.

This approach (which would also have many advantages for OR training in developed countries), is, sadly, the exception not the rule. The rule has been to export Western consultants and their techniques without any apparent consideration of the probability that this transplant will be rejected by the indigenous culture. The result, as a recent study (Kemball-Cook, 1980) shows, is that there appears to be no strategic OR being carried out, and indeed no established health service OR groups functioning in the developing world.

Two contrasting examples from operational research in the developed world will be described here to give a fuller impression of the potential of OR in social planning, as well as indicating some of the disadvantages. These are a British effort to assist in decision-making about the balance between institutional health care and care in the community; and a Canadian project aimed at developing a health planning system for the region surrounding Ottawa.

The Balance of Care model

In 1970 Sir Keith Joseph, then the Secretary of State in charge of the Department of Health and Social Security (DHSS) in the British government, initiated a study of the balance between hospital and other institutional care for patients, and care by community-based services which enabled patients to continue living at home. This study has been carried out by the DHSS's own Operational Research Service, with the cooperation of management consultancies, academic groups and a number of local health authorities. Indeed at the time of writing the project is still continuing and developing; it constitutes a major investment both of intellectual resources (analyst-years well into three figures) and of money. The methods which it has constructed have been applied both for planning at the national and the local levels (see Coverdale and Negrine, 1978; Gibbs, 1978; Klemperer and McClenahan, 1981; McDonald *et al.*, 1974).

The problem was of interest to the government for a number of reasons. Many of the facilities of the National Health Service (NHS) were under strain (due in good part to the consistent under-funding of the NHS – see Thunhurst, 1982). This strain might be reduced if some categories of patients could be treated in a community setting, freeing up resources (beds etc.) for those for whom there was no substitute for institutional care. Or, alternatively, it would enable the Government to keep down the costs of running the NHS, at whatever level of inadequate service was felt to be tolerable.

The problem itself was of daunting complexity. One aspect is the overlap between health services (provided by the NHS) and personal social services (administered by local government authorities) – many categories of patient require services from each. Thus a disabled elderly person living at home may require daily visits from both a nurse and a home help. Withdrawal of either service could force the patient into institutional care. Equally, caring for different groups of patients makes competing demands on the same resources – for example, home helps look after the elderly, the physically handicapped, and maternity cases. Furthermore, each level of the NHS system has some degree of independence. The DHSS issues guidelines and priorities, and allocates funds to regions, and, with varying degrees of conviction, has imposed a formalised cyclical planning system. But regions and districts (and, before the 1982 reorganisation, the intervening 'area' level) have a good measure of discretion over detail, while the actual pattern of care received by patients is determined case-by-case by professional field-workers and clinicians who are jealous of their professional autonomy. So decisions taken by the DHSS cannot directly determine which form of treatment any category of patients receives. But decisions taken by the DHSS (or at intermediate levels in the administrative hierarchy) can set the available resources which constrain the professionals' ability to give ideally preferable treatments to all patients, and so influence their behaviour.

The Balance of Care model was constructed to help administrators assess the consequences of their allocational decisions. It is unclear, however, to what extent the Balance of Care model actually affected strategic decision-making on the issue. Model outputs at best confirmed a previously established national policy of moving away from institutional care and towards community care. (This policy was based on the evidently lower costs to the NHS – though not necessarily to society as a whole – of non-institutional care.) Later work using the model has taken a more modest aim of comparing different ways in which such a change in the balance could be achieved.

Although the model went through a number of phases (which will be discussed below) the basic structure remained unchanged. The client population is divided into six groups (mentally ill, maternity, elderly . . .) which are in turn subdivided into a total of some 150 client categories according to their condition, mental state, housing circumstances, etc. For each client category a number (typically between 1 and 5) of alternative modes of treatment are identified, specifying which is preferred, and which are acceptable but non-preferred. For an elderly client category, modes might be long-stay hospital; acute hospital; acute hospital with early discharge and follow up. . . . For a surgical client the modes might be normal hospital stay, early discharge, day surgery.

Each of these modes of treatment consumes different health service resources. Thirty-eight such resources have been listed – home help, residential home places, day surgery case capacity, psychiatric beds, meals, etc. – and for each mode of treatment the amount of each resource used up by one patient is specified. (There is of course a difference between the amount of a resource 'ideally' required for a patient, and the amount actually received – but for relative simplicity of presentation this complication, and a number of others, will be ignored here.)

The problem is now well on the way to a type of formulation well known in operational research, for which a range of established solution methods exist. We have a number of scarce (health service) resources to be rationed between competing uses (the client categories). This is very like linear programming, and an opportunity to pioneer its application to health services must have seemed very attractive to the DHSS OR Service and its consultants. What is missing, however, is an objective function – something to maximise or minimise. One possibility was to put a unit cost on each resource, and determine what allocation of client categories to acceptable treatment modes would minimise the cost of providing care. This was indeed the nature of the first version of the model produced by the DHSS. However, its formulation cut across certain cherished assumptions about what the National Health Service is for, and how it functions. The NHS is *not* supposed to be aiming to minimise costs, but 'to secure improvement in the physical and mental health of the people'; and the administrative hierarchy is *not* supposed to be able to allocate treatments to patients – that is the job of clinicians. A reformulation was set in motion.

The second version of the model was based on the assumption that professionals would continue to make clinical judgements about treatments; the purpose of the model was to predict what these allocations would be for any proposed change in the resources made available through the administrative system. The problem of prediction, however, is an acute one – after all, professional field-workers make judgements based on far too many and too intangible factors to be represented in neat mathematical equations. The modellers' solution was to hypothesise that, in aggregate, the NHS somehow makes rationing decisions so as to maximise some utility function of its own. This utility function (very much the same as an objective function) could not unfortunately be derived from first principles – anyone who tries to define in measurable, one-dimensional terms what benefits derive from a wide variety of particular client-treatment allocations is asking for a long argument if nothing else. So the utility function would need to be *inferred* from the previous allocational behaviour of the NHS.

This boiled down to a theory that the National Health Service behaves so as to maximise a utility function composed of three factors: (i) the utility of treating a particular number of clients in a given category; (ii) the utility of expending a particular quantity of any given resource in a given mode on a client of a given category; and (iii) the costs of resources used up. These factors have to be added across all combinations of client categories, modes of treatment and resource types. If the OR team could find out what precise function of this kind the NHS *had* been maximising, (or rather had been behaving as if it were maximising), then it could be used to predict how the NHS would use any particular set of resources which might be made available in the future.

To find out what the utility function was, the team had to make assumptions about what mathematical shape each of the factors had and then use historical data to infer the unknown parameters in their equations. These mathematical equations proved to be quite complex (not simple linear expressions like the cost function in the first version of the model) and estimating the parameters proved a major chore. (A tiny change in a parameter could produce large differences in predicted behaviour, an unsatisfactory characteristic for any model based on doubtful data.) However, if one could trust the 'inferred' utility function, then it could be used for prediction of behaviour. For this activity the OR world had available another of its standard techniques, mathematical programming, a generalisation of linear programming, which can cover cases such as this in which the objective function is no longer a linear function of the decision variables.

Once all these steps had been achieved, the model was in principle available as a management tool. It could be run without resource constraints, to observe the ideally preferred pattern and costs; and it could be run with alternative plans for the future provision of resources, to compare the consequences for particular client groups. However there were certain practical problems which limited its usefulness.

There was the problem of data. The model makes formidable demands for quantitative information. It is necessary to have estimates of the number of clients in each category. At the national level these numbers are not known with great confidence; if the model is used at the local level, it is necessary to take a 100% sample of the hospital population, and a substantial sample of those receiving community-based care. Furthermore, forecasts of the change in the size of the client categories are required. It is necessary to have figures on the amount of each of the thirty-eight resources currently and historically available, and how they are allocated to patient categories. There is a need for detailed cost information on the resources employed. It is necessary to set up a professional advisory group which can construct and legitimate the alternative acceptable modes of treatment, and the quantities of resource devoted to each client which they imply. And if the effort of constructing the model is to be of lasting benefit to administrators and planners, this vast data bank will need maintaining and updating at regular intervals.

Another problem is the density and opacity of the model. Partly this was a consequence of the complexity inherent in the project – which is that of gaining centralised conceptual (and then practical) control over a wide range of different health care activities which had previously been administered more autonomously. But a good deal of the trouble lay in the particular formulations adopted. Once the (highly dubious) assumption is made that the NHS must be optimising something, the way is open for concentrically expanding circles of mathematical under-growth. A fearful black box, the mathematical programming computa-tional algorithm, is then wheeled out to perform myriad iterations before announcing 'the answer'. But if the managers who must take operational responsibility (let alone the patients who must suffer the consequences) cannot comprehend the mathematical formulations, or understand the computational pirouettes which find the optimal solu-tion, then they can have little trust in the answer.

For these sorts of reasons version two of the Balance of Care model ran into considerable customer resistance, particularly when attempts were made to apply it at more local levels (areas or districts). This resistance was reinforced by the need to rely on DHSS experts to interpret the results of computer runs, and by the sheer expense of the computer time involved. Work started on the third, 'portable', version of the model. The aim was to provide an economical form of computa-tional assistance, using only the simplest of assumptions. Its purposes were twofold: to show how professional field-workers would be likely to use any given combination of resources made available, and to indicate how planners might search for better combinations of resour-ces to offer. These two functions – 'simulation' of clinician behaviour, and 'optimisation' – are handled separately in the revised version.

Simulation of behaviour is no longer represented by a mathematical programming version of some supposed innate corporate optimising tendency in the NHS. Instead, current behaviour is observed as well as data will permit. If the available quantity of any resource is changed, the elementary assumption is made that the proportion of that resource allocated to any given client category will remain the same. Further, if the population of any category changes, it is assumed that the amount of any resource received by that client category will change in proportion.

Optimisation is also simplified. No trace of mathematical programming remains here either. Instead some idea of 'good buys' of extra resources for the health service is obtained by (for example) observing which resources fall far short of the quantity which would be required if all clients were to be treated in the cheapest acceptable mode. Similar rules are used to highlight what switches of client group to alternative modes of treatment would have a striking cost advantage to the NHS, if professional field-workers could be persuaded to cooperate in changing their priorities for patient allocation. These 'optimisation' routines are relatively 'transparent' – that is, their working is capable of being understood by non-experts. Further, it is possible to run the model on the computer using only the simulation facility, giving the likely consequences for clinician behaviour if alternative amounts of the various resources are made available. That is, it can be used just to answer questions in the form 'what will happen if . . .?'; the posing of questions of the 'what is the best action to take?' type is an optional extra.

The troubled history of the Balance of Care model is instructive, in that it illustrates in its trajectory both many of the pitfalls and some of the potential of OR methods and models. The lessons that can be drawn from this and other experience will be considered further in the final section.

The Ottawa-Carleton Project

District Health Councils (DHCs) are local bodies established since 1974 in the Province of Ontario in Canada to advise the Provincial Minister of Health on matters concerning the organisation and delivery of health care in their districts. DHCs are composed of from fifteen to twenty volunteers, and include health care providers, consumers and elected officials. These volunteers are supported by a small staff. The councils have broad responsibilities to identify and consider alternative methods of meeting community health needs, to plan a comprehensive health care programme, and set priorities consistent with their long-term goals. But they have no direct control over health service budgets, nor do they have authority to implement their plans.

By 1979, twenty-two DHCs had been established, covering populations ranging in size from 20,000 to over 500,000. The first, and largest, was the Ottawa-Carleton Regional District Health Council (OCRDHC), covering eleven municipalities in Eastern Ontario including the national capital. In 1979, the OCRDHC obtained additional funds from the Ministry of Health and the Ottawa-Carleton regional government to support a professional planning team to undertake a two-year Planning Program. This was to be a demonstration project, to discover ways in which DHCs, despite their volunteer composition and limited staff and powers, could plan effectively for the future development and improvement of their communities' health. It is this Planning Program which will be described here; earlier accounts (OCRDHC, 1978a, 1978b, 1979a, 1979b; Best and Rosenhead, 1980; Parston *et al.*, 1981) exist but are not easily accessible.

The initial funding proposal for the Planning Program declared that it would aim to produce a twenty-year comprehensive master plan for the development of the region's health services. But a four month period of 'planning planning' at the onset of the Program led to a very different approach, based on the sort of criticisms of OR-influenced planning which have already been sketched in this chapter. (For a more detailed critique, see Rosenhead, 1978.) This approach treated the Planning Program not as a 'once-and-for-all' exercise, but as the initial stage of an on-going, continuous and effectively unending process of planning. The implementation of early decisions and the passage of time would provide further information to be taken into account in subsequent stages of the planning process. To take these shorter-term decisions with due consideration it would be necessary to assess them in the context of future developments of the health care system. But this analysis of the future need not take the form of a master plan. Because the future state of the health care environment is so uncertain, it would be more appropriate to anticipate a *range* of possible and likely future events. Candidate short-term decisions could then be analysed in terms of both their short-term impact, and their longer-term compatibility with a number of alternative futures any one of which may transpire, that is, for their long-term flexibility.

As an aspiration this was an advance on conventional attitudes. But to make the aspiration effective an operational methodology was required. The building of this methodology was the major enterprise of the Planning Program.

The overall structure of the methodology which was developed during the 'planning planning' period is summarised in Figure 7.2. (In practice further changes in the method were made as experience was gained in using it.) The essential features of the approach can be explained most clearly in terms of the three horizontal planning streams: 'policies and standards', 'demand and performance', and 'futures'. These three streams reflect the multiple emphases of the DHC's Planning Program. Thus, comprehensive health planning was seen to be conducted within the context of provincial and regional government policy, and as a response to community views (policies and standards stream). The intent of planning was seen as to coordinate and

Fig. 7.2   Ottawa – Carleton planning methodology

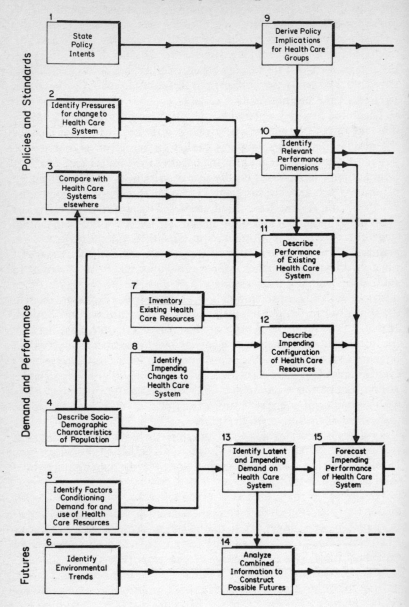

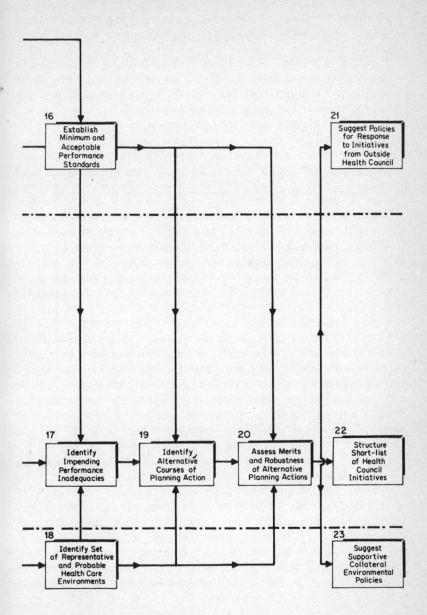

provide direction for the deployment of local health care resources (demand and performance). And it was recognised that planning on the basis of future predictions which may not come true could easily result in an inefficient, inflexible and inappropriate allocation of health care resources (futures).

It is impossible for reasons of space to describe all the constituent activities in adequate detail. Instead, a few will be picked out which demonstrate the differences between the Ottawa-Carleton methodology and more conventional OR-based approaches.

In the Policies and Standards stream shown in Figure 7.2, the Council's stated policies (box 1) are not the only source of objectives. Part of the research effort goes into identifying pressures from community groups for modifications to the health care system (box 2), and part into comparing the region's health services with those achieved elsewhere (box 3). The process establishes not only dimensions and measures of performance, but also acceptable standards of performance on these dimensions (box 16). These standards form the basis for a 'satisficing' approach – in which the search is for solutions which are 'good enough' – rather than an optimising one.

These standards are also used to identify impending inadequacies of performance of the local health care system some three years ahead if actions are not taken now (box 17). For this to be possible quite extensive data collection and modelling activities are required in the Demand and Performance stream (boxes 4, 5, 7, 8, 11–13, 15). These assess the services that are already available from the host of health care providing agencies, or which are currently in the pipeline. This process identifies shortfalls in provision, and these inadequacies, as well as community pressures for change, contribute to the development of candidate actions for short-term implementation. (In practice the process of surveying health care agencies to collect data also produced ideas on possible modifications to the health care system.)

However, the identification of even these shorter-term inadequacies of health care provision can not be carried out without examining possible future changes to the environment in which that health care system would operate. (This applies, of course, still more to the longer-term considerations to which we will turn shortly.) In Ottawa-Carleton establishing these alternative futures (boxes 6, 14, 18) was achieved in part by consulting other agencies for information on housing policies, transport plans, forecasts of employment patterns. In addition, the assistance of over 200 people with expertise relevant to the health field was enlisted for a Delphi analysis.

The Delphi analysis is worth describing in rather more detail. Delphi is a method for eliciting consensus among a panel of experts about relevant aspects of the future. It was an approach inherited from the earlier 'master planning' origins of the Program, for which it was well suited – if you are to construct a master plan for health services twenty years ahead, it is comforting to feel that you have established some certainty about the future in which those health services will be operating. This consensus is engineered by mailing a series of questionnaires to the panel (who never meet as a group) – in this case asking each member to respond on a seven-interval scale to a series of statements about possible changes in the health care environment. How likely was each change, and in what time period? Then the responses are tabulated by the planning team, and the overall results fed back to the experts who are each invited to reassess their answers in this new light. Experience shows that the respondents usually converge on a consensus after only a few 'rounds' of this kind.

Evidently Delphi analysis in this standard form would not have been appropriate to the step-by-step planning approach which replaced the master plan orientation, for this was specifically organised round the essential uncertainty of the future and the consequent need to maintain flexibility. However preparations for the Delphi analysis had achieved considerable organisational momentum, and it could not easily be abandoned.

The solution was to take the responses from an early round of the Delphi, and subject them to cluster analysis. This is a statistical technique which splits the respondents into groups, so that members of each group had responses as similar to each other, and as different from those of other groups, as possible. Subsequent rounds of the Delphi analysis were then performed with each panel member only given feedback on the responses from his or her own group. This amended Delphi method promoted the emergence of a number of significantly different views of the future, which could be combined with other sources of information to construct a set of representative alternative futures for the environment of the Ottawa-Carleton health care system.

The futures which were developed in this way differed on such issues as population distribution, economic growth prospects, changes in methods of health care delivery and in technology, and possible governmental actions (such as revision of the scope of health insurance). They were ultimately condensed into four coherent alternative scenarios. And each scenario was considered with two versions, in which the Province of Quebec either did or did not sever its formal links with the rest of Canada – significant because 18 per cent of the hospital usage in Ottawa-Carleton was by Quebecois. These futures were regarded as not improbable, meaningfully different, and relevant to the outcome of decisions likely to be confronted by the Council.

All these analytic exercises converge on the activity of identifying among the candidate shorter-term action sets those that are 'robust' – that is, which would keep options open for a range of future directions of development for the health care system. (A more extended description of robustness analysis is available in Rosenhead, 1980.) For this to be possible we need to identify not only the possible short-term actions, but also a set of alternative longer-term configurations of the health care system. The configurations are produced by taking, in turn, one of the alternative futures, assessing the likely performance of the existing health care system in that future, and then developing a strategy designed to provide acceptable levels of health care in the light of Council's policies (box 19). For example, a future in which there would be severe economic constraint and continued dominant influence of physicians over health care elicited a configuration with only limited development of non-institutional services. A future in which decreasing use is made of Ottawa-Carleton hospital beds can be expected to generate large-scale conversion of paediatric beds. A future with expanded health insurance suggested increases in long-stay institutional services and use of non-physicians to provide care.

We now have a set of alternative possible configurations of the health care system, each designed to handle one of the possible futures confronting that system. How do we choose? To choose one is to guess at a particular future, which is extremely likely not to occur. The answer is not to choose – that is, not to choose an entire future configuration. This will evolve over time, step by step; the only decisions to be taken *now* are those to be implemented *now*. As the first sentence in the long-term planning report put it: 'This is not a plan' (OCRDHC, 1979b). Consideration of candidate short-term actions within the context of these alternative configurations facilitated a strategic long-term evaluation which would educate current and future decision-making. But beyond that it was possible to identify what these alternative futures for the health care system had in common (box 20). (For example, all futures required at least moderate increases in day-surgery services.) By this means several broad areas of development were identified which could be pursued over the medium-term with some confidence, and thirteen areas were specified in which at least limited development could take place without foreclosing options in such a way as to endanger system performance.

As well as this overall evaluation of health services, the particular problems of care for the elderly were analysed in the first of a series of 'operational plans' (OCRDHC, 1979a). Alternative action-sets were presented in terms both of their effect on short-term performance and of their longer-term viability, against the background of the strategic evaluation. This document served as an agenda for discussion not just on the Council itself. It was widely circulated to community interest groups, cultural and ethnic societies, tenants organisations and many others. Through extensive dissemination (newspapers, libraries) it formed the basis for community-wide debate – an active debate, with public meetings attended by as many as 150 people. It was as the product of these arguments, as well as of the more analytic planning process which had laid the foundations for constructive discourse, that the Council made its eventual recommendations to the Provincial Minister of Health.

For the Council itself, the operational planning process produced outputs of three kinds. One was a shortlist of planning initiatives which the Council itself might take directly or oversee (box 22) – for example increases in day-care places for the elderly, or the establishment of a geriatric assessment unit. The second was the reconsideration of policy guidelines for the gerontology sector, so as to indicate to health care delivery agencies what type of development was likely to receive the Council's recommendation (box 21). The third consisted of proposals which the Council might promote for consideration by agencies which control 'non-health' resources, such as housing and transport authorities (box 23). This was in recognition of the fact that futures do not just 'happen', so that attempts should be made to encourage the development of future environments in which health would be improved and health care provision made easier.

The limitations and potential of OR

Operational research developed its methods and techniques in the context of work for the military and for business, and the techniques which have been transferred to the arena of social planning bear the marks of these origins. Yet the context of social planning has quite distinct characteristics, and some of the dimensions of difference are indicated in Table 7.1 (see Rosenhead 1978, 1981).

Major social planning problems normally have the characteristics of what Ravetz (1971) calls 'practical' (as opposed to 'technical') problems, and what Rittel calls 'wicked' (as opposed to 'tame') ones (Rittel and Webber, 1973). There is not at the inception of a study a clearly enunciated agreed function to be performed for which a best means can be sought by experts. There is, at best, some statement of a purpose to be achieved; there will be alternative formulations of this purpose, each leading to different types of solution. For a 'practical problem', planning has to propose not just a specification of optimal means towards an agreed end, but an argument in favour of accepting both the definition of the problem and the corresponding means of solution. There cannot be the neat separation of ends and means posited by conventional operational research, with its objective function and control variables.

It follows that the 'moon-ghetto metaphor' ('why can't we use the

Table 7.1   **Characteristics of planning environments compared**

Social planning	*Industrial planning*
Powers – indirect, permissive, indicative	Direct powers
Decisions – conditional on those of others	Independent decision-taking, except
– a premium on coordination	on strategic issues
Inertia, lumpiness of projects	Perhaps less marked
Explicit relationship to politics	Non-existent
Multiple interests, recognition of conflict	Consensus assumed; any conflicts resolvable by appeal to authority
Grass-roots protest	Trade unions
Formal participation in planning process	Not as yet

methods which got a man on the moon to solve the problems of the ghetto?') is misconceived. Methods for disentangling technical problems are *not* appropriate for the more argumentative requirements of practical problems. This lesson emerges very clearly from a study of the Rand Corporation's attempt to apply OR/systems analysis methods to the problems of New York City's administration (Greenberger *et al.*, 1976). The methods proved effective where there was a relatively unsophisticated organisation (for example, the fire service), controlled through a quasi-military chain of command and pursuing a single, easily measurable and politically uncontroversial objective. They proved singularly inappropriate where, as in the Health Service Administration, the reverse of these conditions applied.

The use of 'technical' analysis on more complex and ill-defined practical problems may result in the rejection of the analysts by the system they are purporting to study. But an alternative outcome can be that the technical definition of the problem, backed up as it is by techniques which promise to find a scientifically authenticated 'best' answer, may affect the balance of political forces in that system. It may enable the executive, in local or national government, to impose or gain support for its own version of the planning problem; the consequence is usually depoliticisation and an extension of the powers of that executive. This 'technocratic' take-over, based on assumed consensus about ends, has the effect of driving out explicit political debate, which is in good measure about the choice of ends. This is not, of course, to say that the problem formulation and solution are in fact neutral between different interest groups and classes. It is rather that those groups whose interests are dominant in the executive can present their problem as *the* problem.

The mainstream of operational research applications in social planning has the characteristics identified in Table 7.2. (Some of these have been demonstrated in case studies discussed in more or less detail in the previous section.) They constitute a consistent paradigm, which is of a form of planning for a bureaucracy in charge of all relevant aspects of the present and the future. This paradigm is less than adequate for planning in the real world of industry (see Table 7.1) but for social planning environments it is a clear misfit, unless seen as part of a more or less conscious attempt to pacify those environments.

Table 7.2   Characteristics of mainstream OR applications in social planning

1. Problem formulation in terms of a single objective and optimisation. Multiple objectives, if recognised, are subjected to trade-off onto a common scale.
2. Overwhelming data demands, with consequent problems of distortion, data availability and data credibility.
3. Scientisation and depoliticisation, assumed consensus.
4. People are treated as passive objects.
5. Assumption of a single decision-maker with abstract objectives from which concrete actions can be hierarchically deduced.
6. Attempts to abolish future uncertainty, and pre-take future decisions.

This dominant paradigm, despite the planning disasters it has so often fomented, retains its strength at least in part because of the lack of a forceful competing approach which also offers methods for handling complexity and uncertainty. Such an approach cannot be brought into existence by wishful thinking, but only by the mobilisation of client groups with the ability to promote alternative planning methods as part of the pursuit of their own interests. Such groups are only beginning to recognise their need to plan (Rosenhead and Thunhurst, 1982). Nevertheless we can anticipate the characteristics of an alternative methodology as the dialectical opposite of those of the dominant paradigm, as indicated in Table 7.3. Certain aspects of this approach are evident in the case study of health planning in Ottawa-Carleton. Conversely, the eventual reformulation of the Balance of Care model can be seen as a belated response to the inadequacy of the more conventional approach.

Table 7.3   Possible characteristics of an alternative planning methodology

1. Non-optimising; seeks alternative solutions which are acceptable on separate dimensions, without trade-offs.
2. Reduced data demands, achieved by greater integration of hard and soft data with social judgements.
3. Simplicity and transparency, aimed at clarifying the terms of conflict.
4. Offers people roles as active subjects.
5. Facilitates planning from the bottom-up.
6. Accepts uncertainty, and aims to keep options open for later resolution.

This alternative methodology accepts the need, in any viable advanced society, to conduct formal quantitative analyses if the complexity, risk and uncertainty of social organisation is not to overwhelm our ability to make purposeful decisions. What it does not accept is the overlay of jargon and high technique which has accreted as operational research has become part of a project to substitute analysis for societal decision-making. Indeed the complexity of OR's technique is a consequence of its attempt to confine explicit subjectivity to the role of providing initial inputs of quantified value judgements. With a richer and more active *social* process of debate and decision-taking, so ambitious a *technical* process would no longer be necessary. Appropriate technical analysis would then assume its modest but honourable place as an aid to truly democratic planning, and thereby realise operational research's original radical potential.

8 Computers and Social Planning
Tony Cornford

Computers are just one part of a developing technology of information transmission and information processing, which is having an increasing impact on planning techniques. The fundamental function that a computer can perform for a planner is in the storage, manipulation and retrieval of information. There are of course methods for the storage and manipulation of information that require no equipment other than a good memory, or the use of paper and pencil. What the computer can do which unautomated techniques cannot is to store vast amounts of information, retrieve individual items of information and perform enormous numbers of simple manipulations of the items of information stored, all at very high speed. For example, the very fastest types of computer in use today, used for such tasks as long-range weather forecasting, are capable of performing over 140 million multiplications in one second. If this speed were not available, then the models of the world's climate needed for preparing such forecasts could not be constructed.

The ability of this physical equipment to perform these prodigious feats is really of little interest unless it is done to some purpose. The computer itself will always be just a part of an *information system*, and it is this term which is used to identify the totality of the computers, the people and the other items that go to make a useful facility. It is possible to make a general distinction between *information*, which is the useful end product of an information system, and *data* which is the raw material of an information system. For example the raw responses derived from a national census are of minor interest; one response drawn at random would tell you little about the country or its population. Once the responses have been processed by a computer, and tables produced of, for example, numbers of people by sex and age in the various regions of the country, then some useful information has been produced. The computer is able, by aggregation of vast amounts of information, to produce useful information. If a computer is used to store the medical records of individuals it is then possible to search all these records for people who have particular characteristics. Thus a researcher might wish to know all patients who have suffered from a particular disease and been treated with a particular drug. Here the computer is using its speed to filter a large amount of data, producing only that information that is relevant.

To perform such operations would be an enormous task without the help of a computer. The production of the census tables is clearly not a logically very complex task. Each response is looked at in turn, and on the basis of what is recorded there, a count of men and women in each age group and region is incremented by one. What the computer brings to the problem is its ability to go through this simple procedure thousands of times in one second, and thus the useful information may be made available to planners soon enough for them to make constructive use of it.

If a census is processed slowly then each passing month decreases the value of the information to social planners. Since this property of depreciation is common to a very wide class of information the speed and power of the computer within information systems can increase the value of information, and thus the information system.

Social planners necessarily find themselves faced with problems for which information and its processing is potentially the key, and might expect that this technology can contribute by increasing the quality and value of the information they use, as in the example above, and by extending the range of techniques available to them. At the same time, to use computer-based methods in planning will always require a certain amount of effort, and will require that the planner work in collaboration with people trained in the field of computing. If this collaboration is to be fruitful it is a requirement that the social planner can communicate with computing people, and this requires at least some familiarity with the techniques, the machines and the language used.

This chapter concerns itself largely with the computer technology itself, rather than the design and analysis techniques used by information systems designers, but it should be understood that the technology of computers should always be of secondary importance to the information system in which it is incorporated, and that the design, implementation and adaption of information systems is itself a complex discipline.

When first confronted with a computer and the people who work with them, many individuals will be struck at once by the extent to which the area is smothered by jargon, much of it making a mockery of the English language, and no doubt other languages as well. This jargon is nonetheless not so impenetrable as it might at first seem. A number of the technical terms used in this chapter are defined in the text, but it would be very turgid reading if every concept and term were given an exhaustive definition. The reader may like to look up some of these terms in a computer dictionary or any introductory text for a fuller explanation (Chandor, 1977; Hunt and Shelly, 1979; Bishop, 1982).

The principles underlying the operation of computers are relatively simple. The apparent complexity of any particular computer or a computerised information system arises when a large number of these simple, logical and understandable operations take place, which, when viewed in their entirety, are too complex to comprehend. For this reason it is important when approaching computers to use techniques to keep some control over this complexity.

People who work with computers attempt to clear away unneccesary detail when viewing one aspect of any particular system, and simply look at the important features. This is known as the technique of 'abstraction', taking out or abstracting the important details. Computer people talk in terms of 'black boxes' which are procedures or items of equipment whose external characteristics are known, but whose implementation details are not considered. Following this approach, in this chapter we will not look in depth at the details of how a computer works, but concern ourselves with the most important features exhibited by a computer, and the functions it can perform.

A similar process of abstraction in reverse is generally advocated for designing information systems. An overall structure is first arrived at, and subsequently each individual component of this simple structure goes through further refinement and development. This technique is known as structured or top down design. Abstract general components of the system are successively refined until a final, implementable, design is arrived at.

Development of computers

Electronic digital computers were first built in the 1930s, but the concept of an automatic calculating machine is at least 100 years older. The Cambridge mathematician Babbage (1791–1871) attempted during his lifetime to build sophisticated mechanical calculating machines, but was defeated very largely by the lack of engineering skill available to him. By the end of the nineteenth century mechanical precursors to the present day computers existed. The 1890 American Census was in part evaluated using mechanical machines designed by the engineer Herman Hollerith. The Census returns were prepared for the machines by punching holes in cards. These cards were run through the machinery which counted how many holes there were in particular positions on the card. This technique for preparing data for a computer is still in use today, in an adapted form. Figure 8.1 shows a present day punch card on which some details of the author have been punched. (Note that the computer reads the holes, the printing along the top is for humans to read.)

As engineering design and production skills improved, the power of mechanical data processing machinery increased, but it would always

Fig. 8.1 A punched card, used for preparing data and programs for a computer

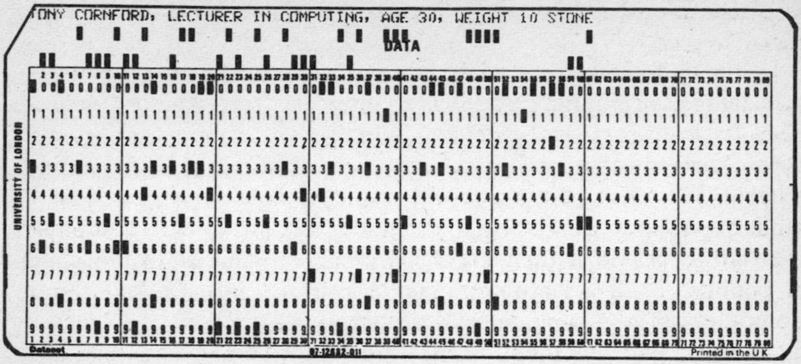

be slow and expensive in comparison to electronic methods. Such equipment is now almost totally superseded by electronic digital computers.

The stimulus of the Second World War led to the construction of the first electronic computers, machines built with very special problems in mind, such as the calibration of weaponry or the decoding of intercepted military signals. People who worked with this equipment became aware that, though these machines had been built to solve particular problems, computers could be built and used as general purpose machines capable of being adapted to tackle a variety of information processing tasks. The technique used to achieve this is to build a machine that requires no physical adaptation to change from task to task, but which simply requires that a different script be followed. This script, or sequence of instructions, is what is now generally called a program. A computer is built with a general set of capabilities for manipulating items of data, in the form of numbers and characters (text), and the ability to use these general capabilities according to any specified sequence of instructions, which the computer itself stores.

A simple analogy is that of a competent cook who, with a basic array of pots and pans, can follow a vast variety of recipes, requiring only that the recipe and the appropriate ingredients be made available. The cook plays the part of the computer, a general apparatus for, in this case cooking; the recipe plays the part of the program, the specific operations to be performed on this occasion; and the ingredients are the raw data which will be processed into some useful product, not information in this case, but food.

The civilian use of these general purpose computers developed in the 1950s and by the end of that decade they were relatively common in large commercial organisations and government in the industrialised world, used particularly for accounting operations and certain areas of research, in pure science and, through censuses and social surveys, in social science.

By the mid-1960s there arrived on the scene third generation machines, families of computers built using integrated transistor technology. The classic example is the IBM 360 range of computers introduced in 1965. These machines were more powerful, cheaper and much more reliable. From this point onwards computers were to infiltrate into all kinds of public sector and commercial organisations. These computers were still large and static items of equipment, costing many thousands of pounds. Such a large computer is referred to as a Mainframe. Computers of this size demand a substantial staff of specialists to maintain and operate them. In the years that have followed there have been many refinements of this type of computer; the power of the machines, the speed at which they operate and the volume of data they can handle have all increased while the size and the price have decreased.

During the 1960s the way in which computers were used started to change. When computers were relatively less powerful, they were simply capable of performing work on one task at a time, and this work was generally presented to the machine punched onto cards or paper tape. A batch of work would be prepared for the computer and presented to the machine. The computer would then work its ways through this. This style of working is known as batch processing. Since the 1960s mainframe computers have been powerful enough to allow them to handle more than one task at the same time, sharing the resources of the machine. This technique is used to allow more efficient batch processing, with multiple tasks being performed by the computer at the same time, or it can be used to allow multiple users to communicate with the machine directly via a terminal, without needing to prepare punched cards or paper tape. This style of computer usage, known as time sharing, multi-access computing or interactive computing, is now common, though punched cards and batch processing are still used for applications that do not require the rapid response of interactive systems.

At the start of the 1970s a further technological advance took place with the introduction of the first microprocessors, very small complex computer components etched on a single slice of silicon crystal less than 0.5 cm square. This microelectronic technology, sometimes referred to as 'the chip' has reduced the cost and size of computers dramatically through the 1970s, and led to their use for information processing in an ever wider range of applications ranging from industrial robots to video games.

This increase in the variety of tasks for which computers are used results from a number of developments. The micro chip makes computers cheaper, smaller and more reliable. These small cheap machines have become available to people who were not brought up using the third generation mainframes, and who did not have preconceived ideas about what was expected of a computer system. This wider, less technical user-community have imposed a new, superior standard on the whole computer community by showing how user-friendly systems can be built, that computers can be useful to a vast variety of people at work, and that the attainment of moderate skill in using computers is within the grasp of almost anyone with secondary level education. (User-friendly is a jargon phrase which indicates a computer program that is helpful to the user and forgiving of mistakes.)

This development of the technology also reduced and even reversed the economies of scale previously seen in the computer industry. Computer installations no longer need to be large to be cost effective. Many organisations which previously shared the use of a large computer are now able to justify the purchase of their own smaller computer.

Microcomputers, the size of a small suitcase, now have computing power equivalent to the largest machines of the early 1960s. These types of machines are sometimes referred to as 'personal computers' since in general they allow only a single person to use them at a time, but more importantly because it is conceived that these machines will become personal items of equipment, like a typewriter or a calculator, used by their owner for a variety of information processing tasks.

Overall structure of a computer

A computer can be described as made up of five simple hardware components. Hardware is the term used for the physical apparatus of a computer. These are input devices, memory devices, a control unit and an arithmetic and logic unit (ALU) together with output devices.

Input devices are the components by which data is passed to the computer. This data may be the program to follow or it may be the data the program will operate upon (in other words the recipe or the ingredients). The most common input devices are punched card readers or a keyboard connected directly to the computer. More elaborate input devices may be used in special applications, such as equipment to read the ticks on a multiple choice questionnaire, or to read information encoded in a magnetic stripe on a bank card or the bar code on a library ticket.

Memory devices are the components that allow the computer to store information and retrieve it at a later time. Most computers will have a variety of memory devices, including a small amount of fast access memory for storing data and programs in current use, and a large amount of memory for the permanent storage of the bulk of information. The small fast memory is referred to as Core or RAM (Random Access Memory). The large capacity memory, referred to as secondary storage or file store, is generally on magnetic tape or magnetic disc. Just as with record players or tape recorders these secondary storage devices generally allow the computer tape or disk to be changed. Thus a particular computer may only have four tape decks for reading and writing on tapes, but may have many thousands of tapes stored in a tape library.

Data is stored on secondary storage devices in files. For example a computerised information system in a hospital will have many files, one containing details of patients, one containing details of drugs in stock, one for doctors and one for nurses. Each file will consist of a number of records and each record will contain the details of one particular person or item. Collectively these files would be referred to as the data base of the system.

The size of the memory components of a computer is measured in units of bytes. One byte is required to store one character, about 4 bytes required to store a decimal number. The random access memory of a computer may vary between 64K bytes or less for a small personal microcomputer to upward of 50M bytes for a large mainframe. (1K bytes = 1024 bytes = 2^{10} bytes; 1M bytes = 2^{20} bytes. The K stands for kilobytes, the M for megabytes.)

The capacity of secondary storage devices varies from 100K bytes for a small floppy disk used with a personal microcomputer, to 500M bytes for a fixed disk on a large mainframe computer. The capacity of a standard sized magnetic tape is upward of 40M bytes. Such a tape is easily capable of holding the entire response from a nationwide household income and expenditure survey.

The control unit coordinates all activities within the machine by following the program instructions. The arithmetic and logic unit (ALU) performs operations on data such as the addition or multiplication of two values or making logical comparisons of two values to find if they are equal. It is here that the user's work is done. The ability of the ALU to make comparisons allows the computer to evaluate conditions and take appropriate action. Thus in the example given earlier of building up a census table of numbers of men and women the computer first checks if an individual is male or female by comparing that persons code for sex against those for male and female. On the basis of this logical comparison the computer will then add 1 either to the count of men or to the count of women. If the code matches neither then the computer program should indicate an error.

The control unit and ALU are combined in many computers on one chip (a microprocessor), but nonetheless their functions of, on the one hand following a program, and on the other performing the actions specified in the program, are distinct.

Output devices allow the machine to display results to users. These devices are generally either some form of printer, or a television-like display, called a VDU (visual display unit). Most output from a computer comes in the form of printed text, but it is increasingly possible to produce graphical output, graphs, charts or pictures, on a screen or printed on paper.

A computer terminal combines both input and output functions in one unit, generally with a keyboard for input and a screen for output. Figure 8.2 shows a simple block diagram of this structure, and Figure 8.3 identifies these components in a small microcomputer using floppy disks as backing store, a television and a printer as output devices, and a keyboard as an input device.

Fig. 8.2   A simple block diagram of the five main components of a computer system

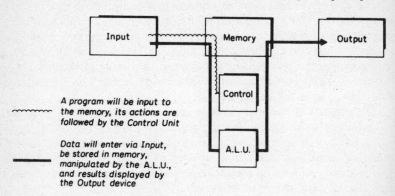

In this chapter we will not be concerned with the exact details of how these components work together, but one should note from Figure 8.2 the typical flow of data through a computer system, from the input devices to memory, subsequent processing in the ALU and finally display of information on an output device. Also important is the typical flow of a program through the computer, from the input device to the memory, from where the control unit will fetch and obey the program instructions one at a time. When a program is read and obeyed it is said to be executed.

Telecommunications allow the input and output devices to be far removed from the rest of the computer. A device known as a modem allows the telephone network to be used for sending and receiving computer data. The simplest and cheapest devices will only permit transmission of data at slow speeds, from 30 to 120 characters per

Fig. 8·3 *A small microcomputer*

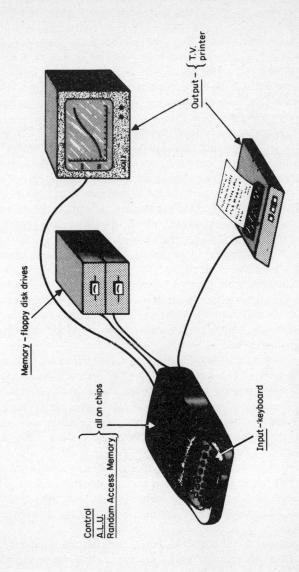

Output – { T.V.
          { printer

Memory – floppy disk drives

all on chips

Control
A.L.U.
Random Access Memory

Input – keyboard

second. More elaborate computer networks are now being built which allow much faster transmission, and it is now becoming common for computers to be linked together by such networks, allowing items from the data base of one computer to be accessed by another.

Software

All this hardware can collectively be called the processor, but users of computers will be more interested in the functions a computer can perform than the processor which performs them. In order for a processor to do work for a computer user it must be told the nature of the task. The general term used for the activity of preparing these instructions is programming.

Processors are thus programmed to perform tasks. The generic term for a class of computing task is an application. Thus 'statistical applications', 'medical applications' or 'social planning applications' may be discussed. Programs are prepared, entered into memory of the computer and then executed. Once a program is in the memory of the computer it can be executed repeatedly. The general term for programs is software, in contrast to the physical components, the hardware.

Some fundamental programs are required for any computer to operate. This basic set of programs is known as the operating system, and is usually provided by the manufacturer of the computer. Additional software can be bought either from the manufacturer or from specialist companies known as software houses. From the user's point of view it is this layer of pre-prepared software which gives the computer its characteristics and enables it to be used by relatively unskilled people.

The primary way to use a computer, given it has already an operating system, is to prepare a program, or set of instructions, using a language that will be understood by the processor (in particular by the control unit). However, most computer users never write programs, they simply use pre-prepared programs. Even professional computer programmers try to reuse existing programs, rather than re-invent the wheel.

The designing, coding, testing and documentation of programs is time consuming and requires a certain amount of skill. The use of a pre-prepared program designed to perform a certain set of tasks can be quicker, cheaper and less demanding. Such programs are referred to as packages.

In some application areas, such as statistical analysis or common accounting operations, packages are widely used. Another area in which packages have been very popular is in providing programs for personal microcomputers, allowing them to be used easily for such processes as word processing (the preparation and editing of documents stored in the computer's memory), maintaining mailing lists or building simple numerical models. In other areas of computer usage the impact of packages has been slight since the concept of a package implies that many people wish to perform the same function in a similar fashion.

A computer package should consist not only of programs, but also of supporting literature to allow users to understand what the programs do, and to learn to use them. Such supporting literature is known as documentation. The quality of the documentation is at least as important as the quality of the program.

Some computer users, such as local authorities, libraries or health service administrations, have at times taken an approach in which organisations cooperate to develop and share computer software. Within the universities and research community much swopping of programs and data takes place.

Techniques used in computing

Systems analysis

The skills required to use computer technology has given rise to the development of a variety of professions or occupations associated with computers.

The systems analyst's task is to analyse an information processing task, design and evaluate solutions, construct and implement a system and maintain or adapt it as time goes on. In order to carry out these functions the systems analyst has at his or her disposal a collection of techniques and methods. These are primarily of use in three main areas: the collection of information about the problem area, the identification and resolution of conflicting interests among users, and the systematic progress from analysis through design to implementation.

There are a variety of methods or styles of systems analysis, and different organisations approach the problems of designing and building information systems from very different angles. These styles may stress the importance of the data flowing through the system, the organisational structure it is to serve, the needs for planning and management information, the necessity for flexibility, adaptation and evolution or the importance of participation of all concerned in the development, use and evolution of a system.

Computer programming

The computer programmer is more concerned with writing the actual programs that are to run on the computer and documenting them as he or she does so. Most programmers work in high level languages, that is languages which generally make some concessions to the humans who will use them. (Some languages make more concession than others.) These languages such as BASIC, FORTRAN, COBOL, PL/I or Pascal are easy to learn and use and are available for use on a vast variety of makes and models of computer. A particular computer can be programmed in more than one high level language because a program written in a high level language is in fact translated by the computer into its own native language before it is executed. If the computer has the appropriate translator program or compiler, then it can understand a program written in that language. A computer thus first sees a program as data requiring manipulation, such as translation; only after this translation process is it able to execute the program. A program written for a microcomputer in the language FORTRAN will run on a large mainframe, with perhaps some small modifications. This portability of programs is of course important for computer users and allows computer packages to be implemented on a variety of different computers.

The programmer's job is in part involved with the technicalities of the machine, but is also to take notice of what the user of the programs requires. Programmers therefore need to have some understanding of the overall system their programs will serve and the people who will use them. This tends to lead to the situation in which specialist computer users, such as social planners or economists, prefer to learn about computing and program their own systems, rather than work with professional computer programmers. This has arisen in part from the lack of skill that technical users tend to have in the specification of what a computer program should do. The more skill planners have in designing and specifying their systems, the more help they can get from professional programmers.

The programming of computers in their own native languages, known as machine codes, which make little or no concession to humans is a much more arcane task, and the programmers who do this, 'systems programmers', are more involved maintaining the internal working of the machine.

Operating computers
Computer operators are the people who actually man a computer, minding the input and output devices, loading and removing disks and tapes from backing storage devices, and managing the day-to-day operations of a computer, such as taking security copies of all the information stored on the machine.

As computers get smaller and smaller, and diffuse more and more into organisations, these job divisions start to break down. The owners of personal microcomputers must be their own systems analyst, programmer and operator. The same is true of most research and education users who must at least act as their own systems analysts and probably their own programmers. The development of packaged software with high quality documentation and high level languages has helped to make this a less daunting prospect.

Modes of operation of computer systems

Information systems come in a number of varieties. Here three are presented, though often a particular system will present features of various types. Within such an information system the computer itself may play a greater or lesser role. The information processing in most organisations, even large technological corporations in the developed world, is mostly still done by traditional methods. A look in any office, at the paper on the desks and the filing cabinets will confirm this.

Data processing

A data processing system is one in which the main aim is to process the day-to-day transactions of an organisation as they arrive and to store information about the operations of the organisations. An example would be the computer programs used by a bank to amend its records when a cheque is presented, or a system used by a wholesaler to process orders and to prepare statements for customers.

Social planners will perhaps seldom be interested in such systems though they may wish to make some use of the information stored within such a system or the standard reports generated by such a system. An example might be information stored by a local authority on the collection of property taxes, or information collected in a hospital about the prescription of drugs.

Information retrieval systems

An information retrieval system, in contrast to a data processing system, is not simply concerned with supporting the day-to-day activities of an organisation, but with providing information about those activities when it is wanted. Within formal organisations this is often referred to as the Management Information System, or MIS. Planning organisations will often have their own equivalent requirement for an information retrieval system capable of accessing their data base.

Another type of information retrieval system is the large computerised bibliographies available, by use of telecommunications, on a worldwide basis, or the information sources on medical drugs, legal information or social and economic statistics which are also available on a similar worldwide basis. If a researcher requires to know the GNP for the OECD countries over the last twenty years, then it is possible to access a computer in France, using a computer network, and extract the information.

Increasingly with microcomputers there is interest in building information retrieval systems for people to use providing information on income and housing support, job vacancies or entitlement to benefits. In the United Kingdom there have been a number of such systems developed, and the concept has been evaluated by a number of organisations, such as the citizens advice bureaux, and recently adopted by the Department of Health and Social Security.

Modelling systems

Modelling systems are those used to forecast or simulate some situation or to estimate the parameters of a model. Though computers are not required for many modelling approaches, they are increasingly used, and techniques such as multiple regression or mathematical programming (see chapter 7) almost always require computers. Examples would be the model of the UK economy maintained by the Treasury, or a demographic model used to predict a country's population in future years.

Researchers and information technologists are interested in developing further modes of operation of information systems. Two that are talked about currently are decision support systems and knowledge based systems.

Decision support systems are information systems that are intended specifically to provide information to decision-makers. This type of system is particularly appropriate for use in situations where complex technical and financial data needs to be reviewed prior to taking action. DSS are intended to allow the investigation of alternative possible actions, using interactive computing techniques.

Information systems can be built to allow for the incremental improvement of their performance, not by adaptation of the programs, but by the successive refinement and extension of the data they retain about their application. Such systems are sometimes known as 'knowledge based systems', and are currently of interest to researchers in artificial intelligence.

Research tools

Social planners are most likely first to encounter computers as a tool in pursuing research. The use of computers in research may require their use in all of the three main styles outlined above, though the end result of research will generally be in using some modelling or information aggregation and retrieval technique.

Packaged software is generally used by social researchers for processing the results of surveys or other statistical investigations. The most common packages used are SPSS (Statistical Package for the Social Sciences), BMDP (Bio Medical Package) and SAS (Statistical Analysis System), though there are a vast number of others, each with their particular advantages. These packages allow both the production of summary descriptive information and the estimation of a variety of statistical models.

Secondary analysis of social surveys is frequently used by social planners to enable them to investigate areas that would be impossible to study by mounting specialist enquiries. The large-scale and wide-ranging surveys undertaken by governments, such as the General Household Survey and the Family Expenditure Survey in Britain, together with the Census, are generally available in machine readable form, such as on computer tapes, ready for use directly with statistical or information retrieval packages. Other planning techniques, such as linear programming or discrete event simulation are also supported by various packages, though there are not such dominant products as are found for statistical computing.

The use of computers in social planning

Computers can be applied to a wide range of social planning and social administration problems. For example in undertaking a survey and processing the results it is possible for the computer to provide help at all stages of the project.

The computer can be of help in preparing sampling frames and generating samples. Standard sampling frames may be available already in a computer readable form; thus a hospital may have records of patients which are usable or a local authority an electoral list. The computer might also print the questionnaires, particularly if they are to be personalised letters addressed to individual people.

Once the survey responses are returned they must be input into a file. This will require either that the replies be punched onto cards and then read into the computer, or that the replies be typed directly into the computer using a keyboard. The computer can be of use at this stage by reporting any reply that is suspect, for example people aged over 100 or families with more than 10 children. Such cases can then be checked and corrected if found to be in error.

Once the data are all in a file on the computer then the analysis phase begins. If a statistical package is used then this will require that the data be read into that package's own internal format, which will allow names to be associated with items of data, thus AGE will refer to the age of a respondent, SEX to their sex and REGION to the region in which they live. The package will allow the specification of tables to be generated or statistical models to be estimated. Figure 8.4 illustrates these stages.

A more substantial illustration is the computing used in the preparation of a study of the distribution and redistribution of income in Britain (Piachaud, 1982).

The computing undertaken for this study demonstrates how the computer can be of use in pursuing research when using secondary analysis techniques. The project was to study the distribution of income in the United Kingdom, making use of the Family Expenditure Survey or FES as it is commonly known.

Fig. 8.4   The stages of preparing and processing a social survey using a computer

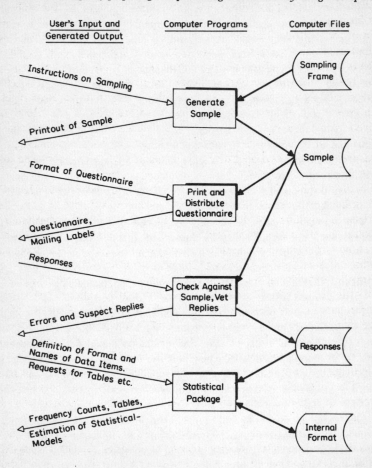

The Social Science Research Council Data Archive at the University of Essex has a national function in Britain for the dissemination of computer-based data. Copies of a vast variety of data sets are held there and are made available to researchers in a machine readable form. In the case of this study only a subset of the FES was required, and once this was specified the Survey Archive could extract the required data and deliver it on a single magnetic tape.

This tape was then used on the University of London Computer Centre computers. Note that although the computers used in London and Essex are of different makes, the format of magnetic tapes is fairly standard and allows the interchange of data using this medium. The data received from Essex included about 180 items of data on each of 20,000 people.

In order to study income distribution it was necessary to alter the format in which the data were presented. The FES is a survey which collects information about people within families, and families within households. For this study it was required to generate a file in which there was one single record for each family, rather than one record for each person. In order to do this some manipulation of the file that arrived from Essex was done using the capabilities of the SPSS package. Once a file of families was created then the analysis of the data began. Measures of income distribution were calculated, and compared to those from other sources.

Finally, the file of families was used to generate answers to 'what if' questions. The income distribution that would result from a 25 per cent increase in pensions, or a doubling of child benefit, could be simulated, as could the effect of a minimum wage or negative income tax. Figure 8.5 shows an example of the instructions given to the SPSS package to produce a table, and the result is shown in Figure 8.6.

Another example of the use of computers in social planning is given by Tottle (1979) who discusses a project to explore the use of small computers in support of the planning and production activities of a large number of small farmers in Kenya and Malaysia. In this project the computer was used for a range of tasks, including building up a data base on the capabilities of individual farms, helping to plan the yearly cycle of activities for each farmer, and to monitor the progress of the plan. The computer was also used to administer loans to farmers for the purchase of seed and fertiliser, and to help with the administration of the marketing of crops.

Clark (1978) and Sparrow (1978) describe a project using computers to produce an integrated medical record of patients' dealings with the National Health Service. The project was carried out in Devon, a rural English county. The system is intended to allow all health services within the region to use a single patient record. Access to this record is made by use of computer terminals placed in a doctor's surgery and terminals in local hospitals. The objectives of the system are better patient care, increased clinical and administrative efficiency and improved facilities for management and research.

One example of the utility of the system was shown when a medical

Fig. 8.5   A simple SPSS program to produce a table. The program uses an SPSS internal format file with the name FAM77 and cross-tabulates two of the variables in this file. These are the type of family TYPEFU – in this case families with children – and the family income expressed as a percentage of supplementary benefit – GFNREL. This output forms the basis of a table in Piachaud, 1982

```
RUN NAME      A SAMPLE TABLE FOR CHAPTER 8
GET FILE      FAM77
CROSSTABS     TYPEFU BY GFNREL
FINISH
```

journal published an article linking a particular drug with breast cancer. A local doctor was able to request a list of all patients receiving the drug, or who had taken it in the past. These patients were then examined and their treatment changed where necessary.

The value and limitations of computers

Computerised information systems have a life cycle, which is in part related to the technology, and only in part to the users' needs. Systems are initiated, designed, implemented, maintained and adapted, but the hardware which supports such systems will have a finite life. University computer users in particular are familiar with the problems that a change of hardware imposes on their computer usage. Other organisations with more stable and predictable workloads can adopt more stable policies and are perhaps more used to long-term planning. However, in planning and developing any major system, particularly one with extensive programming effort, or demanding the creation and maintenance of an extensive data base, planning and design must be carried out in the light both of the system's projected life and of the life of the supporting hardware.

Computerised information systems inevitably raise issues of the security of the information stored in a computer, and the rights of privacy of the people or organisations supplying the data (Sieghart, 1976; Bulmer, 1979). The power of computer technology to transmit, store and organise information, and the ease with which it can be adapted from one task to another, one of the fundamental properties of computers, raise particular concern when computers are used to store personal and sensitive data open to abuse.

Computers highlight this issue in part because of their speed and capacity for storing and retrieving information, but also because of the

Fig. 8.6 Table produced by the SPSS program depicted in Fig. 8.5

GFNREL

TYPEFU	COUNT / ROW PCT / COL PCT / TOT PCT	1.I -90	2.I 90-100	3.I 100-120	4.I 120-140	5.I 140-200	6.I 200-300	7.I 300-400	8.I 400+	ROW TOTAL
5. MC 1 CHILD	COUNT	26	12	42	60	272	373	122	15	922
	ROW PCT	2.8	1.3	4.6	6.5	29.5	40.5	13.2	1.6	32.3
	COL PCT	17.9	14.1	21.1	25.2	28.1	40.7	45.9	36.6	
	TOT PCT	.9	.4	1.5	2.1	9.5	13.1	4.3	.5	
6. MC 2 CHILDREN	COUNT	34	14	62	79	389	394	94	16	1082
	ROW PCT	3.1	1.3	5.7	7.3	36.0	36.4	8.7	1.5	37.9
	COL PCT	23.4	16.5	31.2	33.2	40.2	43.0	35.3	39.0	
	TOT PCT	1.2	.5	2.2	2.8	13.6	13.8	3.3	.6	
7. MC 3 CHILDREN	COUNT	11	6	30	45	152	88	35	7	374
	ROW PCT	2.9	1.6	8.0	12.0	40.6	23.5	9.4	1.9	13.1
	COL PCT	7.6	7.1	15.1	18.9	15.7	9.6	13.2	17.1	
	TOT PCT	.4	.2	1.0	1.6	5.3	3.1	1.2	.2	
8. MC 4 CHILDREN	COUNT	13	7	17	16	58	21	5	0	137
	ROW PCT	9.5	5.1	12.4	11.7	42.3	15.3	3.6	0.0	4.8
	COL PCT	9.0	8.2	8.5	6.7	6.0	2.3	1.9	0.0	
	TOT PCT	.5	.2	.6	.6	2.0	.7	.2	0.0	
9. MC 5+ CHILDREN	COUNT	4	8	5	5	20	6	1	0	49
	ROW PCT	8.2	16.3	10.2	10.2	40.8	12.2	2.0	0.0	1.7
	COL PCT	2.8	9.4	2.5	2.1	2.1	.7	.4	0.0	
	TOT PCT	.1	.3	.2	.2	.7	.2	.0	0.0	
10. ONE PARENT+CHILD	COUNT	57	38	43	33	76	35	9	3	294
	ROW PCT	19.4	12.9	14.6	11.2	25.9	11.9	3.1	1.0	10.3
	COL PCT	39.3	44.7	21.6	13.9	7.9	3.8	3.4	7.3	
	TOT PCT	2.0	1.3	1.5	1.2	2.7	1.2	.3	.1	
COLUMN TOTAL		145	85	199	238	967	917	266	41	2858
		5.1	3.0	7.0	8.3	33.8	32.1	9.3	1.4	100.0

possibility they allow for making connection between separate sets of information stored on separate computer systems. Social scientists can exploit this capability, allowing them to pursue research through the linkage of information stored on one system with information stored on another, but it does imply a risk to the confidentiality implied in almost all data gathering operations.

When completing a tax return, or visiting a doctor, the information that is provided may be stored in a computer system. The thought that this information might be passed to the police or an employer and an individual's details from various sources combined to give a very detailed dossier is profoundly disturbing.

The impact of all this upon social planners is to emphasise the need to apply controls over what exact items of data are stored and who can gain access to them, to explain to the people or organisations providing data the conditions under which data is to be used, and to honour those conditions. There are also aspects of physical security which need to be considered, not only for ethical reasons but also because the power of computers allows people to make very serious and expensive mistakes. If the results of two years' survey work are stored on a magnetic tape with no back-up copy in existence, then the corruption of this tape could be disastrous.

It is possible to see the advent of cheap and reliable computers and their associated technologies as potentially liberating or revolutionary developments. Computers can be seen as removing drudgery from work, allowing automation to replace human operators by machines for dangerous or unpleasant work. The computer can promote efficiency in organisations by providing information which is timely and accurate.

The French study *The Computerisation of Society* by Nora and Minc (1981) is clearly in this vein, but the optimism the authors show and their delight in the technology they describe is only one side of the argument (Barron and Curnow, 1979; Burns, 1981). Using computers for even the simplest project will soon show up not only advantages but also some disadvantages.

Using computers will tend to reorganise working practice, impose requirements for the learning of new skills and possibly reduce the number and the variety of people involved, and thus the number of different viewpoints and interests represented in a project. Computerisation might also remove planners from 'the field', as more and more of the day-to-day work is done through a computer terminal. Ultimately the situation can arise where the sole reality is seen as being in the data stored on the computer, and no further contact with the world outside is necessary (Weizenbaum, 1979). All computer users must be careful to remember that computers cannot solve real problems, all they can do at best is to provide accurate information on the current situation and provide a tool for the investigation of possible futures.

Computer systems, despite their glossy new image, can be profoundly conservative and inimical to change. This is in part because of the isolation they might impose on their users, partly because of the investment that large computerised systems represent, and more interestingly the ability that this developing technology has to provide props or buttresses to large bureaucratic structures that might better be demolished.

Bibliography

Abler, R. *et al.* (1971) *Spatial Organization: The Geographer's View of the World*. Englewood Cliffs, Prentice Hall.

Adelman, I. and Morris, C.T. (1967) *Society, Politics and Economic Development*. Baltimore, Johns Hopkins University Press.

Alinsky, S. (1946) *Reveille for Radicals*. Chicago, University of Chicago Press.

Apthorpe, R. (1970) 'Development Studies and Social Planning' in R. Apthorpe (ed), pp. 1–28.

Apthorpe, R. (ed) (1970) *People, Planning and Development Studies*. London, Frank Cass.

Avison, N.H. (1972) 'Criminal statistics as social indicators' in A. Shonfield and S. Shaw (eds), pp. 33–52.

Bailey, R. and Brake, M. (eds) (1975) *Radical Social Work*. London, Edward Arnold.

Barnes, J.A. (1977) *The Ethics of Inquiry in Social Science*. New Delhi, Oxford University Press.

Barron, I. and Curnow, R. (1979) *The Future of Microelectronics*. Milton Keynes, Open University Press.

Baster, N. (1972) 'Development Indicators: An Introduction' in N. Baster (ed), pp. 1–20.

Baster, N. (1972) 'Development indicators: an introduction' in N. Baster (ed.)

Bauer, R. (ed) (1966) *Social Indicators*. Cambridge, MIT Press.

Baxter, R.S. (1976) *Computers and Statistical Techniques for Planners*. London, Methuen.

Beaumont, J.R. (1980) 'Spatial interaction models and the location-allocation problem', *Journal of Regional Science*, Vol. 20, pp. 37–51.

Beesley, M.E. and Foster, C.D. (1963) 'The Victoria Line: social benefit and finances', *Journal of the Royal Statistical Society*, Series A, Vol. 126, pp. 46–58.

Bennis, W.G. *et al.* (eds) (1961) *The Planning of Change*. New York, Holt, Reinhart and Winston.

Beresford, S.A.A. *et al.* (1978) 'Varicose veins: a comparison of surgery and injection-compression sclerotherapy', *The Lancet*, 29 April, pp. 921–924.

Best, G. and Rosenhead, J. (1980) *Robustness in Practice: The Regional Planning of Health Services*. Paper presented to the Fourth European Congress on Operational Research, Cambridge, July, 1980.

Beyer, J.C. (1973) *Budget Innovations in Developing Countries: The Experience of Nepal*. New York, Praeger.

Bishop, P. (1982) *Computing Science*. London, Nelson.

Boldy, D. (1980) *Operations Research Applied to Health Services*. London, Croom Helm.

Booth, T. (ed) (1979) *Planning for Welfare: Social Policy and the Expenditure Process*. Oxford, Blackwell and Robertson.

Bowlby, S.R. (1979) 'Accessibility, mobility and shopping provision' in B.

Goodhall and A. Kirby (eds) pp. 293–323.

Brand, J. (1978) 'The politics of social indicators' in M. Bulmer (ed), pp. 228–243.

Breheny, M.J. (ed) (1979) *Developments in Urban and Regional Analysis*. London, Pion.

Broady, M. (1968) *Planning for People: Essays on the Social Context of Planning*. London, Bedford Square Press.

Buell, B. *et al*. (1952) *Community Planning for Human Services*. New York, Columbia University Press.

Bulmer, M. (1978) 'Social science research and policy making in Britain', in M. Bulmer (ed), pp. 3–43.

Bulmer, M. (ed) (1978) *Social Policy Research*. London, Macmillan.

Bulmer, M. (ed) (1979) *Censuses, Surveys and Privacy*. London, Macmillan.

Bunge, W. (1962) *Theoretical Geography*. Lund, Gleerup.

Burns, A. (1981) *The Microchip: Appropriate or Inappropriate Technology*. Chichester, Ellis Horwood.

Caiden, N. and Wildavsky, A. (1974) *Planning and Budgeting in Poor Countries*, New York, Wiley.

Campbell, A. and Converse, P.E. (1972) *The Human Meaning of Social Change*. New York, Russell Sage.

Carley, M. (1981) *Social Measurement and Social Indicators: Issues of Policy and Theory*. London, Allen and Unwin.

Carlisle, E. (1972) 'The conceptual structure of social indicators', in A. Shonfield and S. Shaw (eds), pp. 23–32.

Casley, D.J. and Lury, D.A. (1981) *Data Collection in Developing Countries*. Oxford, Clarendon Press.

Cazes, B. (1972) 'The development of social indicators: a survey' in A. Shonfield and S. Shaw (eds), pp. 9–22.

Chambers, R. (1981) 'Rapid rural appraisal: rationale and repertoire', *Public Administration and Development*, Vol. 1, pp. 95–106.

Chandler, A.D. (1977) *The Visible Hand: The Managerial Revolution in American Business*. Cambridge, Harvard University Press.

Chandor, A. (ed) (1977) *The Penguin Dictionary of Computing*. Harmondsworth, Penguin.

Chase, S.B. (ed) (1968) *Problems in Public Expenditure Analysis*. Washington, Brookings.

Chatterjee, B. and Gokhale, S. (eds) (1974) *Social Welfare: Legend and Legacy*. Bombay, Popular Prakashan.

Clark, D.J. (1978) 'A patient data base for the National Health Service', *Computer Bulletin*, Series 2, no. 17, pp. 17–21.

Clark, R.W. (1962) *The Rise of the Boffins*. London, Phoenix House.

Clark, J.A. and Cole, S. (1975) *Global Simulation Models: A Comparative Study*. London, Wiley.

Cole, S. *et al*. (1973) *Thinking about the Future*. London, Chatto and Windus.

Conyers, D. (1982) *An Introduction to Social Planning in the Third World*. Chichester, Wiley.

Coombs, P. (1970) *What is Educational Planning?* Paris, UNESCO.

Coverdale, I.L. and Negrine, S.H. (1978) 'The balance of care project: modelling the allocation of health and personal social services', *Journal of the Operational Research Society*, Vol. 29, pp. 1043–1045.

Crawford, E. and Rokkan, S. (eds) (1976) *Sociological Praxis*. London, Sage.

Crowther, J.G. and Whiddington, R. (1947) *Science at War*. London, HMSO.

Curtis, S.F. (1982) 'Spatial analysis of surgery locations in general practice', *Social Science and Medicine*, Vol. 16, pp. 303–313.

Dasgupta, P. *et al*. (1972) *Guidelines for Project Evaluation*. New York, United Nations Industrial Development Organisation.

Dear, M.J. (1978) 'Planning for mental health care: a reconsideration of public facility location theory', *International Regional Science Review*, Vol. 3, pp. 93–112.

Dear, M.J. (1979) 'Thirteen axioms of a geography of the public sector' in S. Gale and G. Olsson (eds), pp. 53–64.

De Neufville, J.I. (1975) *Social Indicators and Public Policy*. Amsterdam, Elsevier.

Dertouzos, M.L. and Moses, J. (eds) (1979) *The Computer Age: A Twenty Year View*. Cambridge, MIT Press.

Doherty, J. (1973) *The Location of Health Facilities in Tanzania*. Dar-es-Salaam, University of Dar-es-Salaam.

Draper, F.T. and Pitsvada, B.T. (1981) 'ZBB looking back after 10 years', *Public Administration Review*, Vol. 41, pp. 76–83.

Drew, E.B. (1969) 'HEW Grapples with PPBS' in A. Etzioni (ed), pp. 173–185.

Drewnowski, J. (1970) *Studies in the Measurement of Levels of Living and Welfare*. Geneva, United Nations Research Institute for Social Development.

Duhl, L.J. (1963) 'Planning and poverty' in L.J. Duhl (ed), pp. 295–304.

Duhl, L.J. (ed) (1963) *The Urban Condition*. New York, Basic Books.

Duncan, O.D. (1969) *Towards Social Reporting*. New York, Russell Sage.

Ecklein, J.L. and Lauffer, A. (1972) *Community Organizers and Social Planners: A Volume of Case and Illustrative Materials*. New York, Wiley.

Epstein, A.L. (1967) *The Craft of Social Anthropology*. London, Tavistock.

Etzioni, A. (ed) (1969) *Readings in Modern Organizations*. Englewood Cliffs, Prentice Hall.

Falk, N. and Lee, J. (1978) *Planning in the Social Services*. Farnborough, Saxon House.

French, R.A. and Hamilton, F.E.I. (eds) (1979) *The Socialist City: Spatial Structure and Urban Policy*. Chichester, Wiley.

Frieden, B.J. (1967) 'The changing prospects for social planning', *Journal of the American Institute of Planners*, Vol. 33, pp. 311–323.

Frieden, B.J. and Morris, R. (eds) (1968) *Urban Planning and Social Policy*. New York, Basic Books.

Friedmann, J. (1979) *The Good Society: A Personal Account of its Struggle with the World of Social Planning and a Dialectical Enquiry into the Roots of Radical Practice*. Cambridge, MIT Press.

Gale, S. and Olsson, G. (eds) (1979) *Philosophy and Geography*. Dordrecht, Reidel, pp. 53–64.

Gans, H. (1968a) 'Planning, social: regional and urban planning' in D.L. Sills (ed), pp. 129–137.

Gans, H. (1968b) *People and Plans: Essays on Urban Problems and Solutions*. New York, Basic Books.

Gans, H. (1968c) 'Social and physical planning for the elimination of poverty' in B.J. Frieden and R. Morris (eds). pp. 39–54.

Gardner, G. (1978) *Social Surveys for Social Planners*. Milton Keynes, Open

University Press.

Gerima, Y.W. (1973) 'Social planning: a challenge to social work education' in *Proceedings of the XVI Congress of Schools of Social Work*. New York, International Association of Schools of Social Work.

Gibbs, R.J. (1978) 'The use of a strategic planning model for health and personal social services', *Journal of the Operational Research Society*, Vol 29, pp. 875–883.

Gilbert, N. and Specht, H. (1977a) *Dynamics of Community Planning*. Cambridge, Ballinger.

Gilbert, N. and Specht, H. (eds) (1977b) *Planning for Social Welfare*. Englewood Cliffs, Prentice Hall.

Gish, O. (1975) *Planning the Health Sector*. London, Croom Helm.

Glass, R. (1948) *The Social Background of a Plan: A Study of Middlesbrough*. London, Routledge and Kegan Paul.

Glennerster, H. (1975) *Social Service Budgets and Social Policy: British and American Experience*. London, Allen and Unwin.

Glennerster, H. (1980) 'From containment to conflict: social planning in the seventies' *Journal of Social Policy*, Vol. 10, pp. 31–51.

Godlund, S. (1961) *Population, Regional Hospitals, Transport Facilities and Regions*. Lund, Gleerup.

Goodchild, M.F. and Massam, B. (1969) 'Some least-cost models of spatial administrative systems in southern Ontario' *Geografiska Annaler*, Vol. 52, pp. 86–94.

Goodhall, B. and Kirby, A. (eds) (1979) *Resources and Planning*. Oxford, Oxford University Press.

Gould, P. *et al*. (1966) 'An approach to the geographic assignment of hospital services', *Tijdschrift Voor Economische en Sociale Geografie*, Vol. 57, pp. 203–206.

Gouldner, A. (1957) 'Theoretical requirements for the applied social sciences', *American Sociological Review*, Vol. 22, pp. 92–102.

Gouldner, A. (1961) 'Anti-Minotaur: The Myth of a Value Free Sociology' *Social Problems*, Vol. 9, pp. 199–213.

Greater London Council (1978) *Friday Hill Estate: Report of the Housing Appraisal Survey*. London.

Greenberger, M. *et al*. (1976) *Models in the Policy Process*. New York, Russell Sage.

Grindle, M.S. (1980) *Politics and Policy Implementation in the Third World*. Princeton, Princeton University Press.

Grosser, C.F. (1965) 'Community development programs serving the urban poor', *Social Work*, Vol. 10, pp. 15–20.

Grosser, C.F. (1973) *New Directions in Community Organization: From Enabling to Advocacy*. New York, Praeger.

Gulbenkian Foundation (1968) *Community Work and Social Change: A Report on Training*. London, Longman.

Gupta, B.N. (1967) *Government Budgeting with Special Reference to India*. Bombay, Asia Publishing House.

Haggett, P. (1965) *Locational Analysis in Human Geography*. London, Edward Arnold.

Haley, K.B. (ed) (1979) *OR '78*. Amsterdam, North Holland.

Hardiman, M. (1974) *Report on the Household Survey: The Survey and Planning of Maiduguri*. Maiduguri, Max Lock Group.

Hardiman, M. and Midgley, J. (1980) 'Training social planners for social development', *International Social Work*, Vol. 23, pp. 2–15.

Hardiman, M. and Midgley, J. (1982) *The Social Dimensions of Development: Social Policy and Planning in the Third World*. Chichester, Wiley.

Harper, E. and Dunham, A. (eds) (1959) *Community Organization in Action: Basic Literature and Critical Comments*. New York, Association Press.

Haveman, R. and Margolis, J. (eds) (1970) *Public Expenditures and Policy Analysis*. Chicago, Rand McNally.

Heclo, H. and Wildavsky, A. (1974) *The Private Government of Public Money*. London, Macmillan.

Heinemann, M. *et al*. (1982) issue on 'Science at the cross-roads' in *Science for People*, Vol. 51.

Hendriks, G. (1964) *Community Organization*. The Hague, Ministry of Social Work.

Hillman, M. *et al*. (1976) *Transport Realities and Planning Policy*. London, PEP.

Himes, J.S. (1954) *Social Planning in America: A Dynamic Interpretation*. New York, Doubleday.

Hindle, D. (1978) 'Management science in developing countries: adopting the right style', *Omega*, Vol. 6, p. 370.

Hitch, C.J. and McKean, R.M. (1961) *The Economics of Defense in the Nuclear Age*. Cambridge, Harvard University Press.

Hodgart, R.L. (1978) 'Optimising access to public services', *Progress in Human Geography*, Vol. 2, pp. 17–48.

Hogg, J. (1968) 'The siting of fire stations', *Operational Research Quarterly*, Vol. 19, pp. 275–287.

Honda, K.L. (1979) *Programme and Performance Budgeting in the US and Feasibilities for India*. New Delhi, Uppsala.

Hopkins, R.F. and Mitchell, R.C. (1974) 'The validity of survey research in Africa: some propositions', *African Studies Review*, Vol. 17, pp. 567–574.

Hunt, R. and Shelley, J. (1979) *Computers and Commonsense*. London, Prentice Hall.

India, Planning Commission (1980) *Sixth Five Year Plan, 1980–85*. New Delhi.

Isard, W. (1956) *Location and Space Economy*. Cambridge: MIT Press.

Isard, W. (1976) 'Some directions for the extension of dynamic spatial analysis' in I. Masser (ed), pp. 1–10.

Jackson, R. and Sellars, M. (1977) 'The distribution of RSG' *Centre for Environmental Studies Review*, No. 1, pp. 1–10.

Jacobs, A.B. (1976) 'Notes on the value and use of computer models in the practice of city planning', *Design Methods and Theories*, Vol. 10, pp. 21–25.

Janowitz, M. (1971) *Sociological Models and Social Policy*. Morristown, General Learning Press.

Jones, D. and Mayo, M. (eds) (1974) *Community Work Vol 1*, London, Routledge and Kegan Paul.

Jongmans, O.J. and Gutkind, P. (eds) (1967) *Anthropologists in the Field*. Assen, Van Gorkum.

Kahn, A.J. (1963) *Planning Community Services for Children in Trouble*. New York, Columbia University Press.

Kahn, A.J. (1969a) *Theory and Practice of Social Planning*. New York, Russell Sage.

Kahn, A.J. (1969b) *Studies in Social Policy and Planning*. New York, Russell Sage.

Kemball-Cook, D. (1980) *Review: Applications in Health and Population Planning*. Brighton, University of Sussex Developing World OR Group.

Kirk, G. (1980) *Urban Planning in a Capitalist Society*. London, Croom Helm.

Klemperer, P.D. and McClenahan, J.W. (1981) 'Joint strategic planning between health and local authorities', *Omega*, Vol. 9, pp. 481–491.

Koleda, M. (1971) 'A public good model of governmental consolidation' *Urban Studies*, Vol. 8, pp. 103–110.

Kuenstler, P. (ed) (1961) *Community Organization in Britain*. London, Faber.

Lane, R.P. (1939) 'The field of community organization', *Proceedings of the 66th National Conference of Social Work*. New York, National Association of Social Workers.

Lane, R.P. (1940) 'Reports of groups studying community organization process' *Proceedings of the 67th National Conference of Social Work*. New York, National Association of Social Workers.

Lapping, A. (ed) (1970) *Community Action*. London, Fabian Society.

Layard, R. (ed) (1972) *Cost-Benefit Analysis*. Harmondsworth, Penguin.

Lazarsfeld, P. and Reitz, J.G. (1975) *An Introduction to Applied Sociology*. New York, Elsevier.

Leach, E. (1967) 'An anthropologist's reflection on a social survey' in O.J. Jongmans and P. Gutkind (eds), pp. 75–88.

Leonardi, G. (1979) 'A mathematical-programming framework for the general location of spatially interacting activities: theory and algorithms' in M.J. Breheny (ed), pp. 28–47.

Levine, R.A. (1970) *The Poor Ye Need not Have With You: Lessons from the War on Poverty*. Cambridge, MIT Press.

Lindblom, C. (1959) 'The science of muddling through', *Public Administration Review*, Vol. 19, pp. 79–88.

Lippitt, R. *et al*. (1958) *The Dynamics of Planned Change*. New York, Harcourt Brace.

Little, A. and Mabey, C. (1972) 'An index for designation of Educational Priority Areas' in A. Shonfield and S. Shaw (eds), pp. 67–93.

Little, I.M.D. and Mirrlees, J.A. (1974) *Project Appraisal for Developing Countries*. London, Heinemann.

Lohman, R.A. (1980) *Breaking Even: Financial Management in Human Service Organizations*. Philadelphia, Temple University Press.

Luck, G.M. (1979) 'Barefoot ORSA' in K.B. Haley (ed), pp. 213–233.

Lyden, F.J. and Miller, E.G. (eds) (1972) *Planning Programming Budgeting: A Systems Approach to Management*. Chicago, Markham.

Lynd, R. (1939) *Knowledge for What: The Place of Social Science in American Culture*. Princeton, Princeton University Press.

Maas, H. (ed) (1966) *Five Fields of Social Service*. New York, National Association of Social Workers.

McAllister, D.M. (1976) 'Equity and efficiency in public facility location', *Geographical Analysis*, Vol. 8, pp. 47–63.

McDonald, A.G. *et al*. (1974) 'Balance of care: some mathematical models of the National Health Service', *British Medical Bulletin*, Vol. 30, pp. 262–271.

McGranahan, D. (1972) 'Development indicators and development models' in N. Baster (ed). pp. 91–102.

McKean, R.M. (1958) *Efficiency in Government and the Use of Systems Analysis*. New York, Wiley.

Maclaren, A. (1981) 'Area based positive discrimination and the distribution of wellbeing', *Transactions of the Institute of British Geographers*, Vol. 6, pp. 53–67.

McLoughlin, J.B. (1969) *Urban and Regional Planning: A Systems Approach*. London, Faber.

Magee, C.C. and Osmolski, R.S. (1979) *Bridgend Speciality Cost Statement*. Cardiff, University College Cardiff.

Mahadur, P.D. and Rao, K.R. (1974) 'A model for location of service facilities in a non-Western urban environment' in M. Yeats (ed), pp. 164–182.

Marglin, S.A. (1967) *Public Investment Criteria*. London, Allen and Unwin.

Marris, P. and Rein, M. (1967) *Dilemma of Social Reform: Poverty and Community Action in the United States*. London, Routledge and Kegan Paul.

Massam, B. (1975) *Location and Space in Social Administration*. London, Edward Arnold.

Massam, B. (1980) *Spatial Search: Applications to Planning Problems in the Public Sector*. Oxford, Pergamon.

Massam, B. and Bouchard, D. (1977) 'Towards a framework for examining the utilization of a public facility: health care centres in Kuala Lumpur', *Geoforum*, Vol. 8, pp. 113–120.

Masser, I. (ed) (1976) *Theory and Practice of Regional Science*. London, Pion.

Mayer, R. (1972) *Social Planning and Social Change*. Englewood Cliffs, Prentice Hall.

Mayo, M. (1975) 'Community development: a radical alternative' in R. Bailey and M. Brake (eds), pp. 129–143.

Meadows, D.H. *et al.* (1972) *The Limits to Growth*. London, Earth Island.

Mehmet, O. (1978) *Economic Planning and Social Justice in Developing Countries*. London, Croom Helm.

Midgley, J. (1978) 'Developmental roles for social work in the Third World: the prospect of social planning', *Journal of Social Policy*, Vol. 7, pp. 173–188.

Mills, C.W. (1943) 'The professional ideology of social pathologists', *American Journal of Sociology*, Vol. 49, pp. 165–180.

Mills, C.W. (1959) *The Sociological Imagination*. New York, Oxford University Press.

Mishan, E. (1971) *Cost-Benefit Analysis*. London, Allen and Unwin.

Mohan, J.F. (1979) *The Use of Grid Square Census Data in the Location of Hospital Facilities: A Case Study of the Durham Health District*. Durham, Durham University.

Mooney, G. *et al.* (1980) *Choices in Health Care*. London, Macmillan.

Morrill, R.L. (1970) *Spatial Organization of Society*. Belmont, Wadsworth.

Morris, M.D. (1979) *Measuring the Conditions of the World's Poor*. New York, Pergamon.

Morris, R. (ed) (1964) *Centrally Planned Change: Prospects and Concepts*. New York, National Association of Social Workers.

Morris, R. (1966) 'Social planning' in H.S. Maas (ed). pp. 185–208.

Morris, R. and Binstock, R. (1966) *Feasible Planning for Social Change*. New York, Columbia University Press.

Moser, C.A. (1978) 'Social indicators: systems, methods and problems', in M. Bulmer (ed), pp. 203–214.

Moser, C.A. and Kalton, G. (1977) *Survey Methods in Social Investigation*. London, Heinemann.

Moynihan, D.P. (1969) *Maximum Feasible Misunderstanding: Community Action in the War on Poverty*. New York, Free Press.

Myrdal, G. (1953) 'The relation between social theory and social policy', *British Journal of Sociology*. Vol 23, pp. 210–242.

Nora, S. and Minc, A. (1981) *The Computerization of Society*. Cambridge, MIT Press.

North, C.C. (1932) *Social Problems and Social Planning: The Guidance of Social Change*. New York, McGraw Hill.

Novick, D. (1965) *Program Budgeting*. Cambridge, Harvard University Press.

O'Barr, W.M. *et al*. (eds) (1973) *Survey Research in Africa: Its Application and Limits*. Evanston, North Western University Press.

Ogburn, W.F. (1922) *Social Change with Respect to Culture and Original Nature*. New York, Huebsch.

Ohlin, L. (1964) 'Prospects for planning in American social welfare' in R. Morris (ed), pp. 125–136.

Oppenheim, A.N. (1966) *Questionnaire Design and Attitude Measurement*. New York, Basic Books.

Oppong, C. and Church, C. (1980) *The Seven Roles and Status of Women: A Guide to Data Collection and Analysis*. Geneva, ILO.

Organization for Economic Cooperation and Development (1976) *Measuring Social Wellbeing*. Paris

Ottawa-Carleton Regional District Health Council (1978a) *Planning Health Services in Ottawa-Carleton*. Ottawa.

Ottawa-Carleton Regional District Health Council (1978b) *The Future of Community Health Services in Ontario*. Ottawa.

Ottawa-Carleton Regional District Health Council (1979a) *Operational Plan for Gerentology Services*. Ottawa.

Ottawa-Carleton Regional District Health Council (1979b) *Long Term Strategic Evaluation of Health Care Services in Ottawa-Carleton*. Ottawa.

Parston, G. *et al*. (1981) *Multi-Future Strategic Planning*. San Francisco, Western Centre for Health Planning.

Pausewang, S. (1973) *Methods and Concepts of Social Research in a Rural Developing Society*. Munich, Weltforum Verlag.

Peil, M. (1982) *Social Science Research Methods: An African Handbook*. London, Hodder and Stoughton.

Perlman, R. and Gurin, A. (1972) *Community Organization and Social Planning*. New York, Wiley.

Perloff, H.S. (1963) 'Social planning in the metropolis' in L.J. Duhl (ed), pp. 331–347.

Pettit, W. (1928) *Studies in Community Organization*. New York, Appleton, Century Crofts.

Piachaud, D. (1982) *The Distribution and Redistribution of Incomes*. London, Bedford Square Press.

Piachaud, D. and Weddell, J.M. (1972) 'The economics of treating varicose veins', *International Journal of Epidemiology*, Vol. 1, pp. 287–294.

Pinkus, G.E. and Dixson, A. (1981) *Solving Local Government Problems: Practical Applications of Operations Research in Cities and Regions*. London, Allen and Unwin.

Plowden, B. (1967) *Children and their Primary Schools*. London, Central Advisory Council for Education.

Prest, A.R. and Turvey, R. (1965) 'Cost-benefit analysis: a survey', *Economic Journal*, Vol. 75, pp. 685–705.

Psacharopoulos, G. (1975) 'The macro-planning of education: a clarification of issues and a look into the future', *Comparative Education Review*, Vol. 19, pp. 214–224.

Pusic, E. (1965) *Planning the Social Services in Developing Countries*. The Hague, Mouton.

Ravetz, J.R. (1971) *Scientific Knowledge and its Social Problems*. Oxford, Oxford University Press.

Rein, M. (1968) 'Planning, social: social welfare planning' in D.L. Sills (ed), pp. 142–154.

Rittell, H. and Webber, M. (1973) 'Dilemmas in a general theory of planning', *Policy Sciences*, Vol. 4, pp. 155–169.

Rivlin, A.M. (1970) 'The planning, programming and budgeting system of the Department of Health, Education and Welfare: some lessons from experience' in R. Haveman and J. Margolis (eds), pp. 502–517.

Rivlin, A.M. (1971) *Systematic Thinking for Social Action*. Washington, Brookings.

Robertson, I.M.L. (1976) 'Accessibility to services in the Argyll District of Strathclyde: a location model', *Regional Studies*, Vol. 12, pp. 419–428.

Robertson, I.M.L. (1978) 'Planning the location of recreational centres in an urban area: a case study of Glasgow', *Regional Studies*, Vol. 12, pp. 419–428.

Robinson, I. (ed) (1972) *Decision Making in Urban Planning*. Beverly Hills, Sage.

Rosenhead, J. (1978) 'Operational research in health service planning', *European Journal of Operational Research*, Vol. 2, pp. 75–85.

Rosenhead, J. (1980) 'Planning under uncertainty II: a methodology for robustness analysis', *Journal of the Operational Research Society*, Vol. 31, pp. 331–341.

Rosenhead, J. (1981) 'Operational research in urban planning', *Omega*, Vol. 9, pp. 345–364.

Rosenhead, J. (1982) *Why Does Management Need Management Science?* Paper presented to the 26th Annual Meeting of the Society for General Systems Research, Washington, January, 1982.

Rosenhead, J. and Thunhurst, C. (1982) 'A materialist analysis of operational research', *Journal of the Operational Research Society*, Vol. 25, pp. 219–230.

Roskill (1970) *Report of the Commission of the Third London Airport*. London, HMSO.

Ross, M.G. (1955) *Community Organization: Theory and Principles*. New York, Harper.

Ross, M.G. (1958) *Case Histories in Community Organization*. New York, Harper.

Rossi, P.H. (1981) 'Applied sociology' in J.F. Short (ed), pp. 283–299.

Rushton, G. (1969) 'Analysis of spatial behaviour by revealed space preferences', *Annals of the Association of American Geographers*, Vol. 59, pp. 391–400.

Rys, V. (1974) 'Problems of social security planning in industrialized and developing countries', *International Social Security Review*, Vol. 27, pp. 314–346.

Sagasti, F.R. (1974) 'Operations research in the context of underdevelopment: some case studies from Peru', *Operational Research Quarterly*, Vol. 25, pp. 219–230.

Sagasti, F.R. (1976) 'Thoughts on the use (and non-use) of OR/MS in the planning and management of development', *Operations Research Quarterly*, Vol 27, pp. 937–948.

San Fransisco, Department of City Planning (1972) 'The San Francisco Community Renawal Simulation Model' in I. Robinson (ed), pp. 555–595.

Sastry, K.S. (1979) *Performance Budgeting for Planned Development*. New Delhi, Radiant Publishing.

Schultze, C.L. (1968) *The Politics and Economics of Public Spending*. Washington, Brookings.

Selltiz, C. *et al*. (1976) *Research Methods in Social Relations*. New York, Holt, Reinhart and Winston.

Selwyn, P. (1970) 'Social planning for penal systems' in R. Apthorpe (ed), pp. 47–56.

Sheldon, E.B. and Moore, W. (eds) (1968) *Indicators of Social Change: Concepts and Measurements*. New York, Russell Sage.

Schick, A. (1966) 'The road to PPB: stages in budget reform', *Public Administration Review*, Vol. 26, pp. 243–258.

Schick, A. (1973) 'A death in the bureaucracy: the demise of federal PPB', *Public Administration Review*, Vol. 33, pp. 146–156.

Shipman, M.D. (1972) *The Limits to Social Research*. London, Longman.

Shonfield, A. and Shaw, S. (eds) (1972) *Social Indicators and Social Policy*. London, Heinemann.

Short, J.F. (ed) (1981) *The State of Sociology: Problems and Prospects*. London, Sage.

Sieghart, P. (1976) *Privacy and Computers*. London, Latimer.

Sills, D.L. (ed) (1968) *International Encyclopaedia of the Social Sciences*. New York, Macmillan.

Simon, H.A. (1957) *Administrative Behaviour*. Toronto, Collier Macmillan.

Sovani, N. (1974) 'Whither social planners and social planning' in B. Chatterjee and S. Gokhale (eds), pp. 46–68.

Sparrow, J. (1978) 'A primary care computer system', *Computer Bulletin*, Series 2, no. 16, p. 11.

Spradley, J.P. (1980) *Participant Observation*. New York, Holt, Reinhart and Winston.

Streeten, P. (1981) *First Things First: Meeting Basic Needs in Developing Countries*. Oxford, Oxford University Press.

Stretton, H. (1978) *Urban Planning in Rich and Poor Countries*. Oxford University Press.

Stumpf, J. and Granger, B.P. (1973) 'Social welfare planning' in H. Trecker (ed), pp. 97–112.

Sugden, R. and Williams, A. (1978) *The Principles of Practical Cost-Benefit Analysis*. London, Oxford University Press.

Taylor, C.L. (1972) 'Indicators of political development' in N. Baster (ed), pp. 103–109.

Taylor, P.J. (1975) *Distance Decay in Spatial Interactions*. Norwich, Geo Abstracts.

Taylor, J.L. and Williams, D.G. (eds) (1982) *Urban Planning Practice in Developing Countries*. Oxford, Oxford University Press.

Thavaraj, M.J.K. and Iyer, K.B. (1973) *Readings on Performance Budgeting*. New Delhi, Research Publications in Social Science.

Thunhurst, C. (1982) *It Makes You Sick: The Politics of the NHS*. London, Pluto.

Tietze, M.B. (1968) 'Towards a theory of urban public facility location', *Papers of the Regional Science Association*, Vol. 21, pp. 35–51.

Todaro, M.P. (1977) *Economics for a Developing World*. London, Longman.

Tottle, G.P. (1979) 'Computers in support of agriculture in developing countries', *ICL Technical Journal*, Vol. 1, pp. 99–115.

Trecker, H. (ed) (1973) *Goals for Social Welfare, 1973–1999*. New York, Association Press.

United Kingdom, Department of Education and Science (1970) *Output Budgeting for the DES*. London, HMSO.

United Kingdom, Department of Health and Social Security (1976a) *Sharing Resources for Health in England*. London, HMSO.

United Kingdom, Department of Health and Social Security (1976b) *Priorities for Health and Personal Social Services in England: A Consultative Document*. London, HMSO.

United Kingdom, Department of Health and Social Security (1978) *The 1978 Programme Budget: A Description of Methodology*. London, Department of Health and Social Security.

United Kingdom (1982) *The Government's Expenditure Plans, 1982/3 to 1984/5*. London, HMSO, Cmnd. 8494.

United Nations, Economic Commission for Latin America (1962) *A Manual for Programme and Performance Budgeting*. New York.

United Nations (1971) 'Social policy and planning in national development', *International Social Development Review*, Vol. 3, pp. 4–15.

United Nations (1979a) *1978 Report on the World Social Situation*, New York.

United Nations (1979b) *Patterns of Government Expenditure on Social Services*. New York.

United States, President's Research Committee on Social Trends (1933) *Recent Social Trends*. New York, McGraw Hill.

United States, Department of Health, Education and Welfare (1969) *Towards a Social Report*. Washington, Government Printing Office.

Visvanathan, S.S. (1973) *Performance Budgeting in Government: An Illustrated Guide*. New Delhi, Indian Institute of Public Administration.

Wachs, M. (1973) 'Physical accessibility as a social indicator', *Socio-Economic Planning Sciences*, Vol. 7, pp. 437–456.

Waddington, C.H. (1973) *OR in World War 2*. London, Elek Science.

Wallman, S. (ed) (1977) *Perceptions of Development*. Cambridge, Cambridge University Press.

Wallman, S. *et al.* (1980) 'Ethnography by proxy: strategies for research in the inner city', *Ethnos*, Vol. 1–2, pp. 5–38.

Ward, L. (1906) *Applied Sociology: A Treatise on the Conscious Improvement of Society by Society*. Boston, Ginn.

Ward, R.A. (1964) *Operational Research in Local Government*. London, Allen and Unwin.

Warner, A.G. *et al.* (1930) *American Charities and Social Work*. New York, Crowell.

Warren, R.L. (1955) *Studying Your Community*. New York, Russell Sage.

Warwick, D.P. and Osherson, S. (eds) (1973) *Comparative Research Methods*, Englewood Cliffs, Prentice Hall.

Waterston, A. (1965) *Development Planning: Lessons from Experience*. Baltimore, Johns Hopkins University Press.

Weisbrod, B.A. (1968) 'Income redistribution effects and cost-benefit analysis' in S.B. Chase (ed). pp. 177–209.

Weizenbaum, J. (1979) 'Once more: the computer revolution' in M.L. Dertouzos, and J. Moses (eds). pp. 439–458.

Wildavsky, A. (1975) *Budgeting: A Comparative Theory of Budget Processes*. Boston, Little Brown.

Williams, A. (1967) *Output Budgeting and the Contribution of Micro Economics to Efficiency in Government*. London, HMSO.

Williams, A. and Anderson, R. (1975) *Efficiency in the Social Services*. Oxford, Blackwell and Robertson.

Wilson, A.G. (1974) *Urban and Regional Models in Geography and Planning*. London, Wiley.

Wilson, J.Q. (1966) *Urban Renewal: The Record and the Controversy*. Cambridge, MIT Press.

Withanan, R.M. (1973) *The Introduction of Programme and Performance Budgeting in Ceylon*. Colombo, Colombo Agency for Administrative Studies.

Yeats, M. (ed) (1974) *Proceedings of the IGU Conference on Quantitative Geography*. Montreal, McGill.

Young, P. (1956) *Scientific Social Surveys and Research*. Englewood Cliffs, Prentice Hall.

Zaltman, G. *et al.* (eds) (1972) *Creating Social Change*. New York, Holt, Reinhart and Winston.

Zurcher, L.A. and Bonjean, C. (eds) (1970) *Planned Social Intervention*. New York, Chandler.

Index

DATE DUE

DEMCO 38-297